A
Learning Hebrew and

How Biblical Languages Work

Peter James Silzer &
Thomas John Finley

How Biblical Languages Work: A Student's Guide to Learning Greek and Hebrew

Published by Kregel Publications, a division of Kregel, Inc., P.O. Box 2607, Grand Rapids, MI 49501.

Unless otherwise noted, Scripture quotations are from author's own literal translation of the original texts.

Scripture quotations marked NRSV are from the New Revised Standard Version of the Bible, © 1989 by the Division of Christian Education of the National Council of the Churches of Christ in the USA. Used by permission.

Scripture quotations marked NASB are from the *New American Standard Bible.* © The Lockman Foundation 1960, 1962, 1963, 1968, 1971, 1972, 1973, 1975, 1977, 1995.

Scripture quotations marked KJV are from the *King James Version* of the Holy Bible.

Scripture quotations marked NIV are from the *Holy Bible, New International Version®*. © 1973, 1978, 1984 by International Bible Society. Used by permission of Zondervan Publishing House. All rights reserved.

Scripture quotations marked NLT are from the *Holy Bible, New Living Translation,* © 1996. Used by permission of Tyndale House Publishers, Inc., Wheaton, Illinois 60189. All rights reserved.

Library of Congress Cataloging-in-Publication Data
Silzer, Peter James.
How biblical languages work: a student's guide to learning Greek and Hebrew / by Peter James Silzer and Thomas John Finley.
p. cm.
Includes bibliographical references.
1. Hebrew language—Grammar. 2. Greek language, Biblical—Grammar. 3. Bible. O.T.—Language, style.
I. Finley, Thomas John. II. Title.
PJ4556.S55 2003
492.4'82421—dc22 2003021288

ISBN 978-0-8254-2644-5

Printed in the United States of America

4 5 6 7 8 / 12 11 10 09 08

Contents

Illustrations

Tables

Preface

Professors of biblical languages have frequently noted that their students do not have an adequate understanding of basic grammatical concepts, not even those of English. Thus, teachers face the dual task of explaining English grammar as well as that of Hebrew or Greek. Likewise, students complain about all the new terms they have to learn and feel overwhelmed by the complexities of the biblical languages. We have written this book to help you, as a new student of Hebrew or Greek, to understand the basic patterns of the biblical languages before you face too many of the "jots" and "tittles." We have developed this strategy through teaching a course at Biola University and Talbot School of Theology to people just like you. We are both lifelong students of the biblical languages who have benefited from linguistics. We are convinced that you will learn better by first understanding the general truths about human language and then applying your understanding of those facts to the biblical languages.

Our Conviction

For us the Bible is more than just an interesting subject; it is God's inspired revelation to his people. Pete has dedicated his life to the process of getting the Bible into the languages of the world so that people can respond to God's revelation as they receive it in their own language. Tom is firmly committed to training pastors and teachers to use the Hebrew language as a tool for more effective study and communication of the Scriptures to others. When Jesus Christ asked his close disciples whether they were going to turn away from him like many of their less dedicated contemporaries, the apostle Peter answered: "Lord, to whom would we go? You alone have the words that give eternal life" (John 6:68 NLT). That is the way we view the Bible; its words point to Jesus Christ, who alone can give eternal life. It is the inspired and inerrant Word from God to us.

How to Use This Book

This book provides the first practical beginner's guide to the main components of biblical Hebrew and Greek. It will guide you through various key ideas in Hebrew and Greek, using insights gleaned from linguistic studies of languages around the world. The introductory chapter will help you understand how the "big picture" of the biblical languages is similar to all other human languages. It will show you that Hebrew and Greek are organized in the same basic way as other languages.

The next part of the book (chaps. 2–7) describes major features of Hebrew and Greek: how the sounds are pronounced, how words are put together, how phrases and clauses are structured, how words convey meaning, and how languages change. As such, this book serves as an auxiliary tool to supplement the traditional grammars you will use in the classroom. It will help you as you enter the biblical language classroom by explaining the main ideas about language in understandable terms.

In chapter 8 you will find individualized help with how to study Hebrew and Greek based on your personal learning strengths. You are ultimately the one responsible for your success in learning to use the biblical languages. Our hope is that we can encourage and guide you to success.

Finally, we have included a glossary of important linguistic terms that are discussed in this book or that are widely used in standard grammars of Greek and Hebrew. You will want to refer to this glossary frequently as you begin your studies so that you understand the basic principles and concepts about language. The terminology used in standard textbooks has been developed over hundreds of years by many different scholars. We cannot change the fact that you will face the challenge of learning this new "language" of terminology while you also try to learn Hebrew or Greek, but we have tried to explain the ideas in clear language.

We have written this book primarily to help students in beginning classes in the biblical languages. The book relates the biblical languages to the normal characteristics and functions of human language so that you come to a better understanding of how the languages work. We have tried to demystify the biblical languages and to make the main features of each language understandable to you before you tackle the many small details of the exotic sounds, the complicated verbs, and the ways words are put together in Hebrew and Greek.

Our secondary audience includes people who want to study the biblical languages on their own. This book is not meant to replace a complete textbook or formal studies, but it will help you grasp the most important features of the biblical languages.

Learning Aids

When Hebrew or Greek words are used in this book, we have normally used a special set of English letters so that you do not have to know the Hebrew or Greek writing system to benefit from it. We do, however, guide you through the main features of the biblical language alphabets in chapter 2.

To help you process the information in each chapter, we have included exercises and other resources for further study, including, as relevant, Internet sites.

Acknowledgments

Peter J. Silzer

My interest in Koine Greek ("Koine" includes the Greek of the New Testament) goes back to my undergraduate days with Dr. John Schwane at Concordia Lutheran Junior College, Ann Arbor, Michigan. I am thankful for his help as a teacher in those early years and as a friend through the years. Dr. Bob Holst and his love for languages and culture deeply influenced me during my two years at Concordia Lutheran Senior College in Ft. Wayne, Indiana.

My thanks to Dr. Kenneth L. Pike and Dr. George Cowan for the way they exemplified godly scholarship in linguistics, and to my many other teachers and mentors in the Summer Institute of Linguistics through the years, including my wife, Dr. Sheryl Takagi Silzer.

I also want to thank my students at Biola University, who helped shape these notes as we studied the languages of the world together. Dr. Herbert Purnell, as the chair of the Department of TESOL and Applied Linguistics, has been a great encouragement to me as I studied, taught, and wrote on the linguistic aspects of the biblical languages.

Thomas J. Finley

Dr. Charles Lee Feinberg first stirred within me a love for the Old Testament and the Hebrew language. Without his gracious guidance and faith in my abilities, I would not be engaged in Hebrew studies today.

In my postseminary studies, Dr. Georgio Buccellati and Dr. Stanislav Segert greatly influenced my methodological approach to Semitic languages and linguistics. I am deeply grateful for their careful scholarship and excellence in teaching. They have given me a model to emulate throughout my career.

I must thank my many students at Talbot School of Theology for their valuable insights into the biblical text. Their zeal for serving the Lord has been an inspiration for me as well.

Finally, I would like to thank my wife, Anita, for her support and faith in me that has enabled me to carry out my research. She also has helped me to think through my ideas and how to express them more clearly. I am deeply indebted to her.

We both would like to thank Peter Gerhard, Doug Geringer, Dr. Brian O'Herin, Ben Block, David Marrs, John Coghlan, and other readers who gave insightful comments on early drafts of this book. We are also very grateful to the staff of Kregel for their many helpful comments and their support of this project.

1

The Big Picture

An Overview of How Language Works

Language . . . is not an abstract construction of the learned, or of dictionary-makers, but is something arising out of the work, needs, ties, joys, affections, tastes, of long generations of humanity, and has its bases broad and low, close to the ground.[1]

—Walt Whitman (1819–1891),
American poet

How many times have you heard people complain, "It's all Greek to me," when they can't understand something? What is it about Greek that makes people think it is unintelligible? You may have a friend who struggled through Greek in seminary because of all the strange new jargon and pages of strange letters. Many people have had difficulty learning Hebrew for some of the same reasons. Now that you have decided to study Hebrew or Greek, you might be intimidated by these stories. Perhaps you have even glanced through your textbook and seen all sorts of strange and complex charts. Despite what you may have heard about Hebrew and Greek, they are really very similar to English. They may seem exotic and strange, but Hebrew and Greek helped people communicate in their day just as English, Spanish, Korean, and other languages help people communicate today. Every language has to deal with

1. Walt Whitman, "Slang in America," in *The Complete Prose Works of Walt Whitman* (New York: G. P. Putnam's Sons, 1902), 3:151.

the same real-world situations and help people understand what happened, when it happened, and who was involved. This introductory chapter presents an overview of the "big picture" of the world's languages—the ways in which languages are similar.

You are about to launch into the study of biblical Hebrew or Greek. As you cast off from the familiar shores of English, you will do yourself a favor by thinking through what you already know about language. You already have an intuitive grasp that some sounds are English sounds and some are not. You have an insider's awareness of which combinations of sounds are used in English and which are foreign. You already know the basic patterns of how words are made in English and how to understand words that are new to you. You already know the basic ways to put sentences together in English and can understand what most sentences mean, even though you may never have heard them before. All of these skills will help you think about the normal patterns of Hebrew and Greek. As you leave the shores of English, this book will help you predict what you will find in the new country, the foreign and exotic country of the biblical languages. In this book you will find that Hebrew and Greek share many characteristics with the language you already know so well.

In this first chapter you will come to understand five main characteristics of language, eight primary functions of language, and three essential ways to look at language. You will see that Hebrew and Greek are no different from English or other languages in terms of this big-picture view. They share the same basic characteristics and functions common to all languages, and they can be learned and studied in the same ways as other languages. We begin with these universal traits of language so that you can put the many details of the biblical languages in perspective. We believe these introductory points will give you useful conceptual "hooks" to help you organize your studies. You can sort the details of Hebrew and Greek by placing each one under the appropriate general feature of language.

Five Key Characteristics of Language

Many people say, "Language is a tool of communication" or "Language is the way people communicate." English, Hebrew, and Greek are all means of communication. So are American Sign Language, Spanish, and Swahili. David Crystal, a well-known linguist and editor, defines language as follows:

> The systematic, conventional use of sounds, signs or written symbols in a human society for communication and self-expression.[2]

But *how* do languages help us communicate? How do two English speakers understand each other? What is it that makes communication possible when we use a particular language? Expanding on Crystal's definition, we can say that there are five key characteristics of human language that help us understand one another and help us learn other languages. All languages, including biblical Hebrew and Greek, are *systems* of *conventionalized symbols* used by *groups of people* to *communicate* and to *express their identity.* Languages are also *productive* and *creative.* Let's look at these five key characteristics of language, thinking about how English fits each part of the definition:

1. systems
2. of conventionalized symbols
3. used by groups of people
4. to communicate and express their identity
5. in a productive and creative way

Languages Are Organized Systems

First, every language is *systematic.* A language is not an odd collection of unrelated sounds and words. Each language has patterns, and these patterns help us solve the puzzles of a language that is new to us. We need to approach languages as careful observers, looking for these patterns. We can look at language the way a musician listens to a song. By careful listening, a musician can find the melody, recognize themes, transcribe the chords, and eventually convey the same piece or variations of it to others. This is possible because each piece of music has discernible patterns and structures.

Languages also have systems, including systems of sound. English, for example, has about forty-two sounds (not letters) that we use to make thousands of words following a few basic patterns. There are English words such as *say, stay,* and *stray,* but not *srtay.* After an *s* there can be *tr* sounds, but not *rt* sounds. English also has the pattern *splash,* but not *lpsash.* We know many words that end with the *ng* sound *(ring, rang, rung, tongue),* but no English

2. *An Encyclopedic Dictionary of Language and Languages,* ed. David Crystal (Oxford: Blackwell, 1992), s.v. "Language."

word starts with that sound. Of all the possible ways to put sounds together, English speakers choose a limited number of patterns. Hebrew and Greek, of course, may have sounds and patterns that are different from English, but they also choose from a limited set of possibilities. We will look at these sound patterns in chapter 2.

When English speakers form words such as *run, run-ner,* and *runner-s,* they use regular patterns. No English speaker uses the form *run-s-ner.* No one has to tell English speakers not to put the *s* in the middle of *runner;* they just know that the normal pattern has the *s* at the end of the word. We also know that other words can be made using the same patterns:

- *run* *runner* *runners*
- *read* *reader* *readers*
- *teach* *teacher* *teachers*

English speakers also follow patterns when putting words together into phrases and sentences. The phrase *the two good books* is understandable, but not *books the good two* or *the books two good.* An English speaker might say *The child gave the flowers to the teacher* or *The child gave the teacher the flowers* but not *Child the teacher flowers the gave the.* Patterns like these are almost second nature to English speakers and have been picked up either as a child in an English-speaking home or as an adult learner. In the same way, speakers of Hebrew and Greek followed regular patterns when they put sounds together, when they made words, and when they combined words to make sentences. We will look at the major patterns of Hebrew and Greek words, phrases, and clauses in chapters 3–5, but you can already begin to predict that they will use a relatively small set of patterns. As you think about the big picture of language, you also can begin to get an idea of how to talk about the patterns you will see in Hebrew and Greek. Every language, no matter how difficult it may be to learn, operates on the basis of systematic patterns.

Languages Use Conventionalized Symbols

In addition to following systematic patterns, languages also use *sounds, signs,* and *symbols* in a conventional way. That is, there are normal, agreed-upon ways of doing things with language. When we talk, of course, we use sounds. These sounds are conventional within a language group in that only certain sounds out of all possible sounds that a speaker might make will be recognized by other speakers of the language. If I make the sound of a *b,* for example, other speakers of English can connect that sound with a sound used for making words in English. For example, the words *boy, habit,* and *cob* all contain the *b* sound. However, if I make a clicking sound, English speakers will not recognize it as a language sound. There are no English words that are made with a clicking sound. It is possible, however, to make words in other languages with clicking sounds. Bantu languages in Africa, for example, use various clicking sounds in their words.

These conventional sounds are combined into words that indicate some meaning. Sign languages basically convey meaning without sounds by using hand signs (and facial expressions) that enable a user to communicate with another person who understands the same sign language. Written codes for language also have been developed as an attempt to convey meaning by way of agreed-upon (conventional) symbols (e.g., letters or characters). These sounds, signs, and symbols are the way in which we can gain access to the meaning of a story, a text, or a conversation. We will need to decode these messages, especially through the written symbols of the biblical languages, to take part in the communication of the original texts. We will show the writing systems of Hebrew and Greek and how they are related to each other and to English in chapter 2.

The relationship between the sound (or shape) of a word and its meaning is arbitrary. That is, we cannot predict what a word will mean from its sound; there is no exact relationship between the sound of a word and its meaning. There is no logical or scientific link between the sounds of the word *house* and the idea of "house." Nor does the fact that *mouse* and *house* sound similar indicate that they have related meanings. The relation between sounds and meanings is arbitrary, not absolute. Even the rather direct link between the sound a rooster makes and the word used to describe it is arbitrary. English uses *cock-a-doodle-doo* to represent the sound, but Spanish uses *kikiriki,* and Modern Hebrew uses *kukuriku.* The English word is arbitrary in that it does not represent the sound exactly. In the same way, Hebrew and Greek words use an arbitrary combination of sounds to represent meaning. For example, the Hebrew word for *house* sounds something like English *buy it,* and the Greek word, *oikos,* sounds just like it is spelled.

This arbitrary connection between sounds and meaning is another way in which language is conventional. Rather than a direct connection between the sound of a word and its meaning, the connection is instead a convention of culture. Once a group of people agree that a certain word means something (e.g., *house* means "house"), the relationship of sound to meaning becomes, at least temporarily, a social convention. Language, then, is *conventional* because a group of people agree that certain sounds will be used to indicate particular meanings. So, although there is no inherent correspondence between the sound of a word and what it means, people can still communicate if they share the same meaning for that word. English speakers can talk about family relationships such as father, mother, brother, sister, and cousins, because English has associated meaning with these words.

The conventional nature of language is also shown by how language can reflect the world somewhat differently in different societies. For example, Greek combines the idea of brother and cousin in a single word in a way that helps us understand that their society was not as concerned as some other societies to distinguish between two people who are cousins and two people who are children of the same parents. The Hebrew culture used two terms for *father-in-law,* depending on whether it was the husband's father-in-law or the wife's. We will look at more ways in which language is a reflection of culture toward the end of this chapter.

Languages Are Used by Groups of People

We have seen that languages are systematic and conventional; they also are obviously used by groups of people. Who determines the structures of a language? Who gets to choose what a word means? It is *a social group* that takes charge of these matters. That is, it is the aggregate of the people who speak the language. Sections of a society may differ in the way they pronounce words (an accent) or in the words and structures they choose to use (dialects).

The meanings of words can change, creating variations between groups of people. Regional American dialects (e.g., *soda* or *pop*) and the differences between American and British English (*elevator/lift, flashlight/torch,* etc.) illustrate the conventional nature of words. People could tell Peter was from Galilee by the way he spoke (Mark 14:70 as interpreted in the KJV), much as a person from Chicago recognizes that someone from Memphis speaks "with an accent." Paul and Peter used different Greek forms because their backgrounds and education were not the same. We will look at factors like these in chapter 7.

Languages also change over time, with new forms arising to take the place of older forms. Because social groups change over time, words also come and go and change meaning, sometimes very quickly. The music *record* of the 1960s has given way to *CDs*, much as *groovy* has been displaced by a succession of other words. The book of Samuel had to explain that the Hebrew term *nābî* ("prophet") was the contemporary word for *rō᾿eh* ("seer") because Hebrew had changed (1 Sam. 9:9).[3] We will discuss some of these types of changes in chapter 7. Biblical Hebrew and Greek, like all languages, were influenced by societal and historical changes. By considering these factors, we will better understand how the meaning of words and phrases changed over time.

Languages Help People Communicate in Eight Ways

Language is a powerful tool within a society. But what does language actually "do" for a society? Typically, people say that language is a means of *communication.* People explain things to others and tell stories. They ask favors and make demands. Through writing people are able to share their thoughts with other generations and people far across the world. But language serves many powerful functions beyond the simple moving of information from one person to another.

It is helpful to think of the specific work that language does and to identify these functions. Eugene Nida, a noted linguist and Bible translation scholar, suggests that language is used in eight ways: aesthetic, cognitive, emotive, expressive, imperative, informative, interpersonal, and performative.[4] In the next few paragraphs, we will consider these eight functions of language.

Expressing Creativity (Aesthetic)

Poets and advertisers create interesting ways of saying things that capture our attention. We like clever ways of saying things. We value poetry for the non-standard way it expresses ideas and makes us think in new ways. We respect storytellers for their skills in relating well-known stories in entertaining ways. Hebrew and Greek writers also used language in artistic ways. There are puns and poems, alliteration and wordplays throughout Scripture. We will look at some of these creative uses of language in chapters 5 and 6.

---

3. The special characters used to represent Hebrew letters will be explained in chapter 2.
4. Eugene A. Nida, "Sociolinguistics and Translating," in *Sociolinguistics and Communication,* ed. Johannes P. Louw, UBS Monograph Series 1 (London: United Bible Societies, 1986), 15–16.

Think of how powerfully Psalm 23 has comforted and encouraged people for thousands of years. Its message probably could be summed up in a few words, but would it be nearly as effective without the imagery of the shepherd and his rod and staff or of the cup running over with blessing?

Thinking (Cognitive)

We also use words to think. Even in our thoughts and dreams, we have labels with which we identify ideas. A. R. Luria, a researcher in the relation of the brain and language, says:

> Regardless of how primitive or abbreviated language may be, it is pivotal to cognition: by means of it we designate numbers, perform mathematics, calculations, analyze perceptions, distinguish the essential from the nonessential, and form categories of distinct impressions. Apart from being a means of communicating, language is fundamental to perception and memory, thinking and behavior. It organizes our inner life.[5]

At the end of this chapter, we will see that Hebrew and Greek organized the world in different ways than English does.

Stirring Emotions (Emotive)

People use language to influence the emotive state of others. Using "strong" or "loaded" words in an argument is often an attempt to sway people's attitudes and feelings. Ralph Waldo Emerson (1803–82) noted that "Speech is power; speech is to persuade, to convert, to compel." More recently, the American poet Gwendolyn Brooks (1917–2000) has noted:

> Words can do wonderful things. They sound purr. They can urge, they can wheedle, whip, whine. They can sing, sass, singe. They can churn, check, channelize. They can be a hup, 2, 3, 4. They can forge a fiery army out of a hundred languid men.[6]

---

5. A. R. Luria, *The Man with the Shattered World* (Cambridge, Mass.: Harvard University Press, 1972), 32–33.
6. Gwendolyn Brooks, afterword to *Contending Forces,* by Pauline E. Hopkins (n.p., 1968). Cited in Dorothy Winbush Riley, ed., *My Soul Looks Back, 'Less I Forget* (New York: HarperCollins, 1991), 444.

It is important to be able to recognize the emotive power of Hebrew and Greek words, especially because our English translations may not fully convey the same emotional force.

Expressing Emotions (Expressive)

People use language to express their emotions. We have special words such as *Wow!* and *Ouch!* that are used only for this purpose. We also change the loudness of our words or use higher or lower pitch to express our emotions. "I'm *really, really* happy about my new job!" adds an additional positive emphasis to what might be a more prosaic report of the same idea. Each language has ways to express emotional states.

Stimulating Action (Imperative)

If we expand on the general word *communication,* we recognize that language is used to influence behavior and to stimulate action. In English we can use a variety of grammatical forms to get someone to perform an action. We can use an imperative structure, like "Close the door!" but we can also use a question form, like "Could someone please shut the door?" or even a statement, such as "It's too noisy with the door open." When we look at Hebrew and Greek, we need to realize that they also use more than one form to make a command or to suggest that someone else do something.

Informing (Informative)

While conveying information is often seen as the primary function of language, we would rather see it as one of the many uses language has in society. Language helps us to record or document information. Parents inculcate cultural values in their children, and teachers educate children in knowledge of the world around them. Whether in the form of oral literature or in writing, language preserves information from the past and makes it available for the future.

Asking people questions and obtaining information is also part of the informative function of language. Again, we may not always use an interrogative marker or a question structure to do this, as in "Tell me about yourself," "I'd be interested in knowing more about you," or "That's enough about me."

Relating to Others (Interpersonal)

Language is a key in making and maintaining relationships with others. The "How are you?" and "What's up?" that we extend to strangers can be likened to a verbal handshake that initiates the very early stages of relating. As we all know (from our culture), such questions don't expect much information in reply. Language is also essential in deepening a relationship. Asking questions to draw out another, as well as sharing thoughts and feelings "heart to heart," are all done with language.

Language also helps people express their solidarity with others. We choose to speak in particular ways to show who we are. Friends share common phrases. Members of social organizations use "in" terms as a mark of identity. Preachers, we hope, speak differently when they meet fellow ministers over coffee than when they preach. Dialect differences are maintained as ways to identify with others from the same region or social class. Our pronunciation and our choice of words mark us as people from a particular geographical and social group. How an Israelite from ancient times pronounced the word *shibboleth* actually identified who was the enemy in a war, reminding us of the fierce loyalty of one dialect of Hebrew against another dialect within the same language and people (Judg. 12:6).

Language can also be used to distance ourselves from others. Young people create new words and phrases (or at least change the meaning of them) to identify with each other and to keep others out of their group. Church people often exclude others (perhaps not intentionally) by using clichés and words that are understood only by the initiated. We are constantly choosing our words to fit in with others or to exclude others from our circle. We will see that Hebrew and Greek words also have social meaning and that words take on distinctive meanings in particular contexts.

Changing the World Around Us (Performative)

Language actually can make things happen. It can modify the state of the receptors. Thus, a person is sentenced in court when the judge says, "I sentence you to five days in the city jail." We accuse and blame people with the words "I accuse you of . . ." and "I blame you for . . . ," just as we forgive and excuse them with other words. Words perform the action. Of course, the person with the authority to make something happen really performs the action, but he or she uses language to accomplish it. Another example is when the minister says, "I now pronounce you man and wife." With these words the minister legally joins two people as husband and wife. There are dozens of key words in Hebrew and Greek that have this special power to change reality (cf. Lev. 13:6; Matt. 9:2).

Hebrew and Greek served these same eight functions in their society as English does in our world today. It is important to consider these aspects of language as we study the original texts so that we understand the message that is being conveyed.

Language Is Productive and Creative

One key element we can add to Crystal's definition of language is that language is also *productive and creative.* This feature of human language is one of the important things that distinguishes human language from other animal communication.[7] Our ability to use human language creatively and powerfully reflects the creative aspect of the image of God in us. Although every human language uses only a small set of ways to make words and a small set of patterns to combine those words into phrases and clauses, the total set of potential clauses or sentences in a language is virtually infinite. We can always make a new sentence, a sentence that is heard for the very first time in the history of the universe, and still be understood by other speakers of the language. For example, I can say, "At 11:00 A.M. on April 10, 2002, I sat down after walking a mile and felt pretty good about my health." There is little likelihood that anyone ever said this exact sentence before, and yet any speaker of English can understand it. By compounding and embedding phrases within other phrases, we can always produce new utterances. English speakers can say:

- The tree
- The large tree
- The very large tree
- The very large oak tree
- The very large green oak tree
- The very large green oak tree on top of the ridge, etc.

---

7. Cf. Clifford A. Wilson and Donald McKeon, *The Language Gap* (Grand Rapids: Zondervan, 1984).

and keep track of the meaning by following the normal patterns for such phrases. We can use similar productive patterns to decipher Hebrew and Greek sentences to sort out which words belong together and what the sentences mean.

Three Essential Ways to Look at Language

Each language is a complex social tool. To properly understand Hebrew and Greek, we will need to look at language from three different points of view. We need to consider how the *forms* (the words, phrases, and clauses), the *meanings* (semantics), and the *context* (including the linguistic and social aspects) are all involved in any given text. We will look at these three aspects of language throughout the remainder of this book.

The *forms* of a language, no matter how strange they appear to be at first glance, establish a system that encodes meaning. Each language organizes words in predictable ways that native speakers understand and use to communicate with one another. To learn another language, we need to understand these basic patterns. In the biblical languages we face several new concepts, including the fact that Hebrew changes the shape of the verb to indicate whether the subject of a sentence is male or female. In English, of course, we do not change the verb when we say *Paul reads* or *Paula reads.* If English changed the verb to show when the subject (Paul or Paula) was male or female, it might look like this:

- Paul o-reads
- Paula a-reads

In these made-up words, the *o* in front of the verb would show that *Paul* is male, and the *a* would be used for *Paula* because she is female.

The biblical languages also have different ways to indicate when an action took place, somewhat similar to words like *sing/sang/sung* in English, in which the verb changes shape to indicate the time of the action.

In chapters 3–5 we will learn the most common grammatical patterns in Hebrew and Greek and see how these patterns differ from English. In chapter 3 we will look at how Hebrew and Greek form words from smaller parts. In chapter 4 we will examine how these words are put in particular orders to make phrases and sentences. Chapter 5 will look at the way even larger pieces of language are put together. The good news is that each language uses only a relatively small set of patterns; there is not an unbounded set of possible ways to put words and phrases together.

The *meaning* component of language is expressed through the forms. As we come to understand the way meaning is connected to the forms of the biblical languages, we can better understand the message that is being communicated. We will come to understand that there are often several forms that express the same meaning. For example, in English we can say:

- *The teacher taught a Hebrew lesson to the students;* or,
- *The teacher taught the students a Hebrew lesson*

and keep the same meaning. We could say:

- *The teacher taught the lesson after the students arrived;* or,
- *After the students arrived, the teacher taught the lesson;* or even,
- *The students arrived and then the teacher taught the lesson*

and maintain the same message.

Another example of the relationship between form and meaning is words that are used interchangeably (**synonyms**) and words that have related meanings. We can say:

- *The <u>tall</u> mountain,* or
- *The <u>high</u> mountain*

and understand the same message; but when we say

- *He is <u>tall</u>,* and
- *He is <u>high</u>*

we mean something different. The English words *tall* and *high* are not completely synonymous. Their meaning depends on the context.

Since most of our understanding of Hebrew and Greek comes through English translations, we will need to be especially careful to find ways to get inside the original languages to avoid misunderstanding key words and phrases. Imagine what it would be like if our knowledge of the English word *key* came only through Spanish translations of the word. Compare the following two sentences:

- *The key idea of a key to a lock or a key to a code is a key to understanding a key of a piano.*
- *The dominante idea of a llave to a lock or a solución of a code is a clave to understanding a tecla of a piano.*

We see here that the English word *key* has five different forms in Spanish. If we think about the English word, we would realize that it is not really just one word; there are several words that happen to have the same shape in English. There are also various senses of each word. The basic idea of a *key* that opens a lock is extended to mean a solution to a code. The *key* of a piano or a computer is not part of the same idea. We see similar patterns in Hebrew and Greek when we look up words in a concordance. Frequently there are several English words used to translate one Hebrew or Greek word (even in such literal translations as the KJV) and also cases where one English word is used for several Hebrew or Greek words. In chapter 6 we will look at some examples.

Finally, *context* is key to understanding what the form-meaning relationship is in a given sentence. Much as English speakers know that *He is high* cannot refer to a person's physical height, speakers of the biblical languages also used context to interpret the original messages. As outsiders to the biblical languages, we need to learn to think about the context of words and phrases so that we can come to a correct understanding of the original meaning. Context helps us understand the difference between similar words and even between the multiple senses of a word.

How Language and Culture Relate

People have often debated about the relationship between language and culture. Some, such as Sapir and Whorf (in the early twentieth century), hypothesized that language constrains or determines thought and perception. Other people consider language to be merely a mirror of the culture, rather than a "straightjacket" or "blinders." Students of the biblical languages often talk as though the Hebrew or Greek mind worked differently than our English-speaking mind. In this section we want to explore the relationship between language and culture.

Language As a Straightjacket of Thought

Edward Sapir and Benjamin Whorf studied the languages of the native peoples of North America (Amerindian) and noticed that the lexical and grammatical structures were often quite distinct from English and other Indo-European languages. Based on their studies, they proposed that language controls a person's thinking processes in some way. In 1929 Sapir said:

> Human beings . . . are very much at the mercy of the particular language which has become the medium of expression for their society. . . . The "real world" is to a large extent unconsciously built upon the language habits of the group.[8]

That is to say, the way we see the world is limited by the structures and words of our language. Whorf later stated:

> We dissect nature along lines laid down by our native language. The categories and types that we isolate from the world of phenomena we do not find there because they stare every observer in the face; on the contrary, the world is presented in a kaleidoscopic flux of impressions which has to be organized by our minds—this means largely by the linguistic systems of our minds.[9]

These early writers on the relationship between language and thought appear to think that language constrains our thoughts. More recently, Carol Eastman has written about these early theories and observes:

> The views of Sapir and Whorf have been taken to mean that people who speak different languages segment their world differently: thus, the French language structures French reality by constraining what French speakers pay attention to, Swahili does the same for the Swahili "world"—if there's a word for "it" in the language we see "it," if not we don't.[10]

8. Quoted in William O'Grady et al., *Contemporary Linguistics: An Introduction,* 2d ed. (New York: St. Martin's, 1993), 242.
9. Ibid.
10. Carol M. Eastman, *Aspects of Language and Culture,* 2d ed. (Novato, Calif.: Chandler and Sharp, 1990), 103.

The concept of language limiting perception has become known as the "Whorfian Hypothesis" or "linguistic determinism."

The Whorfian Hypothesis has been discussed for many years, but recently a number of scholars, including George Lakoff,[11] have extended the discussion to metaphors as well. Lakoff noted that much of language is metaphorical in nature. There are also countless expressions in language that express a cultural reality in a nonliteral way. English, for example, has many expressions that revolve around the concept that time is a commodity: save time, invest time, lose time, and so on. It is this kind of metaphor that has attracted the attention of linguists and philosophers in the past twenty years. Other "conceptual metaphors" include the idea that good feelings are "up" and negative feelings are "down." Lakoff and Johnson seem to side with the Whorfian understanding of the power of language to control thought:

> Our concepts structure what we perceive, how we get around in the world and how we relate to other people. Our conceptual system thus plays a central role in defining our everyday realities.[12]

A relatively recent book by Howard Rheingold, *They Have a Word for It,* promotes a similar theory that the words of a language constrain how people in that language perceive the world. By adding certain foreign words to English, for example, Rheingold proposes that our way of thinking would be changed (for the better).[13]

Language As a Mirror of Society

Many linguists disagree with the deterministic stand of Sapir and Whorf. The fact that people often have ideas for which they have no adequate words indicates that they use words to label what they see, not that they see what they have words for. Based on Berlin and Kay's in-depth study of color terms in a variety of languages,[14] linguists conclude that frequently used perceptual cat-

---

11. George Lakoff, *Women, Fire and Dangerous Things: What Categories Reveal About the Mind* (Chicago: University of Chicago Press, 1987).
12. George Lakoff and Mark Johnson, *Metaphors We Live By* (Chicago: University of Chicago Press, 1980), 3.
13. Howard Rheingold, *They Have a Word for It: A Lighthearted Lexicon of Untranslatable Words and Phrases* (Los Angeles: Jeremy P. Tarcher, 1988), 1–4.
14. Brent Berlin and Paul Kay, *Basic Color Terms : Their Universality and Evolution* (Berkeley: University of California Press, 1969).

egories receive names or words. Less-frequently-used concepts, while perceived, do not always have separate lexical items. Thus, as the differences between colors, for example, become important to a society, more words will be added to distinguish them. (We can see this in individuals as well if we compare the terms for color used by a graphic artist with those used by someone who does not need to distinguish colors for work or hobby purposes.)

Nida notes:

> Whorf regarded language as largely determinative, but most other scholars have taken the position that the structure of language simply increases the facility with which people recognize certain distinctions; for example, the matter of color contrasts, kinship relations, and classifications of fauna and flora. It is certainly true that language reflects certain aspects of social structure. Relative status, for example, is marked at least in a general way in a number of European languages by means of varying forms of second person pronouns. . . . Language is not, however, a direct inventory of a culture, but rather a kind of index, often based on what one might call "fossilized relics" of the past. For the most part, *language follows society rather than determining it.*[15]

Grammar Does Not Equal Thought

It has sometimes been said that Greek is a more precise language than Hebrew for expressing certain concepts or thoughts that the Greeks had, because Greek has nuances that can be brought out through its many forms of the verb and its multiple case endings, for example. Hebrew, by contrast, has only a limited variety in its verbal system and no case endings. This idea assumes that the grammatical structure of a language somehow relates to how its speakers think, but as James Barr warns us,

> The idea that the grammatical structure of a language reflects the thought structure of those speaking it and that it correspondingly reflects the differences from the thought of those speaking a language with different grammatical structure, has very great difficulties.[16]

15. Nida, "Sociolinguistics and Translating," 11 (emphasis added).
16. James Barr, *The Semantics of Biblical Language* (Oxford: Oxford University Press, 1961), 39.

Since form and meaning are arbitrary for the most part, it is not helpful to interpret a culture through its grammar.

Applying the Language and Culture Connection

When you learn a second language, it is helpful to plan activities to help you understand the culture. The ways in which a society maps out kinship and relationships will provide insights into how people relate to others. Thus, rather than randomly gathering names of objects, you can plan a strategy of learning that helps you understand the major features of a culture. We will look at other helpful strategies for learning a language in chapter 8.

Summary and Preview

In this introductory chapter we have seen that all languages have much in common. English, Hebrew, and Greek have the same basic characteristics and fulfill the same functions within their societies. We have also seen that a language reflects the culture of the people who speak it. Now we will move on to a broad overview of various aspects of the biblical languages. We will start with the sounds and writing systems of Hebrew and Greek in chapter 2.

For Further Study

Barr, James. *The Semantics of Biblical Language.* London: Oxford University Press, 1961.

Black, David Alan. *Linguistics for Students of New Testament Greek.* 2d ed. Grand Rapids: Baker, 1995.

Cotterell, Peter, and Max Turner. *Linguistics and Biblical Interpretation.* Downers Grove, Ill.: InterVarsity, 1989.

Lakoff, George. *Women, Fire and Dangerous Things: What Categories Reveal About the Mind.* Chicago: University of Chicago Press, 1987.

Lakoff, George, and Mark Johnson. *Metaphors We Live By.* Chicago: University of Chicago Press, 1980.

Pike, Kenneth L. "The Linguist and Axioms Concerning the Language of Scripture." *Journal of the American Scientific Affiliation* 26:2 (1974): 47–51.

———. *Linguistic Concepts.* Lincoln, Neb.: University of Nebraska Press, 1982.

Pinker, Steven. *The Language Instinct.* New York: William Morrow and Company, Inc., 1994.

———. *Words and Rules.* New York: Basic Books, 1999.
Schaller, Susan. *A Man Without Words.* Berkeley: University of California Press, 1995.
Silva, Moisés. *God, Language and Scripture: Reading the Bible in the Light of General Linguistics.* Grand Rapids: Zondervan, 1990.
Wilson, Clifford A., and Donald McKeon. *The Language Gap.* Grand Rapids: Zondervan, 1984.

Internet Resources

The Summer Institute of Linguistics (SIL) provides thousands of pages of material on language and linguistics on its web site: http://www.sil.org.

The iLoveLanguages! site contains information about many of the world's languages: http://www.ilovelanguages.com.

Exercises

1. Written, and even "spoken," animal sounds, even though they seem to represent the actual noises made, are still examples of the arbitrary relationship between sound and meaning. In what way are these sounds arbitrary? What do you think language would be like if each word had a direct relationship between its sounds and its meaning?
2. Make a "first in the history of the universe" sentence. Describe how this sentence illustrates language productivity.
3. Describe a way you used language as a form of identity in the last week. How did language help you relate to other people in a positive way? Did you exclude someone by your words? Did you feel excluded by the way someone spoke to you?
4. Write at least three different forms to express the following series of events:

    - *The car was dirty.*
    - *I washed the car.*

    Discuss your answers with a friend. What do these variations indicate about the relationship of form and meaning?
5. Write at least five examples using the word *run* that illustrate different meanings of the word. If you know another language or can ask a speaker

of another language, write the correct way of saying the same meaning(s) in that language. Discuss what you learn about form and meaning between the two languages.

6. Describe the patterns in the following examples from Hebrew and Greek. Don't worry about the special marks used with some of the letters; we will explain them in chapter 2:

Hebrew:	*yōʾmar* "he says"	*yiqrāʾ* "he calls"	*yaʿăśeh* "he makes"
	tōʾmar "she says"	*tiqrāʾ* "she calls"	*taʿăśeh* "she makes"
Greek:	*eipen* "he said"	*ekalesen* "he called"	*epoiēsen* "he made"
	eipan "they said"	*ekalesan* "they called"	*epoiēsan* "they made"

   How are the Hebrew and Greek patterns different from English?

7. Reflect on the productive aspect of language and the "image of God."

   - Do you think that our creation in the "image of God" includes the human capacity to use language?
   - In what ways does our use of language mirror God's use of language?

8. Discuss the concept of linguistic determinism. Explain your own views and give examples to prove your points.

2

Can You Spell That?

Reading and Writing

But because words immediately pass away once they have agitated the air waves, and last no longer than the sound they make, letters were invented as signs of words. Thus spoken utterances can be shown to the eyes, not in themselves, but through what are signs of them. It is not possible, therefore, for these signs to be common to all nations. . . .[1]

—Augustine (354–430)
Christian Doctrine, 2.4

Language is primarily an oral means of communication. Thus, you could learn German or Indonesian without ever mastering the writing system. To learn the biblical languages, however, you need to be able to read the texts.

Most students begin their study of Hebrew or Greek merely by learning the alphabet. We give here more linguistic information than you would find in textbooks of Hebrew or Greek about how the sounds of the biblical languages relate to the letters that represent them. Is this information necessary if you wish only to read the text of the Bible in Hebrew and Greek, not to speak these languages? Many of the details found in standard Hebrew and Greek grammars about how words are formed will make more sense if you understand

1. Quoted from Edmund Hill, trans., *Teaching Christianity (De Doctrina Christiana)* (Hyde Park, N.Y.: New City Press, 1996), 130.

some principles of how language sounds work together to make up words. We are convinced that you will make better and faster progress in understanding how the biblical languages work if you can grasp these big-picture ideas.

This chapter will show how the Hebrew and Greek alphabets represent the sounds of each language. We will begin with an overview of how writing systems work. Then we will explain the sounds of Hebrew and Greek.[2] We will then show how the written symbols relate to the sounds of each language. Finally, we will point out the similarities of the Hebrew, Greek, and English alphabets.

How Writing Works

The fact that some languages have been encoded in writing is a fascinating historical topic. Even to this day, a majority of the world's languages are primarily oral modes of communication. Written forms of language are by nature secondary to oral forms and represent, however inadequately, oral language. Written language generally lacks adequate ways to represent intonation and stress, which are important in communicating meaning and emotion. While words can be underlined and punctuation inserted, the written form of language cannot always convey the full meaning of the original oral communication. Think of how many ways the following sentence might be spoken: *They are good students.* The speaker can emphasize any of the four words to give a different spin or emphasis. The written form cannot adequately reflect these subtle differences.

Of course, some forms of communication are written from the outset, such as letters or legal contracts. Some sections in the Bible were originally written (e.g., Kings and Chronicles, Paul's letters), while others may have moved from oral to written form (e.g., some of the psalms and the teachings of Jesus). This does not negate the primary nature of the oral language. It is still true that we learn to read and write our native tongue only after we have learned how to speak it.

On the positive side, written communication allows a culture to communicate with its ancestors and with later generations. Written communication also can cross physical boundaries, such as mountains or seas. Aquinas noted that

2. Even though you may not need to speak Hebrew and Greek, you still need to learn the sounds of the language. It would be difficult to attach meaning to a word if you didn't know a corresponding sound. Plus, if you want to talk about Hebrew or Greek with anyone else, you need some common agreement about how the words sound.

> the use of writing was necessary so that he [the author] might manifest his conceptions to those who are distant according to place and to those who will come in future time.[3]

It is no easy feat to encode language in static, two-dimensional shapes (i.e., letters or symbols). In fact, the whole process of writing is inexact. No writing system is a perfect representation of the way people speak, despite what some native speakers may claim.

As we approach the biblical languages, of course, we must start with the written symbols and try to understand how they represent the sounds of Hebrew and Greek. We will present the Hebrew and Greek symbols separately, but we will also compare them to each other and to English because, as it turns out, all three writing systems have a common source.

In order to make it easier to follow what is said in the rest of the chapter, we will place tables with the complete alphabets of Hebrew and Greek here, including both the actual Hebrew and Greek forms and their transliterated equivalents (cf. tables 2.1 and 2.2). Transliteration refers to putting the letters of one writing system into the letters of another. In this case we will be putting Hebrew and Greek letters into English letters or modified English letters. The additional letters allow us to write certain Hebrew and Greek sounds that English does not have, and they also allow us to use a distinct transliteration letter for each Hebrew or Greek letter. For example, the symbol *ḥ* (an *h* with a dot under it) represents a sound that is somewhat close to the *ch* sound in the Scottish word *loch*. We use transliteration because it will help you to see how Hebrew works without being confused by the foreign system of writing.

When Hebrew or Greek names are represented in English Bible translations, the results are often inexact and inconsistent. For example, the Hebrew sound represented by the transliteration symbol *ḥ* is spelled with *h* in the name *Noah* but with *e* at the beginning of the name *Eve*.

We will use two transliteration systems here, the SBL (Society of Biblical Literature) and the IPA (International Phonetic Association). The SBL system follows the principle of one symbol per one Hebrew or Greek letter, although it does permit some two-letter symbols for certain Greek letters (*th* for *theta*, *ph* for *phi*, *ch* for *chi*, and *ps* for *psi*). Using the SBL system, one knows exactly which Hebrew or Greek letters to use to write any word, but the SBL system does not always show

3. Aquinas, *Commentary on Aristotle's "On Interpretation"* 1.2.

Table 2.1: The Hebrew Alphabet

Letter Name[4]	Hebrew Letter[5]	SBL Transliteration	IPA Transliteration[6]	Modern Pronunciation
Aleph	א	ʾ	ʔ	sound between "uh-oh"
Bet	ב	b	b	b
Gimel	ג	g	g	g
Dalet	ד	d	d	d
He	ה	h	h	h
Vav/Waw	ו	w	w (v)	v
Zayin	ז	z	z	z
Chet	ח	ḥ	ħ (χ)	ch (loch)
Tet	ט	ṭ	t^{ɣ}(t)	t
Yod	י	y	j	y (yes)
Kaph	כ/ך	k	c (k)	k
Lamed	ל	l	l	l
Mem	מ/ם	m	m	m
Nun	נ/ן	n	n	n
Samekh	ס	s	s	s
Ayin	ע	ʿ	ʕ (ʔ)	sound between "uh-oh"
Pe	פ/ף	p	p	p
Tsade	צ/ץ	ṣ	s^{ɣ} (ts)	ts (gets)
Qoph	ק	q	q	k
Resh	ר	r	r[7]	r
Shin	שׁ	š	ʃ	sh (show)
Sin	שׂ	ś	ɬ (s)	s
Tav/Taw	ת	t	t	t

4. Your instructor will teach you how to pronounce these names.
5. Some Hebrew letters have two forms; the one to the right of the slash is a final form used only at the end of a word. More will be said about these final forms below. Note that Hebrew does not distinguish lowercase (small) and uppercase (capital) letters.
6. This transliteration represents the ancient pronunciations. Modern pronunciations are placed in parentheses.
7. The IPA [r] symbol represents the trilled *r* sound, as in Spanish *perro*, "dog." Scholars disagree on the Ancient Hebrew pronunciation of this letter; Modern Hebrew uses a trill.

Table 2.2: The Greek Alphabet[8]

Letter Name	Greek Letter	SBL Transliteration	Classroom Pronunciation (IPA Transliteration)	Classroom Pronunciation (English Letters)
Alpha	Α α	a	a	a ("ah")
Beta	Β β	b	b	b
Gamma	Γ γ	g	g	g (go)
Delta	Δ δ	d	d	d
Epsilon	Ε ϵ	e	ε	e (extra)
Zeta	Ζ ζ	z	z	z
Eta	Η η	ē	e	ā (say)
Theta	Θ θ	th	θ	th (thin)
Iota	Ι ι	i	ɪ	i (rid)
Kappa	Κ κ	k	k	k
Lambda	Λ λ	l	l	l
Mu	Μ μ	m	m	m
Nu	Ν ν	n	n	n
Xi	Ξ ξ	x	ks	ks
Omicron	Ο ο	o	ɔ	ou (bought)
Pi	Π π	p	p	p
Rho	Ρ ρ	r	r	r
Sigma	Σ σ[9]	s	s	s
Tau	Τ τ	t	t	t
Upsilon	Υ υ	y (u in vowel combinations)	y	ü, in German
Phi	Φ ϕ	ph	f	f
Chi	Χ χ	ch	x	loch
Psi	Ψ ψ	ps	ps	ps (oops)
Omega	Ω ω	ō	o	ō (bone)

8. Note that the Greek alphabet follows a slightly different order than does the English.
9. The form ς is a final form of *sigma,* used only at the end of a word.

the exact sound of a letter.[10] For example, transliterating the Greek vowel *iota* with *i* does not show that this vowel can have more than one pronunciation.

The internationally recognized symbols of the IPA system represent exact pronunciations and can be applied to any language. Any linguist will know immediately exactly how a word is pronounced simply by looking at the IPA transliteration. Any Hebrew or Greek letter that receives more than one sound will have a separate IPA letter for each different sound.

Three Types of Writing Systems

There are three basic types of writing systems: *logographic,* or word writing, *syllabic* writing, and *alphabetic* writing. Syllabic writing has a symbol for each syllable, while alphabetic writing has a symbol for each distinct sound in the language. The word *Hebrew* has two syllables *(He-brew)* and so would require two signs in a syllabic system. The word *Greek* has only one syllable and so would be represented by a single sign in that type of system. Sometimes a fourth system is recognized: *consonantal* writing. We will treat it as a subset of an alphabetic system.

The traditional characters of Chinese (Mandarin) are an example of a logographic writing system. Each symbol represents an idea rather than a sound or a group of sounds. This is something like the use of an octagonal sign at an intersection to indicate that a vehicle should stop. In English the sign says "Stop." Speakers of other languages can "read" the sign even though they would say a different word. The symbols used for numbers are another example of logographs. The symbol *2* means two in English, *zwei* in German, *šnayim* in Hebrew, and so forth. Symbol-based writing allows Mandarin and Cantonese speakers to communicate through writing, even though they would not necessarily be able to understand each other if they spoke. Japanese *kanji* is also an example of logographic writing.

A few languages of the world, including the Japanese *katakana* and *hiragana* systems, use symbols to indicate groups of sounds. One symbol represents one syllable. Thus the word *o-ha-yo* in Japanese would have three symbols, one for each syllable. The Native American language Cherokee also has this kind of syllabary or syllabic writing.

The most common writing system is the alphabet. English, Hebrew, and

10. The SBL system does not show a difference between normal Greek vowels and vowels with a *iota* subscript. For example, *ō* is used for both ω and ῳ.

Greek all use an alphabet. The guiding principle of an alphabet is that one symbol represents one sound. We realize, of course, that English is a poor example of this principle. For one thing, English has only twenty-six symbols (letters), but it has around forty-two sounds in any given dialect. We end up with multiple ways of writing the same sound. For example, the sounds in the word *sea* are represented in other ways in *see, seize,* and *cease.* English also has changed the pronunciation of words over the years but normally left the spelling the same. Thus, we now have "silent" letters in *knife* and *night,* even though older forms of English pronounced each of these letters. Fortunately, the Hebrew and Greek writing systems are not as irregular as English.

As we look at Hebrew and Greek, we will need to appreciate the fact that their alphabets are not an exact fit between the sounds and the symbols. Some sounds actually have more than one symbol (in English, *c/k/ck* all representing the same sound); some symbols have more than one sound (like English *c* in *cease/crease*). We will see that Hebrew and Greek also changed through time, even as English has, and that some words that were once pronounced differently ended up sounding the same (like English *main/mane*).

The alphabet of Hebrew differs from that of Greek and English in that it represents only the consonant sounds of a word. Traditionally, the reader had to figure out the right vowel sounds from the context. As we will see, though, in its later stages writers of Hebrew did develop ways to represent the vowels.

Table 2.3 shows how these four writing systems represent spoken language. Note that Hebrew, Greek, and English all use a system of symbols to represent individual sounds. Our task then is to understand what sound(s) each symbol represents.

The Sounds of Language

To learn the sounds of Hebrew and Greek, you need to think about the various types of sounds in these languages and how they are similar or dissimilar from those in your dialect of English. Fortunately, of all the possible noises humans can make, only a relatively small number are actually used in speech. Unfortunately for some learners, some of the Hebrew sounds are not similar to sounds they already use in English. Why is it important to learn how to pronounce Hebrew and Greek as well as to learn their written symbols?

Table 2.3: Summary of Writing Systems

Writing system	Languages	Strategy	Benefits	Drawbacks
Word-based *logograph*	Chinese Japanese *kanji*	One character = one concept	Different languages can communicate via the same writing system	Readers must recognize thousands of symbols
Syllable-based *syllabary*	Japanese *katakana* and *hiragana*	One character = one syllable	Works well with limited syllable patterns	Not useful in languages with complex syllable patterns
Sound-based *alphabet*	**Greek** **English** Russian Korean	One character = one sound	Easy to learn	Spelling difficulties due to dialect or historical changes
Consonant-based *alphabet*	**Hebrew** Arabic	One character = one consonant sound	Easy to learn	Readers must supply correct vowels

- Languages are learned through speaking, hearing, reading, and writing. You will want to approach the language through as many avenues of learning as possible.
- It is easier to remember a written symbol if you have a pronunciation to attach to it.
- It is easier to remember a word if you have a pronunciation to attach to it.

All human languages use a small set of ways to make speech sounds. We can talk about these sounds more intelligently if we consider just what parts of the mouth (and throat) are used to make the sounds of English, Hebrew, and Greek. In fact, knowing how the sounds are made will help you pronounce them more accurately. You actually already know a lot about how sounds are made. The following notes will give you a few more technical terms we will use in the rest of the chapter.

To understand how speech sounds are made, it is helpful to look at the parts of the mouth and throat that are used. Figure 2.1 shows a cross section of a face with the main places where consonants are made. (We will look at vowels later.)

Figure 2.1: The Speech Apparatus

Places of Articulation

1. Lips—Labial
2. Teeth—Dental
3. Alveolar Ridge—Alveolar
4. Hard Palate—Palatal
5. Soft Palate/Velum—Velar
6. Uvula—Uvular
7. Pharynx—Pharyngeal
8. Glottis—Glottal

Parts of the Tongue

a. Tip
b. Blade
c. Back
d. Root

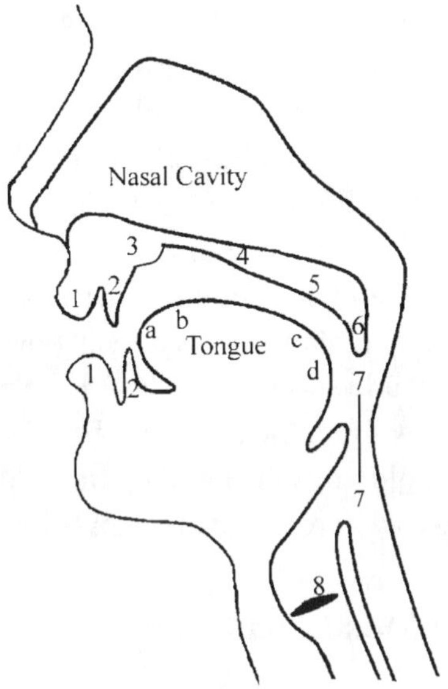

If we start on the left side, at the front of the mouth, we see the lips. (And you thought this was going to be hard.) The sounds made with two lips are called **bilabial**. Just behind the lips, of course, are the teeth. Sounds made with the top teeth touching the bottom lip (you can try it the other way round if you really want to) are called **labiodental** sounds. Sounds made with the tongue between the teeth are **interdental** sounds. The next position along the top of the chart, the alveolar ridge, may be new to you. This is the "bump" just behind your top teeth. Since many sounds are made in this area of the mouth, you will see the word *alveolar* a lot. It is pronounced "al-vee-OH-ler." Behind the alveolar ridge is your hard palate. (Yes, you can check to see if it really is hard. Try tapping your finger against it.) Sounds made on or near the hard palate are called **palatal**. There are also sounds made halfway between the alveolar ridge and the hard palate called **alveopalatals**. Moving back farther in the mouth, we come across the soft palate (yes, it is soft), or velum. Sounds made in this area are called **velar** sounds. About as far back as we can go in the mouth is the uvula (pronounced YOU-view-lah). Some languages make sounds in this area of the mouth; they are called **uvular** (pronounced YOU-view-ler) sounds.

We also must think about several areas inside the throat because some sounds are made there. Actually, the first sound we will discuss has no sound. Sometimes we "make" a sound by stopping the air that is coming out of our lungs by closing the glottis. The glottis is the gap between the vocal folds. You do this every time you hold your breath. The sound is called a **glottal stop.** This is the sound in the middle of *uh-oh.* Above the glottis is the pharynx. Hebrew has two **pharyngeal** sounds, at least in Classical Hebrew. Your teacher will tell you how to deal with these sounds.

The other, and most important, part of the speech mechanism is the tongue. The majority of consonants and all vowels involve some part of the tongue. When we study speech sounds, it is helpful to distinguish which area of the tongue is involved: the tip, blade, back, or root.

You should consult the diagram of the face and the parts of the speech apparatus as you read the material below.

How We Make Consonants

One way to look at sounds is to think of the difference between consonants and vowels. English has about forty-two sounds. The exact number actually differs from one dialect to another. Of these forty-two sounds, most are consonants; the rest are vowels. Vowels are sounds such as *a, e, i, o,* and *u* in English. Think of when the doctor asks you to say "ah" in order to look at the back of your throat. This vowel sound is much better for that purpose than a sound such as *p, t,* or *k* (all consonants). When we make vowel sounds, our tongue doesn't touch anything else in our mouth, and the air we use to make the sound is not stopped or limited in any way. When we talk about vowels, we will use a different set of terms than when we discuss consonants because they are made in different ways. The tables in the following section show the basic consonants and vowels of English. We will start with consonants because they are easier to identify.

We can identify consonants by *where* and *how* the sound is made. The columns of a consonant chart indicate *where* the sound is made. These locations are called places of articulation and have technical names (bilabial, labiodental, etc.) that will help you understand where the sounds are made in the mouth. The names of the columns on the chart relate to the face diagram we just studied. Sounds on the left side of the chart are produced in the front of the mouth (e.g., bilabial sounds) and sounds more to the right are produced further back.

Table 2.4: Where Consonants Are Made in the Mouth and Throat

<table>
<tr><th>Bilabial</th><th>Labiodental</th><th>Interdental</th><th>Alveolar</th><th>Velar</th></tr>
<tr><td>Two lips touch</td><td>Top teeth touch bottom lip</td><td>Tip of tongue is placed between the teeth</td><td>Tip of tongue on or near alveolar ridge</td><td>Back of tongue on or near soft palate (velum)</td></tr>
<tr><td>p b m</td><td>f v</td><td>th</td><td>t d n s z r l</td><td>k g ng</td></tr>
<tr><td colspan="4" rowspan="3">We have modified the usual simple row and column form of this chart into the shape you see here to more clearly indicate that the glottal sounds are made down within the throat, not in the mouth itself.

Also note that the names of the sound types come from their location (bilabial means "two lips," labiodental means "lip and teeth," and interdental means "between teeth").</td><th>Glottal</th></tr>
<tr><td>Space between the vocal folds</td></tr>
<tr><td>h
ʔ (the "sound" in the middle of "uh-oh")</td></tr>
</table>

The first three consonants, *p, b,* and *m,* are all made with both lips touching. All three sounds are formed at that position in the mouth, but there are also differences that distinguish them. These differences fall under the category of *how* the sounds are made rather than *where* they are made. Table 2.5 shows the intersection between the *how* and the *where* questions for each consonant sound. Other positions for making English consonant sounds include the point where the front upper teeth touch the lower lip (labiodental), where the tip of the tongue rests between the teeth (interdental), where the tip of the tongue rests or comes near the area just behind the top front teeth (alveolar), where the tongue rests against or comes near the roof of the mouth toward the back (velar), and where the sound is made as air passes through the vocal folds found in the "voice box," or larynx (behind the "Adam's apple").

As we expand the table of English consonants (table 2.6), remember that the rows indicate *how* the sounds are made. These rows also have technical names such as *stop, fricative,* and so on. Even as the order for the columns signifies moving from the front to the back of the mouth and into the throat, so the order of the rows is significant: sounds toward the top of the table obstruct the airstream more than sounds toward the bottom of the table. Thus, the very top line contains the stop sounds. A stop sound consists of two parts. The air is first completely blocked at the point where the consonant is made and then suddenly released in an "explosion" of air. Because of the sudden release, stops are sometimes also called **plosives.** **Fricatives** allow air to keep escaping and are lower on the chart; **glides** hardly impede the air at all, and are on the very bottom. In fact, the glide consonants are very similar to vowels in this regard. Some people refer to the glides as "semivowels."

Table 2.5: How Consonants Are Made

Sound-Making Process	Description	Example Letters in English
Stop	Air is completely stopped (for at least a moment).	p t k b d g
Nasal	Air is stopped in the mouth, but escapes through the nose.	m n ng
Fricative	Air comes out through a narrow opening.	f s h v z
Affricate	A stop followed by a fricative.	ch (church) j (John)
Lateral	Air comes out over the sides of the tongue.	l
Liquid	Air comes out over the center of the tongue.	r
Glide	Almost a vowel sound, but shorter.	w y

When we put the columns (location) and rows (type of sound) of consonant sounds together, we arrive at table 2.6. We will use symbols from the International Phonetic Alphabet (IPA) rather than English letters because these symbols are internationally understood and are more accurate than using English, Hebrew, or Greek letters to represent particular sounds. Once you learn to recognize these IPA symbols, you can use them to study Hebrew, Greek, or any other language.

Note one more factor: some sounds are **voiceless** and others are **voiced.** This refers to the vibrations of the vocal folds. In sounds such as *v* and *z*, the vocal folds vibrate. These are voiced sounds. Sounds such as *f* and *s* are voiceless. You can determine this for yourself by holding your fingers to your voice box (or near your "Adam's apple") while making the sound. For a voiced consonant, such as *z*, you should be able to feel the vibration.

Table 2.6: Pronouncing English Consonants (Using IPA Symbols)

	Bilabial	Interdental	Labiodental	Alveolar	Palatal	Velar	Glottal
Stop							
Voiceless	p			t		k	ʔ (uh-oh)
Voiced	b			d		g	
Nasal	m			n		ŋ	
Fricative							
Voiceless		θ (thing)	f				
Voiced		ð (the)	v				
Sibilant[11]							
Voiceless				s	ʃ (sh)		
Voiced				z	ʒ (azure)		
Affricate							
Voiceless				ts	tʃ (chap)		
Voiced				dz	dʒ (Joe)		
Liquid				l ɹ			
Glide	w				j (you)		

11. We use the term *sibilant* to distinguish the alveolar and palatal fricatives from other fricative sounds. Your textbook may use other terms.

How We Make Vowels

When we study vowels we need to use a different set of tools. Vowels do not have clear-cut locations such as bilabial or interdental. Vowels do not restrict the air coming out of the mouth the same way that consonants do. Vowels also last relatively longer than consonants. For example, if you say the *ee* sound of *seen* followed by the *ah* sound the doctor likes to hear and keep saying them faster, you will soon be saying *yah.* The *y* sound [j] is a palatal consonant; the *ee* sound is called a vowel. We write the *ee* sound with an [i] in phonetic writing. This same phenomenon occurs between the consonant [w] and the vowel [u].[12]

The vowel chart is divided by how **high** or **low** a vowel is and by whether it is made more toward the **front** or the **back** of the mouth. In fact, all the vowels of English are formed between the palatal and velar areas of the mouth, a rather small space. (See figure 2.1.) Some vowels are considered high *(i, u),* and others are low *(a).* There are also **mid** vowels that are made between these two polar extremes. We can also see that some vowels are made in the front of the mouth *(i, e)* and others in the back *(u, o).* The chart also indicates vowels made in between the front and the back as **central.**

Table 2.7: Pronouncing English Vowels (Using IPA Symbols)

	Front	**Central**	**Back**
High	i "r*ee*d" ɪ "r*i*d"		u "f*oo*d" ʊ "f*oo*t"
Mid	e "r*ai*d" ɛ "r*e*d"	ʌ "r*u*g" (ə "*a*bout")	o "f*oe*" ɔ "f*ough*t'
Low	æ "r*a*d"	a "r*o*d"	

You can feel the movement from high to low if you repeat the following sets of words:

- *reed* [i]
- *rid* [ɪ]
- *raid* [e]

12. A sound placed in square brackets [ ] indicates its actual pronunciation. Hence IPA symbols are used to represent it.

- *red* [ɛ]
- *rad* [æ]

Say just the vowel sounds in these words, and notice how your tongue moves away from the roof of your mouth. You may want to look in a mirror while you do this.

You can feel the movement from front to back if you repeat the following sets of words:

- *feed* *food*
- *raid* *road*

Say just the vowel sounds of these words again, and pay attention to where your tongue is. If you look in a mirror, you should be able to see the front-to-back movement, but when you say the *u* sound, your lips will automatically start to close into a round shape. We call this lip movement *rounding*; the back vowels of English [u, ʊ, o, ɔ] are rounded.

Note: Have you noticed that most of the dialect differences in English involve the vowels? The symbols in table 2.7 can be used to show the different pronunciations in English dialects (British versus American, Texan versus Midwest, etc.). The word *roof,* for example, is pronounced differently in some areas. Some people use the same vowel sound as in *f<u>oo</u>d,* and others use the one in *f<u>oo</u>t.* The IPA symbols for these different pronunciations of *roof* are [ruf]and [rʊf] respectively

When we look at Hebrew and Greek, we will return to these charts of English sounds so that we can learn to make the sounds that are different.

The Sounds of Hebrew

Suppose you were from another country and spoke a foreign language and had no written resources to read about English. How would you go about discovering what the sounds of English are? Which of the following might help you the most: a camera, a record player, or a tape recorder? Would your answer be the same if you were trying to find out about the sounds of an ancient language, like the Hebrew used during the time the Old Testament was written? It can be a challenge to know exactly how letters written in an ancient document sounded. Anyone who has ever studied old literary works in English, such as *Beowulf* or Chaucer's *Canterbury Tales,* knows that the English sounds (and spellings!) have changed considerably over the centuries. The sounds of Hebrew also changed some over time.

How might the following activities help you to discover the ancient pronunciation of Hebrew?

- a visit to a Jewish synagogue
- taping an Israeli reading the book of Genesis
- reading a book about linguistics
- comparing several ancient Hebrew manuscripts of the Bible from different periods of time to see if there are differences between them

As you read through the remainder of the chapter, see if you can discover some insights to help you answer this question.

Getting Started in Reading Hebrew Consonants

Learning how to read and write Hebrew presents some challenges right from the start. Since we don't have tape recordings from the biblical period, we have to rely on various kinds of indirect evidence to decide how the letters were pronounced. Most recent textbooks on biblical Hebrew advocate pronouncing the letters the way people say them in Modern Hebrew, but that leads to some issues that English speakers face when comparing pronunciation with spelling. For example, how is it that English letters like *c* or *g* have more than one pronunciation *(cat* versus *cease* or *get* versus *gem)*? Or that certain combinations involve silent letters, as in *through* or *knight?* Modern Hebrew has combined some sounds into one (*tet* and *tav* both have a *t* sound; *samekh* and *sin* both have the *s* sound), and other letters sometimes become silent *(aleph* and *ayin).*

The Easiest Sounds

The best place to start learning the Hebrew letters is with the sixteen consonant sounds that are most similar to English sounds. Table 2.8 presents a list of these Hebrew consonants with the English sounds following.[13]

13. With some of these letters, the overlap with the English sound is only approximate. For the complete set of Hebrew consonants, see table 2.1.

Table 2.8: Hebrew Consonants with English Correspondents

Hebrew Consonant	English Consonant[14]	Letter Name
ב	b	bet
ג	g	gimel
ד	d	dalet
ה	h	he
ז	z	zayin
י	y	yod
כ ך	k	kaph
ל	l	lamed
מ ם	m	mem
נ ן	n	nun
ס	s	samekh
פ ף	p	pe
ק	k	qoph
ר	r	resh
שׁ	sh	shin
ת	t	tav

We can use these Hebrew consonants to form English words. There are two differences: we do not write any vowels, and Hebrew is written right to left, so it is necessary to reverse the order. Thus,

- *bed*→remove the vowel→*bd*→reverse the order→*db*→בד
- *peg*→remove the vowel→*pg*→reverse the order→*gp*→פג
- *lament*→remove the vowels→*lmnt*→reverse the order→*tnml*→למנת

Table 2.9 shows how Hebrew letters can be used to write English words. Can you think of other words that the letters might represent? Remember,

14. Not the SBL transliteration symbol but the closest equivalent English sound. Cf. table 2.1.

there may be other vowels that could be used to form words with the same consonants.

Table 2.9: Hebrew Letters Used to Write English Words

Hebrew Word (right to left)	מב	פר	סת	ית	גד	דג	דר	זבר	בלנק
Correspond-ing English Consonants (right to left)	bm	rp	ts	ty	dg	gd	rd	rbz	knlb
English Word	mob	par	sit	yet	good	dog	door	zebra	blank

What English words do you think the following could represent?

פפר ____________________ לסת ____________________

בג ____________________ דת ____________________

Six Less Familiar Consonants

The other six letters of the Hebrew alphabet (there are twenty-two letters in all) either are linked to sounds that English speakers don't have or that have undergone some changes over time or both. The details are not important for this book, but we will give a brief overview of some of the most salient features for beginning students of Hebrew.

א

The consonant *aleph* (א) in early Hebrew always had the sound of a glottal stop (IPA ʔ, SBL ʾ, the sound heard in the middle of "uh-oh"). In modern Israeli Hebrew, though, it normally has no sound at all, although in certain circumstances the glottal stop will still be heard.

ו

The *waw* (ו) had the sound of *w* but has shifted to a *v* sound in Modern

Hebrew. You may have noticed that we labeled this sound *vav/waw* in table 2.1 to reflect this change.

ח

The modern sound of *chet* (ח) can be described as a voiceless velar fricative (previously made in the throat). Notice that it looks a lot like *he* (ה) yet with a slight difference. *Chet* has the sound of *ch* in Scottish *loch* or the "hard" sound in German *acht* "eight." Since you now know that velar sounds are made by placing the back part of the tongue near the soft palate (as in *k* and *g* in English), you can try to make this velar fricative sound by saying *aka* several times and then making the middle consonant a fricative sound instead of a stop. It will sound something like a rough *h* sound, but your tongue should be in the same position as it was for *k*. In the IPA system, *chet* is written [x], and it is *ḥ* in the SBL system. The ancient sound was most probably a voiceless pharyngeal fricative, [ħ] in IPA.

ט

The *tet* (ט) currently has the same sound as *tav* (ת), though in biblical times it was slightly different. You can use the English *t* sound for both Hebrew letters.

ע

The original sound of the *ayin* (ע) was a pharyngeal (in the pharynx) fricative, but in Modern Hebrew it is treated very much like the *aleph* (i.e., it is not pronounced or has the sound between "uh-oh"). A pharyngeal sound is made by pulling the root of the tongue back toward the back of the throat (pharynx). English, of course, does not use this sound. It may remind you of choking, but it was a normal speech sound in biblical Hebrew. Again, it is a voiced fricative, so it will sound like a rough or hoarse *h* but with the vocal chords vibrating.

צ

The *tsade* (צ) now has the sound of the affricate *ts* as in the English word *ca*ts, though previously it was a special type of *s* sound.

ש

Finally, the single letter *shin* (ש) can stand for two sounds. One sound is the same as the English *sh (<u>sh</u>oe)*. The SBL symbol is *š;* IPA is [ʃ]. The other sound is difficult to describe. (It is somewhat rare.) It is represented in the SBL system by *ś*, and overlaps in sound with *samekh* (ס) in Modern Hebrew. It was probably a **lateralized** sibilant (IPA [ɬ]) in ancient times. (A lateralized sound is made by forcing the air out over the sides of the tongue rather than across the middle as in a standard *s* sound in English). How do you decide if the sound will be *sh* or *s*? The choice is determined by the word it is in. Thus, *šaʿar* means "gate," while *śaʿar* means "hair." Both words are spelled alike, but scribes who copied the Hebrew Bible by hand during the Middle Ages clarified the choice by placing a dot above the letter. A dot above the right side (שׁ) marks the sound *sh (š)*, while the dot on the left side (שׂ) marks the sound *s (ś)*. Here are the words *gate* and *hair* as they would appear in the Hebrew Bible (without vowels): שׁער—"gate"; שׂער—"hair."

Adding the Vowels in Hebrew

You will want to learn to pronounce the Hebrew vowels according to the way your instructor recommends, but we will mention several facts about Hebrew vowels that will help you learn the details. Even though Hebrew was written originally without vowels, certain Hebrew scribes of the Middle Ages known as "Masoretes" developed a complex system for writing down every slight variation of vowel sounds that they heard when the Hebrew Bible was read in the synagogue. Most writing systems are not so complex when it comes to written symbols for vowels. For example, the English *a* has different sounds in *f<u>a</u>ther, h<u>a</u>d,* and *b<u>a</u>ke.* The system developed by the Masoretes was unlike English in that each vowel symbol tends to represent only a single sound.

The Masoretes distinguished eight vowels in terms of their sound, that is, by the high/low and front/back distinctions illustrated in table 2.7. Table 2.10 shows the approximate value of these eight Masoretic vowels. The SBL transliteration is shown in parentheses. In Modern Hebrew there are seven vowels, including the phonetic sound [ɛ] but not [æ]; also, the low back [ɑ] has shifted to a low central [a].

Classifying vowels as we have done thus far is often called *vowel quality.* Another way to distinguish vowels is by their relative length or *quantity.* Most grammars of biblical Hebrew also classify the vowels as long or short (based on data about the history of the language), but strictly speaking that should

Table 2.10: The Hebrew Vowels as Pronounced by the Masoretes

	Front	Central	Back
High	i *reed* (i)		u *food* (u)
Mid	e *raid* (ē) ɛ *red* (e)	ə *rug* (ĕ)	o *foe* (o)
Low	æ *rad* (a)		ɑ *pod* (ā)[15]

refer only to how long a vowel is given its sound and not to differences in quality. The Masoretes had three additional signs to represent the phonetic sounds [æ], [ɛ], or [ɑ] when they have a very short and quick sound, but otherwise the Masoretic system was based on vowel quality, not quantity.

At an early stage in the history of Hebrew (long before the Masoretes), writers began to use the letter *w* (ו) to stand for the vowel *u* or *o* and the letter *y* (י) to represent *i* or *e*. Thus:

- English *mood* or *mode* could be written *mwd* (מוד).
- English *beet* or *bait* could be written *byt* (בית).

When the Masoretes developed their system for adding vowels to Hebrew manuscripts, they used very small dots and dashes placed above or below a consonant letter to show the vowel sound that would follow that letter (from right to left in the Hebrew form). You will have to look very closely to see these small symbols. We will enlarge the size of the Hebrew examples to help you get started. Here are a few of their symbols with examples (the English equivalent is in parentheses to aid with pronunciation):

- The low back vowel [ɑ] (indicated by *ā* in the SBL system) was a symbol resembling a *t* placed below the consonant:

  מָ = *mā* ("ma"); פָּ = *pā* ("pa")

15. The sound is uncertain. See the chart in the back of Shelomo Morag's book, *The Vocalization Systems of Arabic, Hebrew, and Aramaic: Their Phonetic and Phonemic Principles* (The Netherlands: Mouton & Co., 1962).

- The high front vowel [i] (as in *machine*) was a single dot placed below the consonant.

  מִ = *mi* (“me”); פִּ = *pi* (“pea”); סִ = *si* (“see”)

- The front mid vowel [e] (as in *raid* but without the glide into the [i] sound) was two dots aligned horizontally and placed below the consonant (*ē* in SBL):

  מֵ = *mē* (“may”); פֵּ = *pē* (“pay”); סֵ = *sē* (“say”)

- The back mid vowel [o] (as in *boat* but without the glide into the [u] sound) was a dot placed on the upper left corner of the letter (*ō* in SBL):

  מֹ = *mō* (“Moe”); פֹּ = *pō* (“Poe”); סֹ = *sō* (“so”)

Now you try it. Write the sounds (SBL system) that the following represent:

מָ = *mā*

בִ = ____

דֵ = ____

הָ = ____

כֵ = ____

What happens in the Masoretic system if the word has a *yod* (י) that represents *i* or *e* or a *waw* (ו) for *u* or *o*? In the case of the *yod* (י), the Masoretic symbols for *i* or *e* occur under the consonant, and the *yod* follows with no sign under it. If *yod* is a consonant, then a Masoretic vowel symbol will be placed under it:

כִּי = *kî* (“key”)

נֵי = *nê* ("nay")

יֵי = *yê* ("yea")

In the SBL system the circumflex (^) is used whenever the vowel letter is used. That is, *i* means the vowel *i* with no vowel letter, but *î* means the vowel *i* followed by a *yod.*

If a *waw* (ו) represents the vowel *o*, a dot is placed on top of it for the Hebrew vowel (וֹ); if it stands for *u*, then a dot occurs within it to the left (וּ):

מוּ = *mû* ("moo")

מוֹ = *mô* ("Moe")

You try it:

דֵי = ___

סִי = ___

הוּ = ___

לוֹ = ___

If the last sound in a Hebrew word is the vowel sound [ɑ] (SBL *ā*) as in *p<u>o</u>d,* an *h* may be added to the end of the word to show the vowel, and the previous consonant will have the Masoretic sign for the vowel *ā.* Sarah's name (after it was changed by God) is spelled like this in Masoretic Hebrew:

שָׂרָה

Even though the English spelling often includes the final *h* (Hebrew letter *he*), it is really standing only for the phonetic vowel sound [ɑ]. The transliteration, following the SBL system, is *Śārâ,* the symbol *â,* showing that the word ends with a *he* that represents a vowel, not a consonant.[16]

---

16. SBL system: Masoretic *patach* ([a] as in *h<u>a</u>d*) is *a;* Masoretic *qamets* ([ɑ] as in *p<u>o</u>d*) is *ā;* and Masoretic *qamets* followed by *he* as a vowel indicator is *â.* The vowel *â* can occur only at the end of a word.

With a word like *sûs* or *kōl,* the last letter in the word has no vowel. These words are written like this in the Masoretic system:

- *sûs* = סוּס
- *kōl* = כֹּל.

Table 2.11: The Pronunciation of Hebrew Vowel Letters (Using IPA Symbols)

	Front	Central	Back
High	i = אִי[17]		u = וּ
Mid	e = אֵי		o = וֹ
Low			ɑ = אָה

Classroom Pronunciation

Once you start your study of Hebrew, your instructor will tell you how to pronounce these letters. Some teachers prefer to use the pronunciation of Masoretic Hebrew (how it sounded in synagogues during the Middle Ages); others like to follow Modern Hebrew pronunciation as closely as possible. There are arguments for and against either choice; the important thing is to learn one system well and follow it in your beginning study of Hebrew. You can always learn about alternate pronunciation systems later.

Letters Can Have More Than One Sound

Another thing you need to remember is that the sounds of a language do not always have a single fixed form. Sometimes a sound will be changed by the sounds that are before or after it. For example, the sound *t* in the English phrase *got you* is often pronounced *ch* as in *got chew* in the informal language, but the *t* in *got milk* would not change. Can you see the reason why? (Look at table 2.6 and see where the *ch* [tʃ] sound is in relation to the *t* and *y* [j] sounds.) Even though we often make this change, we prefer to keep the written form the same. This is also true in Hebrew. The letter *b* in Hebrew can sound more like a *v* in certain situations. *Babylon* is spelled *bbl* in Hebrew but sounds like "bavel"

---

17. The *aleph* (א) has been added to three of the vowels to show how the corresponding Masoretic vowel sign fits; it is not part of the vowel.

(cf. "Babel"). Can you think of a reason why the second *b* changes to a *v* sound in this situation? You will encounter other similar phenomena once you begin your study of Hebrew.

Classical Hebrew Versus Modern Hebrew

Hebrew pronunciation has changed over the years, as we will discuss in chapter 7 about language change. Table 2.12 shows how the Hebrew vowels appeared in various stages of Hebrew, including modern Israeli Hebrew.

Table 2.12: The Historic Representation of the Hebrew Vowels

Hebrew Word Transliterated (SBL)	***kôl***	***dibbēr***	***lôʾ* or *lōʾ***
ca. 1000 B.C.	כל	דבר	לא
Dead Sea Scrolls (ca. 200 B.C.–A.D. 135)	כול or כל	דיבר or דבר	לוא or לא
Masoretic Text (ca. A.D. 1000)	כֹּל	דִּבֶּר	לוֹא or לֹא
Modern Newspaper	כול	דיבר or דבר	לוא or לא
English Equivalent	all, every	he spoke	no, not

The time line starts with the earliest stage at the top row and the most recent near the bottom. The top row gives the word's pronunciation according to the SBL transliteration from the Masoretic vowels. The SBL system is used because it is rapidly becoming a standard in all publications related to the Bible, including studies in Greek and Hebrew. If you read transliterated Hebrew in commentaries or journal articles, it will most likely be in the SBL form. Remember: the SBL system helps you to see exactly which Hebrew or Greek letter is used; the IPA system shows you exact pronunciation. Also remember that although the transliterated forms are read from left to right the Hebrew words are read from right to left.

Table 2.13 shows the classical pronunciation of the Hebrew consonants as depicted in a linguistic chart of consonants according to place of articulation in the mouth, manner of articulation, and the factors of voicing and **velarization.** Velarization occurs when the back part of the tongue touches the back part of the roof of the mouth (velum). For the pronunciation of modern Hebrew, see table 2.1.

Table 2.13: Classical Hebrew Pronunciation (Using IPA and Hebrew Letters)

	Bilabial	Alveolar	Palatal	Velar	Pharyn-geal	Glottal
Stop						
Voiceless	p פּ	t תּ	c כּ	k ק		ʔ א
Voiced	b בּ	d ד		g ג		
Velarized		tˠ ט				
Nasal	m מ	n נ				
Fricative						
Voiceless					ħ ח	h ה
Voiced					ʕ ע	
Sibilant						
Voiceless		s ס	ʃ שׁ			
Voiced		z ז				
Velarized		sˠ צ				
Lateralized		ɬ שׂ				
Liquid		l ל ɹ ר[18]				
Glide	w ו		j י			

Transliterated Hebrew

English letters can be used to transliterate the sixteen Hebrew letters with sounds that overlap English. We could use the IPA symbols for the additional letters, but since most students are probably not familiar with IPA, the system recommended by the Society for Biblical Literature (SBL) will be used instead. Most textbooks use a similar system. Table 2.1 includes both the SBL and the IPA symbols, the Hebrew letter, and the name of the letter. The letters follow the order of the Hebrew alphabet. You will need to learn this order to find words in dictionaries.

Five of the Hebrew letters have two shapes. The one to the right of the slash (in table 2.1) in each case represents a final form. This is the way the letter looks when it occurs at the end of a word (i.e., the far left). There is no need to

18. The IPA symbol [ɹ] represents the sound used in the beginning of such English words as *run* and *red*.

Table 2.14: Transliteration of Hebrew Vowels

Masoretic Name	SBL Transliteration	IPA Transliteration (Modern Hebrew)
Chireq	i	i
Chireq-Yod	î	i
Tsere	ē	e
Tsere-Yod	ê	e
Segol	e	ɛ
Chateph-Segol	ĕ	ɛ
Qamets	ā	ɑ
Qamets-He	â	ɑ
Patach	a	ɑ
Chateph-Patach	ă	ɑ
Shureq	û	u
Qibbuts	u	u
Cholem	ō	o
Qamets-Chatuph	o	o
Chateph-Qamets	ŏ	o
Shewa (vocal)	ĕ	ə

distinguish final forms in transliteration, since they are always at the end of a word. They may be followed by a vowel, though. Thus סוּסֶךָ is transliterated as *sûsekā.*

Actually, the nonfinal, or "medial," forms of the letters appeared later in history than the final forms. Two forces may have worked in tandem to bring about the use of an alternate form of certain letters. One would be the tendency to write an individual word quickly. This led to forms that were more easily drawn within each word. At the end of the word, there would be a natural tendency to pause anyway. The second force would be the need to distinguish the ends of words. Many Hebrew words end with one of these five letters that have a distinctive final form, so having a distinct shape at the end of the word clearly demarcates where one word ended and another began. A quick survey showed forty-one instances of a word with one of these final letters out of the 115 words in Genesis 1:1–10. That is, about 36 percent of the words end with a final form of the letter. This contrasts with Greek, where only the letter *sigma* has a final form (σ is medial, ς is final).

In the rest of the book, the vowels of the Masoretic system will be transliterated according to the SBL system. The IPA symbol will be used when there is a need to represent the pronunciation according to modern Israeli Hebrew (Sephardi). As was mentioned above, the Masoretic system has many more symbols for vowels than is normally expected in a writing system. English has only six *(a, e, i, o, u, y)* and Greek only seven (see table 2.16), while the Masoretic vowel system for Hebrew has a total of eleven signs plus additional combinations with the letters *yod, waw,* or *he.*

The Sounds of Greek

The Greek of the New Testament is now about two thousand years away from our present day. Once again, as with Hebrew, we will consider how the language may have sounded a long time ago and compare that with the writing system. As with Hebrew it is difficult to go back in time to determine the exact pronunciation of New Testament Greek. You can also imagine that since Greek was a widely used language at the time of the New Testament, people also had different ways of pronouncing words, much as the pronunciation of English varies from New York to Texas to London to New Delhi. We can, however, still hear Greek spoken in the ancient rites of a Greek Orthodox church service and hear Modern Greek in many areas of the world.

In one sense Greek letters are already more familiar to most English speakers than Hebrew letters since they are often used in mathematics, logic, and even in the names of fraternities and sororities. Even our English word *alphabet* reminds us of the names of the first two letters of the Greek alphabet: *alpha* and *beta.*

Greek has twenty-five letters: eighteen consonants and seven vowels. As with English and Hebrew, the Greek letters do not all have only one sound per letter; some letters have more than one sound. At least that was true for Classical Greek. Under the modern system of pronunciation that many teachers follow, most of the letters have only one sound.

You will need to learn the order of the Greek alphabet in order to find words in dictionaries. Fortunately, the majority of the letters appear in the same order as you are used to in English.

Getting Started in Reading Greek Consonants

Since you have seen most Greek letters already somewhere in your education, we will start with the small (lowercase) and capital (uppercase) consonants. These are found in table 2.15.

The only additional element to the table concerns the consonant *h*. It has a shape in Greek that resembles an opening single quote mark (ʽ) and it may be added above a vowel that starts a word.[19] If a vowel starts a word without an *h* sound, then a separate sign, ʼ, appears above the vowel.[20] Here are some examples:

- ἀγαπη: *agapē,* "love"
- ἁγιος: *hagios,* "holy"
- Ἠλιας: *Ēlias,* "Elias" (Elijah)
- Ἡρωδης: *Hērōdēs,* "Herod"

Table 2.15 shows the IPA symbol for each of the Greek consonants as they are spoken in Modern Greek. The lowercase letters are followed by the uppercase, separated by the slash. The pronunciation of Greek during New Testament times was different, but few teachers use these older pronunciations in class.

The Vowels of Greek

The Greek letters that are used for vowels are also familiar to English speakers. In table 2.16 the lowercase Greek letter is on the left followed by the uppercase form.

Already by the time of the New Testament, some of the Greek vowels had merged into a single vowel. Most teachers of Greek will recommend various ways to distinguish the different vowels in pronunciation, making it easier to hear the difference between words. For the sake of completeness, we will give here the full range of vowels as they existed historically, but it will not be important for the beginning student to try to connect each vowel (shown by its IPA symbol) with a specific Greek letter.

---

19. It will appear to the left of an uppercase vowel. Some grammars call this sign a *rough breathing* mark, as in <u>wh</u>*enever.*
20. Some grammars call this sign a *smooth breathing* mark.

Table 2.15: Greek Consonants (Classroom Pronunciation with IPA Symbols)

	Bilabial	Inter-dental	Labio-dental	Alveolar	Palatal	Velar	Glottal
Stop							
Voiceless	**p** π / Π			**t** τ / T		**k** κ / K	
Voiced	**b** β / B			**d** δ / Δ		**g** γ / Γ	
Nasal	**m** μ / M			**n** ν / N			
Fricative							
Voiceless		**θ** θ / Θ	**f** φ / Φ			**χ** χ / X	**h** ῾
Voiced							
Sibilant							
Voiceless				**s** σ / Σ			
Voiced							
Affricate[21]	**ps** ψ / Ψ			**dz** ζ / Z		**ks** ξ / Ξ	
Liquid				**l** λ / Λ **ɹ**[22] ρ / P			
Glide	**w** υ / Υ				**j** ι / I		

Table 2.16: Greek Letters for the Vowels

English Letter	Greek Letter	Name of Greek Vowel	SBL Transliteration
a	α / A	alpha	a
e	ϵ / E	epsilon	e
e	η / H	eta	ē
i	ι / I	iota	i
o	ο / O	omicron	o
o	ω / Ω	omega	ō
u	υ / Υ	upsilon	u

21. An affricate is a combination of a stop and a fricative. We use the term here in its broadest sense. Some people limit the term to sounds that are pronounced in the same place of articulation, such as [ts] and [dz].

22. The IPA symbol [ɹ] represents the sound used in the beginning of such English words as *run* and *red*.

Table 2.17: A Historical Reconstruction of the Greek Vowels

	Front	Central	Back
High	[i] ι / I [ɪ]		[u] υ / Υ [ʊ]
Mid	[e] η / H [ɛ] ε / E		[o] ω / Ω [ɔ] ο / O
Low		[a] α / A	

Spelling English Words with Greek Letters

It is often possible to spell English words, especially those with a Greek origin, in Greek. Here are some examples. See if you can fill in the English word in the last two column.

Table 2.18: English Words Spelled in Greek

Greek Spelling	αλφαβετ	φιλοσοφι	φιλαδελφια	θοραξ	φιλλιπ
English Word	alphabet	philosophy	Philadelphia		

Accent Marks in Greek

Greek also has markings called accents that are written above vowel letters. At one time these markings indicated how the words were pronounced. Your instructor will probably not have you use the accent marks this way, but you do need to remember where they occur because they sometimes indicate the difference between words that sound the same.

The Semitic Origin of the Greek and English Alphabets

The Greek alphabet actually derives from a Semitic alphabet, possibly Phoenician, which was fairly close to the alphabet used by writers of Hebrew in Old Testament times. The names of the letters of the Greek alphabet closely resemble the Hebrew names. Also, the early shapes of some Greek letters closely resemble their early Hebrew counterparts. The chart below illustrates the interrelatedness of the Hebrew and the Greek alphabets. The archaic Hebrew letters (technically Early Canaanite) look different than the much later printed forms that were presented above. Try to determine how the shape of each Archaic Hebrew letter relates to the meaning listed in table 2.19 below.

Table 2.19: Greek Letters and Archaic Hebrew Letters

Archaic Hebrew Letter	Standard Hebrew Letter	Hebrew Name	Meaning	Greek Letter	Greek Name
𐤀	א	aleph	ox	A	alpha
𐤉	י	yod	hand	I	iota
𐤊	כ	kaph	palm of hand	K	kappa
𐤓	ר	resh	head	P	rho

The Shapes of Hebrew, Greek, and English Letters

Now that we have seen how the Greek alphabet is actually derived from an alphabet that was very similar to Hebrew, we can compare the shapes of the Hebrew and Greek letters. You will notice in table 2.20 that sometimes there is some similarity in shape, even with English letters.

Summary and Preview

Seeing how the writing systems of Greek and Hebrew actually work gives you a better perspective about the language than if you simply memorize the different alphabets. You know that the written language is an imperfect reflection of the spoken language but that it does give adequate information for recording texts for future generations. Knowing how the different sounds relate to each other also will help you to understand changes that take place within words, which is the topic of the next chapter. Reflection on how the sounds have changed over time also should give you insight into why some sounds have merged into a single sound (e.g., the Hebrew *aleph* and *ayin* or the *samekh* and *sin*).

Table 2.20: English Letters Compared to Hebrew and Greek

English		Hebrew (Modern)	Greek
a	A	א	α / Α
b	B	ב	β / Β
c	C	כ	κ / Κ
d	D	ד	δ / Δ
e	E	י	η / Η or ϵ / Ε
f	F	[variant of פ]	ϕ / Φ
g	G	ג	γ / Γ
h	H	ה	ʽ
i	I	י	ι / Ι
k	K	כ	κ / Κ
l	L	ל	λ / Λ
m	M	מ	μ / Μ
n	N	נ	ν / Ν
o	O	ו	ω / Ω or ο / Ο
p	P	פ	π / Π
q	Q	ק	
r	R	ר	ρ / Ρ
s	S	ס or שׂ	σ / Σ
t	T	ת or ט	τ / Τ
u	U	ו	υ / Υ
v	V	ו or variant of ב	
w	W	ו	
x	X		ξ / Ξ
y	Y	י	ι / Ι
z	Z	ז	ζ / Ζ

For Further Study

Campbell, George L. *Handbook of Scripts and Alphabets.* London: Routledge, 1997.

Coulmas, Florian. *The Writing Systems of the World.* Oxford: Basil Blackwell, 1991.

Daniels, Peter T., and William Bright, eds. *The World's Writing Systems.* New York: Oxford University Press, 1996.

Diringer, David. *The Alphabet: A Key to the History of Mankind.* 2 vols. 3d ed. New York: Funk & Wagnalls, 1968.

Internet Resources

Omniglot provides online examples of hundreds of writing systems, including a variety of alphabets and syllabaries: www.omniglot.com/writing/.

The Museum of the Alphabet in Waxhaw, North Carolina illustrates many of the major developments in writing systems. Visit their web site at www.jaars.org/museum/alphabet.

Exercises

1. Look at an article or book about the history of writing, and make your own chart of how the Hebrew letters developed from archaic forms to later forms.
2. Look at a modern version of Psalm 119. In Hebrew the first word of each section begins with a different Hebrew letter, in alphabetical order. If your Bible shows these Hebrew letters, observe the order of the Hebrew alphabet.
3. Practice writing Hebrew/Greek letters until the motions are easy. Be sure to check with your instructor or textbook to see how the letters should be formed.
4. Write simple Hebrew/Greek words on small cards and practice reading them.
5. If English were written without vowels what might *b-t-r* mean in the following sentences? (Hint: the *t* could be doubled in some of these forms.)

- They were *b-t-r.*
- They were *b-t-r* than the others.
- They were more *b-t-r* than the others.
- Put the *b-t-r* on the table.

How did you decide what *b-t-r* meant in each sentence? Did you sometimes have a choice of more than one word?

3

Putting It into Words

How Words Are Made

> *Now the promises were spoken to Abraham and to his seed. He does not say, "And to seeds," as referring to many, but rather to one, "And to your seed," that is, Christ.*
>
> —Galatians 3:16 NASB

People often think of words as the smallest unit of grammar. We think in words. We converse in words. We write words. Yet the word is not actually the smallest grammatical unit.

Why isn't the word the smallest unit? Most languages construct words from smaller meaningful parts. These smaller parts are not always spoken on their own; some may occur only as a part of a larger unit, the word. In this chapter we will look at these smaller units and see how they are combined to make words. We will call these small meaningful parts **morphemes.** We will again look at how forms have particular meaning in context. We will note that Hebrew and Greek have preferred patterns for constructing words and that these patterns are relatively few in number.

Please note that it is not our purpose here to actually teach you all the patterns of Greek and Hebrew. Rather, we want to give you some context for the many grammatical patterns and facts that you will encounter in your study of the biblical languages. Hopefully when you hear terms such as *object pronoun* or *second person singular* or *imperfect verb*, they will not seem so strange to you after having read this chapter. What you get here will be a representative sample of Hebrew and Greek to illustrate certain points of grammar.

In this chapter we will first survey how English, Hebrew, and Greek form words from smaller parts. Then we will consider the different kinds of parts that languages use to make words. Finally, we will see how we can classify languages by how they make words.

How We Can Understand Words

To understand what a word means, we must first know how it is made and how the various parts of the word fit together. The study of the structure of words is called **morphology.** We will use morphology to help us see the patterns in Hebrew and Greek words and to see how they compare to the way English words are made.

Words are normally made up of more than one part. We realize that words have a number of sounds (*cat* has three sounds) and perhaps even several syllables (*category* has four syllables). Words also can have several parts to their meaning. A morpheme is the minimal linguistic unit of a language that has meaning. The English word *houses,* for example, consists of two morphemes: *house+s.* The *-s* adds the idea of "plural." (It also adds a syllable of sound.) Similarly, *walked* is made up of *walk+ed* (*-ed* is pronounced [t] in this case). The idea of past tense is not even a separate syllable (in the spoken form). Morphemes may be as short as one sound *(walk-s)* or the change of a single sound *(sing, sang, sung).*

How do we find morphemes in Hebrew and Greek? We can compare similar words in the language and see what part of the word (which *form*) changes the meaning. One simple way to start looking for morphemes is:

1. *collect* similar words (e.g., plural forms of nouns),
2. *compare* changes in the form of the words with changes in meaning,
3. *draw lines* to indicate the parts of words that stay the same and the parts that change, and
4. *define* each part of the word (the morphemes).

Let's apply these steps to the following examples. First, we collect data that are similar. A Spanish language example is:

- *amigo* "male friend" *amigos* "male friends"
- *amiga* "female friend" *amigas* "female friends"

Second, we need to compare what has changed in the data with changes in the English meaning. We note that the two words that end in an *-s* both have a plural meaning. We also note that the top two words both include a "male" meaning and the bottom two words refer to females.

Third, we can draw lines between the parts to show what we hypothesize are morpheme boundaries or breaks:

- *amig-o* "male friend" *amig-o-s* "male friends"
- *amig-a* "female friend" *amig-a-s* "female friends"

Fourth, we define the morphemes by making a hypothesis about what the parts or morphemes of the word mean. In this case, we might say that *-o* indicates "male" and *-a* indicates "female." We could also hypothesize that *-s* in Spanish indicates "plural" (similar to English *boy—boys, girl—girls*).

Now let's consider some examples from Hebrew and Greek.

The following two words in Hebrew have slightly different forms and slightly different meanings. The first word refers to a male and the second to a female. Hebrew changes the shape of the word (here, a verb) to show the difference.[1]

- *higgaʿtā̲* "You (masculine) arrived"
- *higgaʿt* "You (feminine) arrived"

In Hebrew the difference between "you (masculine) arrived" and "you (feminine) arrived" is indicated by a change in the final vowel of the verb. When "you (feminine)" do something, the final vowel is missing. Now look at the following plural forms of Hebrew verbs. What patterns do you see?

- *higgaʿt<u>em</u>* "You (plural masculine) arrived"
- *higgaʿt<u>en</u>* "You (plural feminine) arrived"

When these same words have a plural *you* the ending changes again to indicate whether the subject (doer of the action) is male or female. In Hebrew we will need to think about this gender difference in all verbs. The endings (suffixes) will indicate whether the subject is masculine or feminine.

1. Hebrew and Greek words will be shown using the SBL transliteration system that was discussed in chapter 2.

This is, of course, very different from English verbs, but it is not difficult to understand.

What happens to Greek verbs? How do they change when the subject changes or the tense changes? Let's consider several examples. Look at each set and see whether the change in the form of the Greek word has a corresponding change in what the word means.

- *luō* "I loose/untie"
- *lueis* "You (singular) loose"

The idea of "I" versus "you (singular)" is indicated by a change in the ending of the verb from *-ō* to *-eis*. *You* has to be defined as singular (sg.) or plural (pl.), because in modern English *you* is ambiguous with respect to singular or plural.[2] In the next pair of Greek verbs, the endings stay the same, but an *-s-* is added between the first part of the verb and the ending.

- *lusō* "I *will* loose"
- *luseis* "You (singular) *will* loose"

The *-s-* in these verbs indicates future tense, and the *-ō* and *-eis* endings still indicate that either "I" or "you (singular)" did the action (i.e., they indicate or "mark" the subject of the verb).

In Greek we will need to pay attention to these and other endings on the verb because they tell us about the subject and the tense of the action.

In the examples above, there were letters or groups of letters that had a particular meaning. As you recall, these small units are called morphemes. A morpheme may be more than one syllable. In English, for example, some morphemes have two syllables:

- *un-fortune-ate-ly*
- *un-gentle-man-li-ness*

Here the dash (-) indicates a morpheme break. Note that some of the morphemes have more than one syllable *(fortune, gentle)*.

2. In the English of the King James Version (KJV), the forms that begin with *th* are singular *(thou, thee, thy, thine)*, while those that begin with *y* are plural *(ye, you, your)*.

Some words appear to have smaller parts but are really only one morpheme. In English:

- *hammer* is not *ham+mer*
- *finger* is not *fing+er*

There are also words that have more than one meaning component without a clear separation between the several parts. In English, many verbs have a past tense morpheme written *-ed: walk-ed, rant-ed.* Other verbs do not show a separate *-ed* morpheme when they are in the past tense:

- *teach* > *taught*
- *am* > *was*
- *go* > *went*

We refer to these latter kinds of words as **suppletive** forms. One form of the word is *supplemented* from another root in order to show a variation in the form.

How We Classify Morphemes

Morphemes can be grouped in several ways. One way is by whether the morpheme is the primary component of the word (a **root**) or a less basic part (an **affix**). Affixes are further divided by where they occur in relationship to the root.

A morpheme that occurs before the root is a **prefix.**

- X-ROOT: *un-happy, pre-history, sub-standard*

A morpheme that occurs after the root is a *suffix.*

- ROOT-X: *happi-ness, happi-ly, book-s, look-s*

Sometimes a morpheme might have parts that occur in a constant order but are broken up as they mesh with another morpheme, like clasping your hands together by interlocking the fingers. Linguists call this a **discontinuous morpheme.** Such morphemes are especially common in the Hebrew verb. Hebrew roots normally have three consonants, and a verb pattern or template can be superimposed on the root as in the following:

- *ktb* a root meaning "to write"
- *kātab* "he wrote"
- *kĕtōb* "(you) write"

The pattern of vowels inserted on either side of the *t* (middle root letter) determines whether the form is a past tense or an imperative (form for issuing a command). This vowel pattern could also be considered an **infix** in that it is inserted inside the root. The three letters of the root are discontinuous because they do not occur together but are separated by the pattern vowels. The same holds true for the infix or pattern vowels. They are discontinuous because they are separated by the middle root letter.

A morpheme that occurs both before and after a root is a **circumfix.** Again, there is no example of a circumfix in English, but it is common in Hebrew. In the following example, the root consists of the three consonants *k-t-b.* The circumfix *ti—î* adds the meaning "you feminine singular future tense."

- X-ROOT-X: *ti-ktb-î* "you (feminine singular) will write"

Morphemes that are not affixes are roots. We normally think of roots as words that can stand on their own. For example, in English, *tree, run, good, well,* and *me* are all roots.

Another way to look at morphemes is whether they can occur by themselves **(free)** or only connected to other morphemes **(bound).** Affixes are always bound. Most roots in English are free forms. Some roots are bound. For example, *huckleberry* consists of two parts, *huckle* and *berry. Berry* can occur on its own as a root, but *huckle* can't, so we would say that *huckle* is a **bound morpheme.**

A Hebrew verb root can be thought of as bound to its pattern. Thus:

- *k̲āt̲ab̲,* "he wrote"; *š̲ām̲ar̲,* "he watched"; *p̲āq̲ad̲,* "he cared for"
- *yik̲t̲ōb̲,* "he will write"; *yiš̲m̲ōr̲,* "he will watch"; *yip̲q̲ōd̲,* "he will care for"
- *k̲ōt̲ēb̲,* "one who writes"; *š̲ōm̲ēr̲,* "one who watches"; *p̲ōq̲ēd̲,* "one who cares for"

These three roots *(ktb, šmr,* and *pqd)* occur in three different patterns. The pattern for "he did something" has the vowel *ā* inserted between the first and second root letters and the vowel *a* inserted between the second and third root letters (a discontinuous morpheme). In a similar way, the pattern for "he will do something" includes the prefix *yi-*, no vowel between the first and second root letters, and the vowel *ō* between the second and third root letters. Finally, the pattern for "one who does something" has the vowel *ō* between the first and second root letters and the vowel *ē* between the second and third root letters.

One other way to think about morphemes is to ask whether they convey *content* or grammatical *function* information. For this discussion we will consider only roots since affixes by definition do not add content, only grammatical information.

Distinguishing Roots and Words

For the moment let's think about the difference between roots and words. So far we have seen roots and affixes. When a root can occur on its own, it is also a word. In English, for example, we can have the root *walk* as in *I walk,* or we can have the root followed by an affix: *walk-s* as in *she walks.* English words, then, can be either a simple root or a root with one or more affixes. We will see more ways to build words a little later, but for now we will think only about the differences between various types of words.

Every language has a variety of types of words. One obvious contrast is the difference between a noun (e.g., *person*) and an adjective (e.g., *happy*). Note that these classes of words must be defined by linguistic factors, not just by their meaning. Even in English it is sometimes hard to talk about whether a particular root is "really" a noun or a verb. When we say "I walk" or "I took a walk," the word *walk* functions as a verb in the first sentence and as a noun in the second. The fact that *walk* occurs after the word *a* in the second example *(a walk)* shows that it is a noun.

We can also say, "It is large" and "I'll have a large." In this case the word *large* is an adjective in the first sentence and a noun in the second. We could also change the first sentence to "It is *larger,*" because adjectives in English can be modified with the *-er* ending to make a comparison. We do not, however, add the *-er* ending in "I'll have a large," because *large* is a noun in this sentence.

It is important to recognize how various types of words act as we study Hebrew and Greek. We cannot merely assume that a Hebrew or Greek word is, for example, an adjective just because it refers to an idea that is expressed as an adjective in English. Some languages do not have a class of adjectives but express ideas such as "old" and "tall" with verbs or nouns. We need to look at how these ideas are packaged in each language, not just how they are translated into English.

Table 3.1 illustrates the differences between various types of English words according to traditional labels for the categories (noun, pronoun, etc.).

Table 3.1: Types of English Words and Their Functions

Type of Word	Function(s)	Examples
Noun	Identifies people, objects, ideas	David, palace, reign
Pronoun	Takes the place of a noun or a group of words	he, she, it, which, that
Adjective	Tells more about a noun	green, large, holy
Determiner	Identifies a particular noun	a, the
Verb	Tells about an action or state	go, know
Adverb	Tells more about a verb, adjective, or adverb	quickly, also, not, very
Conjunction	Connects other words or groups of words	and, but, so that, because
Preposition	Indicates a relationship between words	to, by, under, of, over

These word types are also called **word classes** or **parts of speech.**

Roots with an Independent Meaning

Some roots or words refer to people, things, ideas, actions, qualities, or quantities. These differ from words that have a meaning only in relation to the grammar of the language that uses them. In more technical language, the former are lexical **content roots/words,** while the latter are **function words.** In English some examples of lexical content roots are nouns, verbs, adjectives, numerals, and adverbs, such as:

- **Nouns:** *leg, belief, beauty*
- **Verbs:** *eat, blink, go*
- **Adjectives:** *tall, old, blue, wise*
- **Numerals:** *one, two, three*
- **Adverbs:** *slowly, soon, clearly*

A language can have and even add as many lexical content words as it needs to communicate the realities of its culture, and in this sense it can be thought of as an **open class.** There are unlimited possibilities.

Roots with Grammatical Meaning

Function words do not refer to any sort of reality outside of the grammatical relations of the language. They are typically limited in number and form a **closed class;** there are only limited possibilities. Some examples in English are:

- **Pronouns:** *I, you, she, we*
- **Conjunctions:** *and, but*
- **Prepositions:** *to, from, in*
- **Determiners:** *a, the*

Why is the distinction between lexical content roots and function words important? When you learn vocabulary, you should pay special attention to the function words, because they will help you make sense out of the sentences and paragraphs. Looked at another way, the function words will usually help you to see structural relations between various parts of the biblical text. Also it will be a help to learn vocabulary within its particular category of noun, verb, and so forth. Table 3.2 summarizes the various types of morphemes (forms) that we have discussed above, plus a few additional ones (see also the Glossary):

Table 3.2: Types of Morphemes with English Examples

Free	**Lexical Content Words**		**Function Words**
	Nouns *(tree, love)* Verbs *(eat, cry, think)* Adjectives *(tall, large)* Adverbs *(sadly, wisely)*		Pronouns *(I, you, they)* Conjunctions *(and, because)* Determiners *(a, the, these)* Prepositions *(in, from, with)*
Bound	**Lexical Content Roots**		**Affixes**
	Bound Roots (*cran*-berry) Contractions[3] (we'*ll*, I'*d*, you'*ve*)		Prefixes (*im*-polite) Suffixes (book-*s*) Infixes (N/A) Circumfixes (N/A)

3. The shortened forms of *will, had,* and *have* are also called *clitics.*

How Morphemes Add Meaning

Certain affixes added to a word will change the word from one category to another. For example, adding the suffix *-ate* to some nouns can change them to verbs: *vaccine* becomes *vaccinate* and *décor* becomes *decorate.* Or, the suffix *-er* can change a verb to a noun: *bake* becomes *baker; kill* becomes *killer;* and *give* becomes *giver.* This type of affix is called **derivational.** A second type of affix has more to do with adding certain grammatical information about a word without changing its function. This includes things like the suffix *-s* that makes a noun plural or the suffix *-ed* that changes a verb to the past tense. These **inflectional** affixes will be discussed in the next section.

Affixes That Derive Words from Other Words

Derivational affixes tend to be irregular in how they affect meaning and work only with a limited set of words. Thus, the *-ate* suffix that changes *vaccine* to *vaccinate* does not work with many other nouns. For example, English speakers do not use the form *pill-ate* to refer to giving someone a pill. It is difficult to determine the combined meaning of derived forms and to predict which derivational affix will be used. Table 3.3 shows some characteristics of derivational affixes.

Table 3.3: Characteristics of Derivational Affixes

	Derivational Affixes	**English Example**	**Comment**
Word Class	Typically change class of word	*depend > dependable*	The suffix changes the verb to an adjective.
Function	Indicate relations within the word	*bake > baker*	A baker is one who bakes.
Productivity	Typically limited	*boy > boyish;* but not *youth > youthish*	Affixes can only be used with a small set of words.
Position	Typically close to the root	*bake > bake-r > bake-r-s*	The derivational suffix comes right after the root and before the suffix for the plural.
Meaning	Irregular	*bake > baker; toast > toaster*	A baker is a person, but a toaster is a machine.

English has many derivational affixes. Many of them change one type of word into another type of word. These derivational affixes are limited in their use; they only occur with a small set of words. Note the following English examples:

Nouns Changed to Adjectives

- *affection-ate,* but not *love-ate*
- *alcohol-ic,* but not *water-ic*
- *boy-ish,* but not *youth-ish*
- *man-ly,* but not *boy-ly*
- *Elizabeth-an*
- *health-ful*
- *life-like*
- *pictur-esque*
- *virtu-ous*

Verbs Changed to Nouns

- *accus-ation*
- *acquitt-al*
- *broil-er* ("tool that broils something" rather than "person who broils something")
- *clear-ance*
- *confer-ence*
- *conform-ist*
- *free*-dom, but not *captive-dom*
- *predict-ion*
- *sing-er*

Adjectives Changed to Adverbs

- *exact-ly*
- *quiet-ly*

Nouns Changed to Verbs

- *vaccin-ate, pollin-ate*
- *idol-ize, jeopard-ize*

Some Limitations on Deriving Words from Other Words

In addition to the limitations of derivational affixes mentioned above (not productive, irregular in changing the meaning), there are also many examples of words in which roots can occur only *with* a derivational affix; the roots are bound and cannot occur on their own. In English, for example, we can only say "I was disgruntled"; we cannot say "I was gruntled." Other examples in English include:

- *dis-consolate,* but not *consolate*
- *non-chalant,* but not *chalant*
- *non-descript,* but not *descript*
- *un-gainly,* but not *gainly*

Notice that all of these examples begin with a prefix indicating negation.

Affixes That Add Grammatical Information to a Word

Some affixes add grammatical information to a word without changing its category. As mentioned above, these are called inflectional affixes, and they differ from derivational affixes in a number of ways. Aside from not changing the word category, they also are very productive and their meaning is regular or fixed. That is, a certain affix can always be associated with a specific meaning (e.g., *-s* with the plural of a noun; *-ed* with the past tense of a verb). Comparing table 3.3 with table 3.4 should help you to understand the differences between inflectional and derivational affixes.

English uses only a limited number of inflectional affixes, especially in comparison with Greek and Hebrew. English nouns use the suffix *-s* to show that a noun is plural *(teacher, teacher-s)* and *-'s* to show that it possesses something *(Mary's book)* or has some relationship to something else *(Isaac's father)*. English verbs use the suffix *-s* to show that only one person does the action *(David*

Table 3.4: Characteristics of Inflectional Affixes

	Inflectional Affixes	English Example	Comment
Word Class	Do not change class of word	*teacher* > *teacher-s*	Both words are nouns; the suffix makes the noun plural.
Function	Indicate relations between words	*teacher* > *teacher's*	The suffix relates the noun to something that is possessed.
Productivity	Normally very productive	*teacher-s* *tree-s* *idea-s*	The plural suffix can be added to most nouns.
Position	Typically at edges of word	*teach-er-s*	The plural suffix must occur at the end after any derivational affixes
Meaning	Regular	*walk-ed* *talk-ed* *yield-ed*	The suffix always indicates the past tense on any verb to which it attaches.

walk-s to school) as opposed to more than one *(David and Paul walk to school)*. There can also be inflection on English adjectives, as in *old, old-er, old-est*.

English has only eight inflectional affixes (listed in table 3.5), and all of them are suffixes. Two of these affixes are attached to nouns, four to verbs, and two to adjectives.

Table 3.5: Inflectional Affixes in English

Suffix	Meaning	Word Class
-s	plural	nouns
-'s	possessive	nouns
-s	3d person singular, present	verbs
-ed	past	verbs
-ing	progressive	verbs
-en	past participle	verbs
-er	comparative	adjectives
-est	superlative	adjectives

Note that three of the eight English inflectional affixes have the same phonetic shape: *s*.

Questions That Languages Ask About Nouns and Pronouns

Languages often ask the following questions about nouns and pronouns:

- How many are there?
- What kind of thing is it? Is it "male" or "female"?
- How does it relate to me? Is it about me? about you? about someone else?
- What is it doing in this sentence? Is it the subject? the object?

To answer these questions about nouns and pronouns, English changes the form of nouns and pronouns in one of two ways. For some words the answers to the questions are indicated or "marked" through inflection, as discussed above (*-s* for the plural, etc.). Another way is to use forms from different roots. This tends to happen more with pronouns than with nouns (*I* for the singular but *we* for the plural; *he/she* for the singular but *they* for the plural). As noted earlier, the technical term for this type of change is *suppletion.* Regardless of whether the changes that take place are marked through inflection or through suppletion, your Hebrew or Greek textbook will use terms like those found in table 3.6 to talk about these kinds of changes. The changes in English nouns are inflectional, while changes in the pronouns involve suppletion.

Table 3.6: Grammatical Questions for Nouns and Pronouns in English

Question	Term	Types of Answers	Nouns	Pronouns
How many?	number	singular plural	*tree* *trees*	*I* *we*
Male/female?	gender	masculine feminine neuter	N/A	*he* *she* *it*
Relation to me?	person	first (the speaker) second (the person addressed) third (the person talked about)	N/A	*we* *you* *they*
What is it doing?	case	nominative (doing the action) accusative (receiving the action) genitive (possesses something)	*child* *child* *child's*	*we* *us* *our*

Some of the terminology used in these inflectional processes may be new to some students. Let's look at these terms one by one to get used to what they mean.

Number

Nouns can be either singular (just one) or plural (more than one) in English. English pronouns are marked as being singular or plural, except for *you.* We refer to this distinction as **number.**

Gender

English pronouns also distinguish the **gender** of the referent, at least for *he, she,* and *it.* These are referred to as the masculine, feminine, and neuter respectively. Since some languages attribute gender to all nouns, regardless of whether there are natural sexual distinctions, we could also think about these morphemes as marking three *classes* of nouns. The real issue here is the way in which the gender or class of nouns relate to verbs, adjectives, and pronouns. In Hebrew, for example, a noun that has the gender (or class) "masculine" requires an adjective that describes it to have a similar form. Thus, the masculine noun *bayit* ("house") requires the masculine form of the adjective *gādôl* ("large") in the expression "large house," but the feminine noun *ʾēlâ* ("oak tree") in the phrase "large oak tree" requires the feminine form of the adjective, which is *gĕdôlâ.*

Person

A third factor in English pronouns is the relationship between the speaker (me) and others. The pronouns *I, me, my,* and *mine* are referred to as first-person pronouns; *you, your,* and *yours* are second person; and *he, she, it, they, them* are third person.

Case

The last question about nouns and pronouns in English relates to what the word is doing in the sentence. The only inflection on English nouns is the **genitive,** which typically indicates that a noun is in some relationship to another noun. We might call this possessive, but the relationship does not always include ownership. For example, *Jan's house* indicates a different relationship than *Jan's parents* and *Jan's church.* Jan does not "own" her parents or a church. English pronouns change in more ways than nouns. When I do something, the pronoun is said to be in the **nominative** case. When something is done to me, the pronoun is in the **accusative** case. Pronouns such as *my* and *their* are in the genitive case. Table 3.6 summarizes these cases in English, table 3.9 shows Hebrew affixes, and table 3.12 shows case in Greek nouns.

When we combine these four categories, we can talk quite specifically about a pronoun in English. The pronoun *he*, for example, is a third person singular masculine nominative pronoun. The pronoun *them* is third person plural accusative. Note that English indicates gender only when the pronoun is a third-person singular pronoun.

Table 3.7: The Terms *Nominative, Accusative,* and *Genitive*

Term	Explanation	English Examples
Nominative	The noun or pronoun is the subject of the sentence	*She* sees the boy.
Accusative	The noun or pronoun is the object of the sentence	Sam sees *her.*
Genitive	The noun or pronoun "possesses" something	That is *her* book. That book is *Sally's.*

In biblical studies, the changes in nouns and pronouns are referred to as **declension.** This term is not used for the changes that occur with verbs. Changes in verb forms in the biblical languages are referred to as **conjugation.**

Questions That Languages Ask About Verbs

When languages use verbs, they answer some questions that are the same as for nouns and some that are unique to verbs.

- How many "actors" are there?
- Is the actor "male" or "female"?
- How does it relate to me?

- When did this happen?
- Is it completed or ongoing?
- Does someone control this action?
- How many "objects" are there?
- Is it "real" or imagined?

To talk about verbs we need to add a few more terms, which are described in table 3.8.

Table 3.8: Grammatical Questions for Verbs in English

Question	Term	Types of Answers	English Examples
How many?	number	singular, plural	*he walks/they walk*
Male/female?	gender	masculine, feminine, neuter	N/A
Relation to me?	person	first, second, third	only *he/she/it* take the *walk-s* form
When?	tense	present, past	*walk/walked* (inflection) *goes/went* (suppletion)
Completed?	aspect	completed, incompleted, durative	*eat-en* *walk-ing*
Control?	voice	active, passive	*eat* *eaten*
Objects?	transitivity	intransitive, transitive, bitransitive	N/A
Real?	mood	indicative, subjunctive, optative	*I was* *if I were*

Several of the questions above do not involve inflectional affixes or suppletive forms in English. Instead, English uses other devices like helping verbs (especially forms of *be* and *have*). These and even additional questions are handled with inflectional affixes in Greek and Hebrew, so it is important to think beyond the categories of English.

One of the topics that you will need to study is the difference between **tense** and **aspect.** Linguists use the term *tense* to refer to the time a verb takes place in relation to the time of speaking or writing. Thus, a verb may be in the *past,* the *present,* or the *future* relative to the time of speaking or writing. Languages also have ways to indicate the "internal" time of a verb. The term *aspect* is used to describe the internal time nature of the event or action; whether it is seen as completed or ongoing. Thomas Payne explains ten potential aspects: perfective, imperfective, perfect, pluperfect, completive, inceptive, continuative/progressive, punctual, iterative, and habitual.[4] Outside of linguistic writing, some of these terms are treated as tense rather than aspect. Thus, in Greek textbooks you may find reference to the "perfect tense." See the Glossary for definitions of these terms.

Hebrew Morphology

What follows here is a sample of some of the basic elements of how Hebrew puts words together. In this section we will give Hebrew equivalents for some of the morphological issues discussed above. Just a reminder—this presentation is not meant to take the place of a grammar book. Our hope is that the discussion will give some broader context to the details of Hebrew grammar that would be found in a standard textbook, so that you will be able to understand how what happens in Hebrew relates to what happens in your own language.

Hebrew Nouns

To begin with, let's look at how Hebrew deals with nouns. Hebrew has forms that answer the same general questions that you saw above for English, as shown in table 3.6.

Hebrew adds the ending *-îm* to a noun to make it plural, and it also adds *-â* to make a masculine noun feminine. Hebrew lacks a neuter form, meaning that all nouns must be classified as either masculine or feminine.

Some of the pronouns in Hebrew are formed by suppletion rather than inflection, but Hebrew is different from English and Greek in that there are special forms of pronouns that are suffixed to nouns and prepositions. This can happen with a Hebrew pronoun in any function that it has in the sentence: subject (nominative), object (accusative) of a verb, or possessor (genitive). However, for the possessor function it is the only way the pronoun will occur. As table 3.10 illustrates, when a pronoun suffix is added to a noun, the pronoun indicates the possessor, but when it attaches to a preposition, it shows the object of that preposition.

4. Thomas Payne, *Describing Morphosyntax* (Cambridge: Cambridge University Press, 1997), 238–41.

Table 3.9: Basic Questions for Hebrew Nouns and Pronouns

Question	Term	Types of Answers	Hebrew Nouns	Hebrew Pronouns
How many?	number	singular plural[5]	*sûs* ("horse") *sûs-îm* ("horses")	*ʾănî* ("I") *ʾănaḥnû* ("we")
Male/ female?	gender	masculine feminine (no neuter forms)	*naʿar* ("boy") *naʿăr-â* ("girl")	*hûʾ* ("he") *hîʾ* ("she")
Relation to me?	person	first second third	N/A	*ʾănî* ("I") *ʾattâ* ("you") *hûʾ* ("he")
What is it doing?	case	nominative (subject) accusative (object) genitive (possessor)	N/A	*ʾănî* ("I") *ʾōtî* ("me") *sûs-î* ("my [horse]")[6]

The pronoun that translates as "me" in table 3.9 *(ʾōtî)* is actually a combination of suppletion and inflection. In relation to the subject pronouns, it is based on a separate root (suppletion). In relation to changes of person within the object pronoun *(me, you, he),* however, it is based on inflection. The different inflectional endings that mark person and gender for the object pronoun are all added to the root *ʾōt,* which is a bound morpheme (see above). Table 3.10 illustrates the issue of pronoun affixes for Hebrew nouns, prepositions, and the root for the object pronoun.

As table 3.10 shows, endings like *-î* ("my" or "me") or *-ĕkā,* ("your" or "you") have to be translated differently when attached to a preposition than when attached to a noun. The table also shows that unlike English and Greek, Hebrew distinguishes gender in the forms for *you/your.* Thus the form *sûs-ēk* ("your horse") would be appropriate when talking to a woman but not when talking to a man. To talk to a man we would have to use the form *sûs-ĕkā* ("your horse").

Quite often Hebrew has a phrase in which a noun modifies another noun. In an English phrase like *the king of England,* the noun *England* modifies *king.*

5. Hebrew also has a dual, which indicates two of something. It occurs only with nouns of time (two days, two years) and with nouns that occur naturally in pairs (two feet, two hands). The dual form serves as the normal plural for nouns that occur in pairs (*raglayim* = "two feet" or "feet"). Additionally, the dual form occurs with some numbers (two, two hundred, two thousand).
6. Rather than a separate word for the possessor pronoun *my,* the suffix *-î* is added to the end of the noun. The noun *sûs,* "horse," has been used for the illustration.

Table 3.10: Hebrew Pronouns Suffixed to Prepositions and Nouns

Function of Inflectional Marker	The Noun *sûs* ("horse")	Root for Object Pronoun *ʾōt-*	Preposition *l-* ("to")
1st person singular	*sûs-î* ("my horse")	*ʾōt-î* ("me")	*l-î* ("to me")
2d person singular, masculine	*sûs-ĕkā* ("your horse")	*ʾōt-ĕkā* ("you")	*l-ĕkā* ("to you")
2d person singular, feminine	*sûs-ēk* ("your horse")	*ʾōt-āk* ("you")	*l-āk* ("to you")
3d person singular, masculine	*sûs-ô* ("his horse")	*ʾōt-ô* ("him")	*l-ô* ("to him")
3d person singular, feminine	*sûs-āh* ("her horse")	*ʾōt-āh* ("her")	*l-āh* ("to her")

If I say, "I met the king of England," it is clear that I met the king, not England. *England* functions only to specify which king I met. In English the noun that modifies *(England)* either occurs after the preposition *of* or receives a suffix to mark it as the modifier *(England's king).* In this example we would say that *king* is the "controlling" or "head" noun. It "controls" the main idea in the phrase *the king of England.* In biblical Hebrew it is the controlling noun that is marked, while the modifier has no indication that it is the modifier other than its position in the phrase. Such marking of the controlling noun in a structure like this is different from the way that English and Greek handle the possessive relationship. The special form that the controlling noun takes in this pattern is called by most Hebrew grammars the **construct state.**

Here are several ways in which the controlling noun is marked or identified:

- It is always the first noun in the phrase; it is marked by position.

  melek ("king"); *Yiśrāʾēl* ("Israel")
  melek Yiśrāʾēl ("the king of Israel")

- In marked feminine nouns, *the feminine marker changes* from *-â* to *-at:*

  malk-â ("queen"); *Šĕbāʾ* ("Sheba")
  malk-at Šĕbāʾ ("the queen of Sheba")

- It is not allowed to receive a specificity marker, such as the definite article. Rather, specificity is indicated on the second noun that further describes the controlling noun.

  ha-mmelek ("the king"); *hā-ʾāreṣ* ("the land")[7]
  melek hā-ʾāreṣ ("the king of the land")

- Sometimes the vowels of the controlling noun are changed. This occurs only with nouns that have certain types of vowels:

  dābār ("word"); *ha-mmelek* ("the king")
  dĕbar ha-mmelek ("the king's word")

Hebrew Verbs

Hebrew, in contrast to Greek and English, has two different ways to show a change in person *(I, you, he/she),* gender (masculine or feminine), and number (singular or plural) in verbs. One verb form uses only suffixes to show the various changes in person, gender, and number; and a second form uses prefixes or a combination of prefix and suffix (a circumfix)to show those changes.[8] The first form is sometimes called the **suffix conjugation** and the second the **prefix conjugation.**[9] While the suffix conjugation often refers to action in the past and the prefix conjugation to action in the future, the situation is actually more complex than that. The precise nature of the Hebrew verb system is a matter of some debate among scholars, and it will be enough to say here that it is probably focused more on aspect than on tense.[10]

The example of *kātab* and *kātĕḇ-û* in row one of table 3.11 shows that adding the vowel *û* as a suffix indicates a plural form of the third person on a verb in the past tense. The root *(k-t-b)* doesn't change, although the vowel between the second and third root consonants changes slightly.

7. The definite article ("the") appears as a prefixed *ha-* or *hā-*. When it is *ha-*, the first letter of the Hebrew noun will be doubled.
8. Remember that a combination of a prefix and a suffix surrounding the root is called a *circumfix.*
9. Many Hebrew grammars call the suffix conjugation the perfect and the prefix conjugation the imperfect.
10. Aspect refers to whether the speaker chooses to refer to the way an action or situation develops or unfolds ("imperfective aspect") or chooses simply to state the action or situation without any reference to its development ("perfective aspect"). For example, "he

Table 3.11: Basic Questions for Hebrew Verbs

Question	Term	Types of Answers	Hebrew Example
How many?	number	singular plural	*kātab* ("he wrote") *kātĕb-û* ("they wrote")
Male/female?	gender/class	masculine feminine (no neuter forms)	*kātab* ("he wrote") *kātĕb-â* ("she wrote")
Relation to me?	person	first second third	*kātab-tî* ("I wrote") *kātab-tā* ("you [masc. sing.] wrote") *kātab* ("he wrote")
When?	tense	past present/future	*kātab-tî* ("I wrote") *ʾe-ktōb* ("I write," "I will write")
Completed?	aspect	completed incompleted	*kātab-tî* ("I wrote") *ʾe-ktōb* ("I was writing")[11]
Control?	voice	active passive	*kātab* ("he wrote") *ni-ktab* ("it was written")
Objects?	transitivity	intransitive transitive bitransitive	*hālak-tî* ("I went") *kātab-tî ʾōtô* ("I wrote it") *ha-rʾê-nî ʾet kᵉbōd-ekâ* ("show-me obj. glory-your" = "show me Your glory")
Reality?	mood	indicative jussive	*ya-ʿăśeh* ("he will do") *ya-ʿăś* ("let him do," "may he do")

was singing" brings out the fact that the action of singing was not only in the past but also occurred over a period of time. "He sang," however, simply states that the action took place in the past but makes no reference to the issue of extension over time. "He was singing" would then be imperfective, while "he sang" would be perfective. A simplified way of looking at aspect is to say that the perfective aspect is "completed" action, and the imperfective aspect is "incompleted" action.

11. The same form serves for present/future and also for incompleted action. If it is clear from the context that the action happened in the past, then a translation like "I was writing" or "I used to write" must be used.

In a similar way, the contrast between the forms *kātab* and *kātĕb-â* illustrates the vowel *â* as a suffix that shows that the gender of the form is feminine rather than masculine. The form *kātab* ("he wrote") has no marker for person, while the forms *kātab-tî* ("I wrote") and *kātab-tā* ("you wrote") have a suffix that marks the first person or the second person, respectively. Because the third person is the form that is not marked, many Hebrew grammars will arrange the order of the **paradigm** for the Hebrew verb in the order third person, second person, and first person.

Looking at the forms *kātab-tî* ("I wrote") and *ʾe-ktōb* ("I write," "I will write"), you can see that tense (past/present/future) and aspect (completed/incompleted) are shown by whether a suffix or a prefix is used to mark the person (as well as the gender and number). The form with a suffix shows that the verb is past tense or completed aspect, while the form with a prefix shows that it is either future tense or incompleted aspect.

While the suffixes and prefixes used for person, gender, and number are inflectional affixes, the example of *kātab* ("he wrote") versus *ni-ktab* ("it was written") in row five illustrates a derivational affix in Hebrew. The derivational prefix *ni-* changes the meaning of a verb from *active (voice)* to *passive (voice).* In the example of Hebrew *kātab,* we would say that "he" performed the action of writing. A passive verb changes its forms in relation to whoever or whatever receives the action. Thus *ni-ktab* refers to what was written—for example a letter or a book. In this case the letter or book does not control the action. More will be said about active and passive in chapter 6.

Some actions have an affect or impact on a person or thing that we call the **object.** In the Hebrew example *kātab-tî ʾōtô* ("I wrote it") in table 3.11, the action of the verb *kātab-tî* applies to *ʾōtô,* "it." The verb root *ktb* is said to be **transitive;** it "transfers" the action from the doer to the object. The verb *hālak-tî* ("I went") is **intransitive** because there is no transfer of the action to an object. Although I can say "I went to school," the school is not changed or affected by the action; it is simply the location toward which I am headed. Hebrew does not, in general, show the difference between transitive and intransitive verbs through changes in form, although there are some ways it can do that which we will not discuss here.

The example above of *ha-rʾê-nî ʾet kĕbōd-ekâ* ("show me Your glory") illustrates the use of another derivational affix to mark a verb as **causative** (A causes B to happen). Let's try to unpack the example:

ha-r'ê-nî *'et* *kĕbōd-ekâ*
show-me object *glory-your*
"Show me your glory."

The verb root *r'h*[12] ("see") is transitive. Adding the derivational prefix *h-* indicates the meaning "show," "cause to see," a verb that takes a double object. The pronoun object "me" occurs as *-nî* added to the verb;[13] it is the first object. The second object is *kĕbōd-ekâ* ("your glory"), and the Hebrew word *('et)* placed in front of (to the left of) it is like a signpost that says, "The following word is an object." The term *'et* is often called an "object marker" or "accusative case marker" in Hebrew grammars.

The last example in table 3.11 illustrates how some verbs can have a special form for the **jussive** mood when the action or state is "not yet a reality." Most Hebrew verbs do not have a separate form for the jussive. A form like *yi-ktōb* can be used either for the **indicative** mood ("he will write") or for the jussive mood ("let him write"). However, if the third root position is filled by a vowel rather than a consonant, then there is a form for the third person singular that is different for the jussive mood. The form *ya-ʿăśeh* in the table has the letter *h* in the third position, but it stands for a vowel, not a consonant. That is, we could transliterate the form with *ya-ʿăśe* if we wanted to show just the sound of the form and not its spelling. The final vowel has dropped in the jussive form *ya-ʿăś*.

While the Hebrew language has some ways to mark things like tense, aspect, and mood, you will need to pick up a lot of clues from the context. In this sense the Hebrew verb is less distinctive than the Greek verb, which gives a lot of information directly through changes in the form. In English the main verb has even fewer markings than the Hebrew verb, but a great variety of **auxiliary verbs** will give the details about tense, aspect, and mood. With a form like *yiktōb* you will need to discover from the surrounding context whether to translate *he will write, let him write, may he write, he could write, he must write,* etc.

12. The *h* does not appear in the form. This is a type of root where the third root letter is a vowel, not a consonant. As a result, that third letter can change easily from one vowel to another or even drop out.

13. Most Hebrew grammar books call *-nî* a suffix, but linguists prefer to call it an **enclitic.** It is not a morpheme that adds information to the root like gender or number, but a morpheme that is more like a separate word that has simply become attached to the end of another word.

Greek Morphology

We include here, as we did for Hebrew, a brief survey of some types of morphological issues that students of Greek will encounter. We will begin with Greek nouns, pronouns, and adjectives. We will see that these words receive regular inflectional affixes to indicate number, gender, and case. This process is called **declension** in most textbooks. Then we will look at the Greek verb inflection (also called **conjugation**). Here we will see that Greek verbs can have inflectional affixes that indicate many different things (e.g., number, gender, person, tense, aspect, voice, and mood).

Greek Nouns and Pronouns

Here are the same types of questions we asked for English and Hebrew nouns and pronouns but now ask about Greek nouns and pronouns. Notice that Greek uses inflection to show changes in the third-person pronouns, whereas English and Hebrew use suppletion.

Many Indo-European languages use inflection to mark case on nouns (e.g., German, Russian, Greek). Old English used to have case endings on nouns,

Table 3.12: Grammatical Questions for Greek Nouns and Pronouns

Question	Term	Types of Answers	Nouns	Pronouns
How many?	number	singular plural	*anthrōp-os* ("man") *anthrōp-oi* ("men")	*egō* ("I") *hēmeis* ("we")
What kind?	gender	masculine feminine neuter	*adelphos / adelphē*[14] ("brother"/"sister")	*aut-os* ("he") *aut-ē* ("she") *aut-o* ("it")
Relation to me?	person	first second third	N/A	*egō* ("I") *su* ("you," sing.) *autos* ("he")
What is it doing?	case	nominative accusative dative genitive	*anthrōp-os* ("man") *anthrōp-on* ("man") *anthrōp-ō* ("[to a] man") *anthrōp-ou* ("man's")	*egō* ("I") *me* ("me") *moi* ("[to] me") *mou* ("my")

14. Nouns do have gender in Greek: masculine, feminine, or neuter. However, the gender is related more to the individual vocabulary word than to the inflectional affixes.

but they were dropped before Middle English. (The possessive marker *-s* is a remnant of this pattern.) Greek of the New Testament period (Koine Greek) has inflectional affixes that mark case on nouns, pronouns, adjectives, and determiners. Nouns belong to one of three classes, called **declensions** in Greek studies, each of which has a separate set of case endings. The noun classes are somewhat similar to the fact that in English some nouns take a different plural suffix. We "know" that *child* becomes *children* and *ox* becomes *oxen* because that is the "right" plural marker for those words. In Greek we have to remember which noun class takes which endings, not only for number, but also for gender and case. Table 3.13 shows the different patterns for singular nouns.

Table 3.13: Greek Case Endings on Singular Nouns

	Class I	Class II	Class III
Nominative	*fōn-ē* ("voice")	*anthrōp-os* ("man")	*sōm-a* ("body")
Accusative	*fōn-ēn*	*anthrōp-on*	*sōm-a*
Dative	*fōn-ē*[15]	*anthrōp-ō*	*sōm-ati*
Genitive	*fōn-ēs*	*anthrōp-ou*	*sōm-atos*

Notice that Class I nouns have different suffixes than nouns of Classes II and III. If you see a noun that ends in *-ēs,* you will know that it is a Class I noun and can figure out the other singular endings by following the pattern for that class. We already have defined nominative, accusative, and genitive in our discussion of English, but we now need to define **dative.** In Greek when a noun (or pronoun) receives something (as in *I gave the book* <u>*to the man*</u>), it uses the dative form *(anthrōpō).* Greek does not need to use a preposition ("to") in front of the noun because the noun has the dative marker on it already.

Greek Adjectives

The adjective in Koine Greek changes for these same categories and "agrees" (shows **concord**) with the noun it modifies; in other words, the adjective receives the same case markings that the noun does. Thus, a Greek adjective

15. Although the SBL transliteration of the final sound of the nominative and the dative are the same, the Greek letters are η and ῃ, respectively.

changes shape to agree with a masculine, feminine, or neuter noun. This is similar to Spanish, which also shows number and gender on adjectives. For example, *hermano bueno* "good brother" versus *hermana buena* "good sister." The following table illustrates this agreement:

Table 3.14: Case Agreement in Greek Nouns and Adjectives

Question	Term	Types of Answers	Greek Example
How many?	number	singular plural	*anthrōp-os agath-os* ("good person") *anthrōp-oi agath-oi* ("good people")
Male/female?	gender/class	masculine feminine neuter	*anthrōp-os agath-os* ("good person") *fōn-ē agath-ē* ("good sound") *dōr-on agath-on* ("good gift")
What is it doing?	case	nominative accusative dative genitive	*anthrōp-os agath-os* *anthrōp-on agath-on* *anthrōp-ō agath-ō* *anthrōp-ou agath-ou*

Greek Articles

Greek also has a systematic way to indicate person, number, gender, and case on the word we translate as "the" in English. This word changes shape to agree with the person, number, gender, and case of the noun to which it relates. Note the changes in the following singular and plural nominative forms:

- "the man" *ho anthropos* "the men" *hoi anthropoi*
- "the woman" *hē gunē* "the women" *hai gunai*
- "the child" *to teknon* "the children" *ta tekna*

Greek Participles

We need to look at Greek **participles** before we move on to Greek verbs. In Greek, a participle combines verb and adjective components. The verb side of a participle is that it can be inflected for tense; the adjective side of a participle shows up in the inflectional affixes for gender, number, and case. A participle looks like an adjective because it agrees with the noun it modifies in these three areas. Thus, a participle will have different suffixes when it modifies a masculine, feminine, or neuter noun. Note how the form of the participle changes:

- *philōn:* "(the) loving person (masculine)"
- *philousa:* "(the) loving person (feminine)"
- *philoun:* "(the) loving one (neuter)"

These three examples are all in the present tense and nominative case. Participles can also be in other tenses and in other cases (e.g., genitive, dative, accusative).

Greek nouns, pronouns, adjectives, articles, and participles are inflected for many more things than their English equivalents. You will need to think about these words in terms of the Greek patterns (declensions) and not limit yourself to English patterns.

Greek Verbs

Greek verbs can have hundreds of different shapes. You will see large charts of these verb conjugations in your textbook. The form of the verb changes to indicate changes in meaning. The good news is that we can again look for patterns and use our knowledge of how languages work to master these new forms. Let's look at the normal questions that are addressed within the Greek verb forms. (See table 3.15).

The example of *lu-ō* ("I loose") and *lu-omen* ("we loose") in table 3.15 illustrates the singular and the plural forms of the first person as they occur for present tense verbs. The root does not change; instead the suffix changes from *-ō* for the singular ("I") to *-omen* for the plural ("we"). Like English but unlike Hebrew, the Greek verb does not have a way to mark changes in gender from masculine to feminine. The verb *leg-ei* can be used either for "he says" or for "she says."

Changes in the person for the present tense are shown by varying the ending from *-ō* ("I") to *-eis* ("you") and *-ei* ("he, she, or it"). When we also vary the tense or the aspect, the endings for person, gender, and number change along with other specific markers for tense/aspect. The past tense or completed aspect (usually called *aorist* in Greek grammars), is marked by the prefix *e-* and the

Table 3.15: Basic Questions for Greek Verbs

Question	Term	Types of Answers	Greek Examples
How many?	number	singular plural	*lu-ō* ("I loose") *lu-omen* ("we loose")
Male/female?	gender	masculine feminine neuter	N/A
Relation to me?	person	first second third	*lu-ō* ("I loose") *lu-eis* ("you [sing.] loose") *lu-ei* ("he/she/it looses")
When?	tense[16]	present past future	*lu-ō* ("I loose") *e-lu-s-a* ("I loosed") *lu-s-ō* ("I will loose")
Completed?	aspect	completed incompleted	*e-lu-s-a* ("I loosed") *e-lu-on* ("I was loosing")
Control?	voice	active passive	*lu-ō* ("I loose") *lu-omai* ("I am loosed")
Objects?	transitivity	intransitive transitive ditransitive	*peripat-oumen* ("we walk") *lu-s-ate auton* ("loose it") *e-deix-en autois tas cheiras* ("he showed them his hands")
Reality?	mood	indicative subjunctive optative imperative	*lu-eis* ("you [sing.] loose") *lu-ēs* ("you [sing.] might loose") *lu-ois* ("you [sing.] should loose") *lu-e* ("Loose!")

suffix *-s* and also by the change of the suffix for "I" (from *-ō* for the present tense to *-a* for the past tense or completed aspect). The future has the suffix *-s* and the same endings for person, gender, and number as for the present tense.[17]

---

16. Scholars disagree on the distinction between *tense* and *aspect* in New Testament Greek. For a summary of recent discussions see part 1 of Stanley E. Porter and D. A. Carson, eds., *Biblical Greek Language and Linguistics: Open Questions in Current Research,* Journal for the Study of the New Testament, Supplement Series 80 (Sheffield: JSOT Press, 1993), 18–82.
17. The aorist and future morpheme *-s* is a suffix, not an infix, even though it is followed by another suffix. To be an infix a morpheme must appear within the root.

The difference between the form of the verb for which the doer of the action is the grammatical subject and the form for which the receiver of the action is the subject appears as the difference between the endings *-ō* and *-omai.* Once again, this set of endings for when the subject is "I" will vary if the tense or aspect is changed.

The second-to-last row in table 3.15 contains an example of each of the three types of verbs: intransitive, transitive, and bitransitive. When someone *walks,* he or she does not affect anything, so *walk* is an intransitive verb. The Greek pronoun *auton,* which follows *lusate,* is in the accusative case, and it stands for the thing that is affected by the action of loosing. A different situation arises for the sentence *edeixen autois tas cheiras* ("he showed them his hands"). In this example *tas cheiras* ("his hands") has the form of the accusative, while the pronoun *autois* ("them") is in the dative case. When the object with a verb of this type is a person rather than a thing, then it will normally require the dative case. The sentence could be paraphrased: "He showed his hands to them."

Greek verbs also are marked for one of four **moods:** indicative, subjunctive, optative, or imperative. These moods relate to the speaker's attitude toward how the verb relates to reality; that is, whether the action or state is real or not yet a reality. The **indicative** mood is used more than 15,000 times in the New Testament and is the only mood that handles "real" situations. The subjunctive, optative, and imperative moods all refer to actions or states that are not (yet) a reality. The subjunctive and imperative mood are each used in less than ten percent of the verbs in the New Testament, and the optative is used with less than half of one percent of all verbs in the New Testament. The **subjunctive** mood refers to the potential or probability of a verb; it *might* take place. The **optative** mood indicates something the speaker hopes will occur; it *may* take place. The **imperative** mood reflects the speaker's desire that something happen; it *should* take place. We are used to the imperative in English commands.

The various affixes of the Greek verb are placed in a specific order before and after the verb root. In figure 3.1 we see five of these positions. Note that the term *ending* refers to several pieces of meaning at once: the person and number of the subject and some tense information.

Figure 3.1: Five Affix Positions for the Greek Verb

1	2	3	4	5
PAST TIME	ROOT	PASSIVE	FUTURE TIME	ENDING

We will illustrate this scheme with the common verb *luø* ("I loose").

Figure 3.2: Affix Positions for the Greek Verb *Luō*

1	2	3	4	5	
PAST TIME	ROOT	PASSIVE	FUTURE TIME	ENDING	
	lu			*-ō*	"I loose"
	lu		*-s*	*-ō*	"I will loose"
	lu	*-thē*	*-s*	*-omai*	"I will be loosed"
e-	*lu*			*-on*	"I was loosing"

The Greek verb forms in figure 3.2 indicate different meanings. In the first form, only the root and the ending positions are used. The particular ending *-ō* conveys the fact that it is "I" (first person singular) who is the subject and that the action is happening now (in the present tense). The addition of the *-s* future tense affix in the second example changes the meaning of the verb from present to future. The third example includes the passive suffix *-thē* before the future suffix *-s*. Putting the various morphemes together the word means "I will be loosed." The fourth example has a prefix in the past time position and a suffix *-on* that indicates that the action was seen as an ongoing action and that it was first person. Thus, this example means "I was loosing."

Greek uses different basic forms of a verb to construct the many inflected forms. These forms are called the **principal parts** of the verb. In English, the present, simple past, and the past participle are the three principal parts of a verb; for example, *eat, ate, eaten; sing, sang, sung.* Greek verbs have six principal parts: present, future, aorist, perfect active, perfect middle, and aorist passive. Most textbooks list these forms for the common verbs. You will need to remember these forms in order to master the conjugation of each verb. Here is one example, the verb *luō* ("to loose"):

- **Present:** *luō*
- **Future:** *lusō*
- **Aorist:** *elusa*
- **Perfect Active:** *leluka*
- **Perfect Middle:** *lelumai*
- **Aorist Passive:** *eluthēn*

Notice the *lu-* root in all these forms. In the two aorist forms (aorist and aorist passive) there is a prefix *e-*. In the two perfect forms (perfect active and perfect middle) there is a prefix *le-* (the actual shape of the prefix is based on the initial sound of the root; in this case, an *l*).

Comparing Hebrew, Greek, and English Morphology

Let's look back at the various ways Hebrew, Greek, and English words are changed to indicate grammatical information (inflection). Table 3.16 indicates which types of words (noun, pronoun, or adjective) in each of the three languages change in some way to reflect the features listed in the first column.

Hebrew, Greek, and English all modify nouns and pronouns to indicate how many things are involved (number). Hebrew and Greek also include number on adjectives, and both indicate grammatical gender on nouns (i.e., gender based on grammatical agreement with other words rather than the natural division of male/female), whereas English does not normally do so. (The limited set of gender-specific nouns in English such as *waiter/waitress* has always been relatively small and is decreasing.) Hebrew and Greek also indicate gender on more pronouns than English, which indicates this only in the third person singular *(he, she, it).* Plus, they also indicate gender on adjectives. All three languages keep track of the person of each pronoun, as is common for all languages. Greek has the most ways to keep track of the role of words within a clause (case), marking each noun, pronoun, and adjective in one of four ways (nominative, accusative, dative, or genitive). Hebrew does not mark nouns

Table 3.16: Inflecting Nouns, Pronouns, and Adjectives

	Hebrew	Greek	English
Number	Noun Pronoun Adjective	Noun Pronoun Adjective	Noun Pronoun N/A
Gender	Noun Pronoun (only 2d and 3d person) Adjective	Noun Pronoun Adjective	N/A Pronoun (only 3d person singular) N/A
Person	Pronoun	Pronoun	Pronoun
Case	N/A Pronoun N/A	Noun Pronoun Adjective	Noun (only Genitive) Pronoun N/A

or adjectives for case, and English has only the genitive marker on nouns, typically called **possessive.**

Table 3.17 compares how verbs in each language have separate forms for the features indicated in the first column. Where the feature applies to only a part of the possible forms, the specific forms to which it relates are given. For the categories listed, English is the most limited in how it varies the forms of the verbs. This is partly because it uses forms of the verbs *have* and *be* as "helping" verbs.

Putting Inflection and Derivation Together

Before we consider how to combine the language processes of inflection and derivation, we will summarize the main differences between **derivational** and **inflectional** affixes in table 3.18.

Morphemes with More Than One Form

Morphemes may have more than one form. These variant forms are called *allomorphs* and can be explained either in terms of the way they interact with the sounds around them (phonetic environment) or in terms of the different kinds of words they modify (lexical environment). The English plural suffix *-s,*

Table 3.17: How Verbs Are Changed

	Hebrew	Greek	English
Number	separate forms	separate forms	only 3d singular
Gender	2d and 3d person	N/A[18]	N/A
Person	separate forms	separate forms	only 3d singular
Tense	Past Future	Past Future	Past
Aspect	Completed Incompleted	Completed Progressive	Progressive
Voice	Active Passive	Active Middle Passive	N/A

for example, changes in pronunciation depending on the phonetic qualities of the final sound of the noun root (see table 3.19). The fact that *child* becomes *children* rather than *childs* in the plural form illustrates a lexically determined allomorph of the plural in English. Each of these patterns of change reminds us of the principle that linguistic units can have variations.

Allomorphs Determined by Sounds

The English plural suffix on words like *cats, dogs,* and *roses* changes its phonetic shape due to the sound that immediately precedes it. Table 3.19 shows the last sound of each of the following singular forms and the sound of the plural ending.

Why does the sound, consistently spelled with *s,* change its pronunciation? The key lies in the difference between sounds that are voiced versus those that are voiceless (see chap. 2). The final sounds of *tab, pod,* and *bag* are all voiced stops, and the plural morpheme has a voiced allomorph *z.* When the final sound of the noun is a voiceless stop (see table 2.6), the plural morpheme has a voiceless pronunciation. When the final sound of the noun is a sibilant (e.g.,

18. The Greek participle does have gender distinctions. We have not considered it here because the participle does not have any distinctive person markings and actually has features of both nouns and verbs.

Table 3.18: Derivational Affixes Versus Inflectional Affixes

	Derivational Affixes	Inflectional Affixes
Word Class	Typically change class of word (*depend-able:* the suffix changes the verb to an adjective)	Do not change class of word (*language-s:* the plural doesn't change the fact that it is a noun)
Function	Indicate relations within the word (*teach—teach-er,* "one who teaches")	Indicate relations between words (*student-'s:* the suffix relates the pronoun to something else that is possessed)
Productivity	Typically limited (*wonder-ful, marvel-ous,* but not *marvel-ful)*	Normally very productive (the plural suffix can be added to most nouns)
Position	Typically close to the root (*sing-er-s:* the *-er* derivational suffix comes before the inflectional plural suffix)	Typically at edges of the word (*read-er-s:* the inflectional plural suffix comes after the *-er* derivational suffix)
Meaning	Irregular (*deliver-ance,* "the act of delivering," but *entr-ance,* "a place of entering" or "the act of entering")	Regular (*walk-ed:* the past tense suffix always indicates the same meaning)

s or *z*), the plural morpheme takes on yet another phonetic shape: a vowel plus the voiced sound *z.* By definition a vowel is voiced, so the voiced sound *z* follows a vowel. Yet all three variant pronunciations have the same meaning. They comprise one morpheme with three allomorphs.

Languages have rules that apply to certain phonetic changes that may take place in morphemes. These are called *morphophonemic rules.* Hebrew also has morphemes with more than one form that are caused by the nature of the sounds around them, as illustrated in the table 3.20. Note that the explanations derive from how Hebrew sounded during the time of the Masoretes (Middle Ages) and not from Modern Hebrew.

To express the future tense of a Hebrew verb, we add prefixes to show changes for the person (*I, you, he,* etc.). In table 3.20 the root *šmr* ("watch") has been chosen. To say "he will watch," we add the consonant *y* followed by the vowel *i (yi-šmōr).* If the first consonant of the root is an *ayin* (ע), then the vowel changes to *a* instead of *i.* This has happened in the form *ya-ʿbōd* ("he will serve").

Table 3.19: Allomorphs of the English Plural

Singular	Plural	Final Sounds
tab	*tabs*	bz
pod	*pods*	dz
bag	*bags*	gz
cup	*cups*	ps
pot	*pots*	ts
book	*books*	ks
class	*classes*	sez
rose	*roses*	zez
toe	*toes*	z

Because *ayin* is a "laryngeal" and pronounced in the throat, the front vowel *i* changes to the vowel *a*, which is pronounced farther back in the mouth.

The second example in column 2 deals with adding the definite article to a noun. In Hebrew this is done by prefixing the consonant *he (h)* followed by the vowel *a*. In addition, the consonant with which the noun begins is then

Table 3.20: Hebrew Examples of Phonetically Determined Allomorphs

Standard Hebrew Form	Form with Allomorph	Reason for the Allomorph
yi-šmōr ("he *will* watch")	*ya-ʿbōd* ("he *will* serve")	The sound of the *ayin* (ʿ), made in the throat, causes the front vowel *i* to shift to a back vowel *a*.
ha-mmelek ("*the* king")	*hā-ʾādām* ("*the* man")	The definite article normally causes the consonant to double; but the *aleph* (glottal stop, ʾ) cannot double, and the *a* vowel lengthens instead to *ā*.
mi-ppĕrî ("*from* fruit")	*mē-ʾîš* ("*from* a man")	The preposition *mi-* ("from") normally prefixes to a noun and causes the first consonant of the noun to double; but the *aleph* (glottal stop, ʾ) cannot double, and the *i* vowel lengthens instead to *ē*.

doubled. There are some consonants, like the *aleph (ʾ),* that cannot double. When the definite article is added to a noun like *ʾādām* ("man"), the *aleph* does not double but the prefix becomes *hā-* instead of *ha-*.

The third example is similar to the second. The English word *from* in Hebrew is the prefix *mi-* with the first consonant doubled in the word to which it attaches. Hebrew *ʾîš* ("man") begins with *aleph,* which cannot double. In this case the vowel *i* changes to *ē,* giving the form *mē-ʾîš* ("from a man").[19]

Greek, like English and Hebrew, also has phonologically determined allomorphs. For example, the preposition *sun* ("with") may attach to a word or root as a derivational prefix:

- *sun-elthein* "to come together"
- *sun-trechō* "I run together with"
- *sun-eudokeō* "I agree with"

If the first letter of the word to which it attaches is a labial (formed with the lips), then the form *sun* changes to *sum:*

- *sum-bouleuō* "I advise"
- *sum-mathētēs* "fellow-disciple"

The same meaning ("with") is expressed in several different forms (allomorphs) depending on the phonetic context.

Allomorphs Determined by the Vocabulary

English nouns normally make their plural with the *-s* ending discussed above. There are a number of words, however, that take other endings. These endings are specific to certain words. Since linguists refer to the sum total of the vocabulary of a language as its **lexicon,** the technical term for this type of allomorph is *lexically determined allomorph*. Some English examples include:

- *child* *children*
- *ox* *oxen*

19. Note as well that Hebrew does not have any equivalent form for the English *a* or *an*. *ʾîš* means either "man" or "a man."

English also has nouns that are borrowed from Latin and still maintain Latin plural inflectional markers:

- *alumnus* (singular) *alumni* (plural)
- *datum* (singular) *data* (plural)

Hebrew also has some examples of lexically determined allomorphs. All nouns in Hebrew must be classified as either masculine or feminine, even nouns for which there is no biological basis for a gender distinction. This reflects the fact that adjectives must have a feminine form when used with a feminine noun and a masculine form when used with a masculine noun. Likewise, verbs must have a form that corresponds in gender with a noun that refers to the doer of the action. For singular nouns a suffixed *-â* normally shows that the noun is feminine, and the masculine singular noun does not have any ending. There are, however, some feminine nouns that do not have the suffix *-â;* the fact that they are feminine has to be learned when the noun is learned as vocabulary. We could say, then, that the ending *-â* is a suffix for a feminine noun, which has an allomorph of no ending. The allomorph is used only for particular vocabulary words.

A masculine noun receives a suffix *-îm* that shows it is plural, and a feminine noun in the plural will have a suffix *-ôt.* In some cases, though, a masculine noun will add the suffix *-ôt* in the plural, and sometimes a feminine noun will have the suffix *-îm* for its plural. Such cases are rare and have to be memorized for each noun for which the unusual suffix applies. The student of Hebrew must simply learn which forms are nonstandard, much as a student of English needs to learn that the plural of *woman* is not *womans* but *women.* Table 3.21 shows the basic facts for Hebrew.

The first four rows show the standard or normal way that nouns occur in the singular or plural. We intend for you to focus on the suffixes rather than on vowel changes that take place inside of a noun. The nouns *ʾāb* ("father"), *dôr* ("generation"), and *māʾôr* ("light") form their plurals by attaching the suffix *-ôt,* which is usually the suffix for feminine plurals. Nevertheless, both nouns are still masculine even though the ending does not appear to follow the normal rule that the masculine plural has the suffix *-îm.* We know this because an adjective, which always forms its masculine plural with *-îm,* has

Table 3.21: Hebrew Nouns According to Gender and Number

Masculine Singular Nouns	Masculine Plural Nouns	Feminine Singular Nouns	Feminine Plural Nouns
sûs ("horse")	*sûs-îm* ("horses")	*sûs-â* ("mare")	*sûs-ôt* ("mares")
melek ("king")	*mĕlāk-îm* ("kings")	*malk-â* ("queen")	*mĕlāk-ôt* ("queens")
dābār ("word")	*dĕbār-îm* ("words")	*tôr-â* ("law")	*tôr-ôt* ("laws")
har ("mountain")	*hār-îm* ("mountains")	*mišpāḥ-â* ("family")	*mišpāḥ-ôt* ("families")
ʾāb ("father")	*ʾāb-ôt* ("fathers")	*ʾēm* ("mother")	*ʾimm-ôt* ("mothers")
ʾîš ("man")	*ʾănāš-îm* ("men")	*ʾîšš-â* ("woman")	*nāš-îm* ("women")
dôr ("generation")	*dôr-ôt* ("generations")	*ʾereṣ* ("land")	*ʾărāṣ-ôt* ("lands")
māʾôr ("light")	*mĕʾôr-ôt* ("lights")	*ʿîr* ("city")	*ʿār-îm* ("cities")

the masculine form when it occurs with one of these nouns (*ha-mmĕʾôr-ôt ha-ggĕdôl-îm,* "the great lights"). Or, if one of these nouns occurs as the subject of a verb, the verb will have the masculine form.

The noun *ʾîš* ("man") does have the standard *-îm* suffix for its plural, but it also has an additional letter *(n)* added inside of it. This is probably an example of a second root used for the plural (suppletion). The root for "woman" *(ʾišš)* has the standard suffix *-â* attached to it, but the plural appears to have a supplementary root as well as the suffix *-îm* instead of an expected *-ôt.* The feminine nouns for "mother" *(ʾēm)* and "land" *(ʾereṣ)* both have a singular form without the suffix *-â* but also normal plurals that end with *-ôt.* The feminine noun *ʿîr* ("city") has a singular with no suffix and a plural that has the suffix -*îm.* Even so, its feminine gender is established by phrases like *ʿār-îm gĕdô-lôt* ("large cities").

Koine Greek case endings are another example of lexically determined allomorphs; the shape of the case marker depends on the class of the root noun (see table 3.13).

Classifying Languages

Thus far we have looked at a variety of ways English, Hebrew, and Greek form words. We have noted that they each address basic questions about number, gender, and so on in slightly different, yet systematic, ways. We will now look at these three languages in a "big picture" way that allows us to compare them with the other languages of the world. Languages can be grouped by the way they handle morphology.

Analytic/Isolating Languages

Some languages have few or no words that contain more than one morpheme; each word consists of just one morpheme. Such languages are called **analytic** or **isolating.** These languages use separate words, rather than affixes, to indicate concepts such as time and number. Mandarin is a very clear example of an isolating language. Look at the following sentence and notice the verb:

Ta	*chi*	*fan*	*le*
he	eat	meal	past

"He ate the meal."[20]

Although the sentence talks about the past tense, the Mandarin verb does not change. Rather, a separate word is added to the sentence to indicate this part of the meaning.

In many ways, English is like Mandarin. English has only eight inflectional affixes (all suffixes).

Agglutinating Languages

Languages that typically construct words from clearly defined morphemes are called **agglutinating** languages. In these languages, the breaks between morphemes (e.g., between root and affix) are usually easy to identify. You might remember the word *agglutinating* by imagining strips of wood "glued" together to make a cutting board. The lines or breaks between the strips of wood are

---

20. Data from William O'Grady et al., *Contemporary Linguistics: An Introduction*, 2d ed. (New York: St. Martin's, 1993), 314.

like morpheme boundaries, nice and clear. Turkish is a good example of this kind of language.[21]

- *ev* "house"
- *ev-ler* "house-s"
- *ev-ler-de* "in the house-s"
- *ev-ler-den* "from the house-s"

Notice that the plural morpheme and the ideas of *in* and *from* are clearly seen, and each morpheme indicates only one small part of the overall meaning. This is in contrast to our final general type of languages in which one morpheme may combine a number of meanings.

Fusional Languages

Other languages construct words by using morphemes that often indicate more than one grammatical idea at the same time; for example, tense and number might be indicated with the same suffix. We see this **fusional** pattern in Spanish verbs, such as *habl-o* ("I speak"), in which the suffix *-o* indicates that it is a first person singular subject and that the action of the verb is in the present tense. Hebrew and Greek also fit this fusional category.

Koine Greek combines tense, mood, person, and number into fused verb endings. The following table shows the present tense, active, indicative forms of *lu-* ("to loose"). Note that the endings also show number (singular/plural) and person (first, second, third).

Table 3.22: Greek Verbs Show Fusional Patterns

Number	Greek Verb	English Translation
Singular	*lu-ō*	"I loose"
	lu-eis	"you (sg.) loose"
	lu-ei	"he/she looses"
Plural	*lu-omen*	"we loose"
	lu-ete	"you (pl.) loose"
	lu-ousi(n)	"they loose"

21. Ibid.

Hebrew combines the category of aspect with the person, gender, number affixes. When the affix is prefixed, the aspect is imperfective; when the affix is suffixed, the aspect is perfective.

ti-šmōr—"she will watch" (imperfective)
šāmr-â—"she watched" (perfective)

Summary and Preview

In this chapter we have seen how words are made from morphemes, and we have examined root morphemes and various types of affixes. Additionally, we have looked at how nouns, pronouns, and verbs undergo changes in their form based on how they relate to issues such as number (singular, plural), gender (masculine, feminine, neuter), person (first, second, third), or tense (past, present, future). English deals with these issues in ways that are both similar to and different from Hebrew and Greek, as a survey of some of the more outstanding features of these three languages shows.

Now that you have some idea about forming words in Hebrew and Greek, it is time to move on to using those words to form phrases and sentences. Knowing about words is interesting, but words are, after all, only the building blocks for the larger structures of language, where communication actually takes place. As you learn how Greek and Hebrew communicate through their particular structures, you will begin to experience the great reward that awaits those who study the Bible in its original languages.

For Further Study

Long, Gary A. *Grammatical Concepts 101 for Biblical Hebrew: Learning Biblical Hebrew Grammatical Concepts Through English Grammar.* Peabody, Mass.: Hendrickson, 2002.

Matthews, Peter H. *Morphology: An Introduction to the Theory of Word Structure.* 2d ed. Cambridge: Cambridge University Press, 1991.

Trask, R. L., and Bill Mayblin. *Introducing Linguistics.* New York: Totem Books, 2001.

EXERCISES

1. Identify the morphemes in the following English words.

    - Example: *dishonesty: dis-* derivational prefix; *honest* root; *-y* derivational suffix

    charity
    Christianity
    reflections
    rearranging
    real
    unreasonableness
    immortality
    philosophical
    unfriendly
    underpinnings

2. State whether the underlined segment in each of the following English words is an affix:

    houses
    bus
    butter
    better
    biter
    unwise
    selfish
    shellfish
    cranberry

3. State whether the underlined segment in each of the following English words is a derivational or an inflectional suffix:

    sells
    bigger
    digger

bells
ringing
ringlike
comical
dog's
children
wisdom

4. Examine the following Hebrew data, and see if you can determine the set of inflectional affixes for the past tense of the Hebrew verb.

kātĕbû hayĕlādîm — “The boys wrote.”
kātabnû — “We wrote.”
hayĕlādîm kĕtabtem — “Boys, you wrote.”
katĕbâ hayyaldâ — “The girl wrote.”
Abrāhām, kātabtā — “Abraham, you wrote.”
kātabtî — “I wrote.”
kātĕbâ — “She wrote.”
kātĕbû hayĕlādôt — “The girls wrote.”
hayĕlādôt kĕtabten — “Girls, you wrote.”
Śārâ kātabt — “Sarah, you wrote.”
Abrāhām wĕŚārâ kĕtabtem — “Abraham and Sarah, you wrote.”
Śārâ wĕRibkâ kĕtabten — “Sarah and Rebekah, you wrote.”

4

Putting Words Together

Phrases and Clauses

Thus for loved the God the world, that the Son the unique gave, that every the believing in him not perish but have life eternal.

—John 3:16
in literal English translation

Words seem to be the building blocks of language, but in this chapter we will show that words really occur in groups, not just in isolation. People often think of sentences as being a string of words, much like a string of pearls on a necklace. In fact, sentences are not strings of words; they are combinations of phrases. A sentence might be compared instead with a line of people waiting to enter an amusement park. Each person in line could represent a word or perhaps a morpheme, but there would also be groupings within the line. There might be several families in the line, and they could stand for certain types of phrases. Some people would be there by themselves and would represent phrases that consist of a single word. Perhaps a teacher has brought her class for an outing, and all the children plus the teacher would make up another type of phrase. Let's meet some of these groups in the line and get to know them.

That line of people tells us that there must be some basic organizing principles that the people are following. They didn't simply arrive randomly and start milling around the entrance; they got into an organized line or possibly even several lines. The factors that helped them to organize might include social norms that people form a line rather than try to push and shove their way in randomly. Perhaps also there are signs that give some directions, and of course families and students from a class would have their own internal inclinations to stay together.

Putting Words in Groups

Syntax is like the principles that cause people to organize into lines; it is the study of how phrases, clauses, and sentences are formed from words. Syntax is a subset of grammar; **grammar** can be defined more widely as the overall patterns of a language, including morphology, syntax, and other aspects.

In the last chapter we talked about the basic kinds of words.

- **Nouns** identify people, objects, or ideas.
- **Pronouns** take the place of a noun or a group of words.
- **Adjectives** tell more about a noun.
- **Determiners** identify a particular noun.
- **Verbs** tell about an action or state.
- **Adverbs** tell more about a verb, an adjective, or another adverb.
- **Conjunctions** connect other words or groups of words.
- **Prepositions** indicate a relationship between words.

Now we will see that many of these word types can also be expanded into the next larger unit of syntax: the phrase. Once we have studied the phrase types of English, Hebrew, and Greek, we will see that clauses or sentences are really groups of phrases, not words.

Syntax studies how phrases and clauses are constructed—the order of the words, how various groups of words are connected, which words are most essential to a phrase, and so on. Thus, in English we can say:

the big old black bear but not *the black big old bear.*

We can relate the same information in several ways. For example,

John gave Mary the book; or *John gave the book to Mary;*
but not
John Mary the book gave.

Word order is important in English grammar because it tells us who did what to whom. If *John* is in front of the verb *gave* and *Mary* is after the verb, we know that John was the one who gave the book and Mary was the person who received it. In Hebrew and Greek there are other ways of indicating who gave what to whom. Although word order is important to understanding phrases and clauses, we also need to recognize which words belong together.

Defining Phrases

Phrases are groups of words that function as a unit. In English, for example, a **noun phrase** (NP) is a noun plus other words that are related to the noun in some way. Each of the following comprises a single noun phrase:

- students
- the students
- the diligent students
- the three diligent students

We know that each one is a phrase because of how it functions in relation to other parts of a clause or sentence. For example, each of the above could be followed by "study the biblical languages every day."

There are also **verb phrases, prepositional phrases,** and **adjective phrases** (and others) in which the obligatory element is a verb, a preposition, or an adjective, respectively. We will look more at phrases later in this chapter.

Defining Clauses

Clauses are groups of phrases that include at least one verb phrase (or, for languages other than English, at least one predicate phrase).[1] The following table (4.1) illustrates the most basic type of clause, consisting of a noun phrase and a verb phrase. The verb phrase includes not only the verb itself but also the other parts of the phrase that answer various questions about the verb, such as:

- What was affected by the action?
- Where did the action take place?

1. Roughly speaking, a **predicate** is something that is said about the subject of the clause. Usually the predicate will be less defined than the subject, because the predicate is the new information. See also the Glossary in this volume.

- When did the action occur?
- What was the goal of the action?
- To what degree is the action carried out?

Table 4.1: The Simple English Clause

Noun Phrase	Verb Phrase
The students	were diligent.
The students	came.
The students	studied hard.
The students	studied Greek.
The students	sat near the front of the class.
The students	gave the teacher good evaluations.
The students	always appreciated learning more about linguistics.

We will look at the various types of clauses in English, Hebrew, and Greek later in this chapter.

Analyzing Phrases and Clauses

Phrases and clauses (and even larger units such as paragraphs) are made up of smaller pieces or units, not simply of words. Syntax studies the way that these units are arranged on a hierarchy that begins with the words and moves up to various types of phrases and finally to the clause. The clause or sentence is on the top of the hierarchy, and the individual words are on the bottom. Phrases fall somewhere in between as illustrated in figure 4.1.

Figure 4.1: Hierarchy of Clauses and Phrases

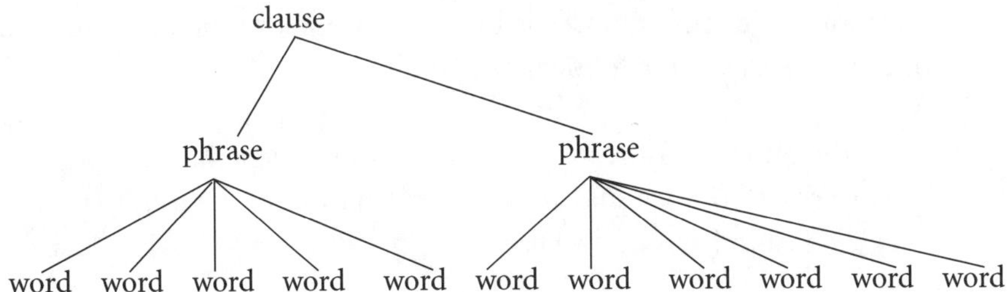

Looking for the Boundaries

To discover the boundaries of the various units of a phrase or clause, a linguist performs appropriate tests. These tests relate to how phrases and clauses are used in particular environments or locations. To return to the analogy of the lines at the amusement park, if we find a father and a mother together, we expect to find their children with them. Perhaps the teacher has arranged for all of her pupils to wear shirts of the same color so that it will be easier to keep track of them. In a similar way the linguist looks for the **head,** or controlling word of a phrase or for certain similarities in shape that show which words belong together.

In the clause

the rather well-dressed students sat in front of the class

we recognize that some words fit together with each other. One way to see which words form a group (a **constituent**) is to ask a question about the clause.

- *Who* sat in the front of the classroom? *(the rather well-dressed students)*
- *Where* did the well-dressed students sit? *(in front of the class)*
- *What* did the well-dressed students do? *(sat in front of the class)*

The answers to these questions show us that certain words really are acting as a group, a phrase. Thus, we have the following phrases:

- *the rather well-dressed students*
- *sat in front of the class*
- *in front of the class*

Another way to identify phrases is by substituting a pronoun or another word for the phrase as in the following examples:

- *They* (the rather well-dressed students) *sat in front of the class*
- *The rather well-dressed students sat there* (in front of the class)
- *They did* (sat in front of the class)

Each language has specific constituents that can be combined to make phrases and clauses. We will look at some of the basic patterns of English, Hebrew, and Greek phrases and clauses in this chapter.

Arranging the Hierarchy

Phrases and clauses are not strings of words; they have an internal structure. We also recognize again that smaller units can be combined to make larger units, just as in phonology and morphology. In this chapter we will see how words can be combined to form phrases and phrases to form clauses. We also could study combinations of clauses as sentences and higher structures such as paragraphs and episodes, but we will leave this for the discussion in chapter 5 on discourse.

The hierarchical nature of language is somewhat like a pyramid: each piece of language on the lower levels is a part of some larger unit. Thus, the words *the rather well-dressed students* combine to make a noun phrase that in turn combines with the verb phrase "sat in front of the class" to make a **clause.**

Figure 4.2: Making a Clause from a Noun Phrase and a Verb Phrase

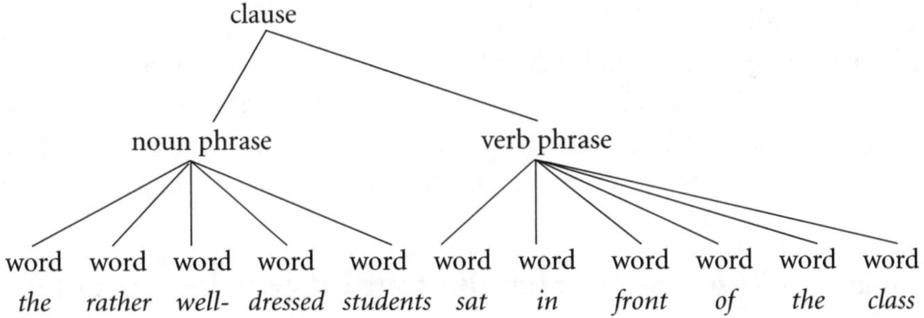

Even within these two phrases, we can recognize smaller groups of words (phrases), such as *rather well-dressed,* an adjective phrase, and *in front of the class,* a prepositional phrase.

Determining the Linear Order

Each language has a limited set of syntactic patterns it uses to make phrases and clauses. Noun phrases, for example, may either have the noun followed by an adjective (as in Spanish *casa blanca*) or vice versa (as in English *white house*); the pattern will not keep changing. Hebrew and Greek both prefer putting the noun before the adjective as in Spanish, as seen in table 4.6. Likewise, some languages may prefer the subject of the clause to precede the verb (as in English, *the student studied*), while other languages will prefer the subject to follow the verb. Hebrew prefers the pattern with the subject after the verb:

bārāʾ *ʾĕlōhîm*
created God
"God created"

At the end of this chapter we will see how these word order preferences follow general patterns in a language.

Picturing Phrases and Clauses

Tree diagrams are graphic ways to show the syntactic relationships within a phrase or clause. The highest element in the hierarchy is placed on top, with the next highest on the second level and lower elements on successively lower levels. Lines are drawn between each higher node and its constituents immediately below it.

Tree diagrams are useful because they can clarify the meaning of ambiguous sentences. For example, the phrase *large circles and squares* is ambiguous. The reader does not know whether both the circles and squares are large or only the circles. A tree diagram will illustrate these two meanings since it can

Figure 4.3: Two Tree Diagrams Illustrate Different Interpretations

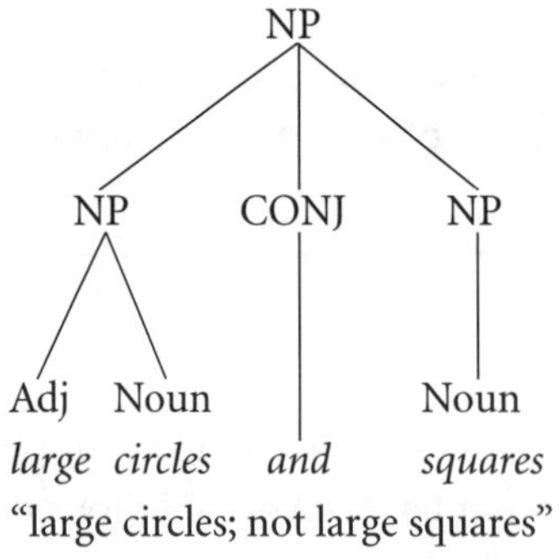

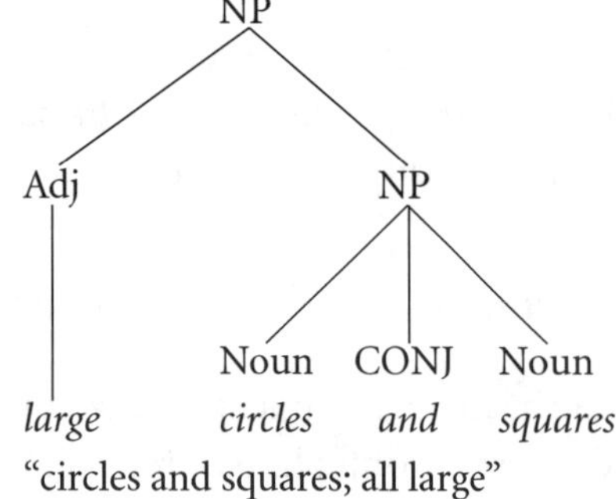

only represent one analysis of the constituents at a time. On the left side of figure 4.3, only the circles are large, while on the right side the circles and the squares are both large.

The left side of figure 4.3 shows that the word *large* modifies only the term *circles* and does not apply to the term *squares*. It can also be represented as follows: *large circles | and squares*. The right side shows the complete phrase broken up into only an adjective modifying a noun phrase *(circles and squares)*. This could also be represented another way: *large | circles and squares*.

The last noun phrase in Genesis 10:21 is analyzed differently by the English versions, and the choice relates to a controversy about whether Shem was the oldest son or not.

ʾăḥî	*Yepet*	*haggādôl*
brother-of	Japheth	the elder/older

The KJV makes Shem "the brother of Japheth the elder." Virtually all other English versions make Shem "the older brother of Japheth."

The problem lies in the fact that in the Hebrew the term "elder/older" must follow the phrase "the brother of Japheth" (a construct phrase; see chap. 3) regardless of whether it applies to *brother* or *Japheth*. The two tree diagrams in figure 4.4 should clarify the issue. The top analysis shows that the Hebrew adjective *haggādôl ("older")* applies to Japheth's brother. Another way to show this is *the brother of Japheth | the older*. The bottom analysis applies the adjective to Japheth, not to his brother. This can be represented by *the brother of | Japheth the elder*.

Forming Phrases

Sentences are composed of units, such as noun phrases or verb phrases, placed together in particular ways that are determined by the grammar of the language. The way the units are structured and put together into sentences varies from language to language. We will look now at how phrases are put together.

Certain "rules" in a given language spell out how the phrases in the language will be put together or structured. These rules are called **phrase structure rules.** When linguists talk about rules, they refer to how native speakers say things (or write them down).

Figure 4.4: Tree Diagrams for Genesis 10:21

Analysis A: *the older brother of Japheth*

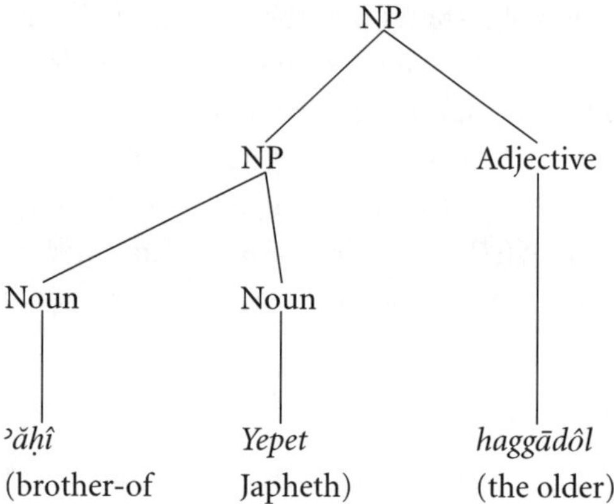

Analysis B: *the brother of Japheth the elder*

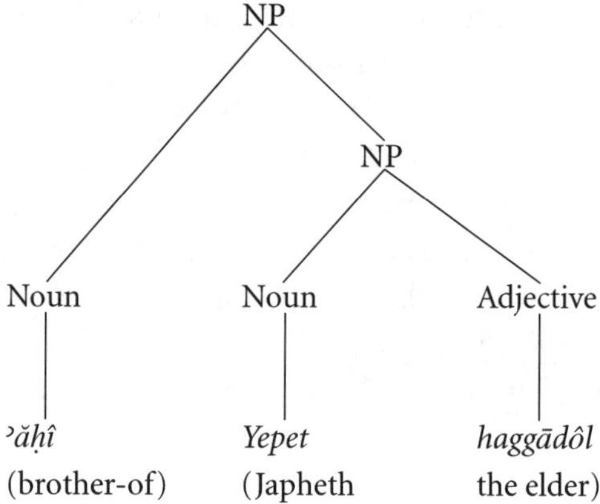

Noun Phrases

One of the rules of English is that in a noun phrase the article always precedes the noun. We could represent this graphically like this: NP → Art N. This tells us that a noun phrase is an article *(a, an,* or *the)* followed by the noun. An example would be *the students* or *an apple.* English does not use the order noun–article, so *students the* and *apple an* are not grammatical in English.

Expanding on this rule for English, a noun phrase that contains a noun described by an adjective has the following shape: NP → Art Adj N. That is, the article must occur before the adjective and the adjective must occur before the noun as in the following examples:

- the good students
- a delicious apple

Hebrew and Greek both put the adjective after the noun. The following rule summarizes Hebrew and Greek noun phrases in this regard:

NP → Art N Art Adj

That is, a Hebrew or Greek noun phrase can be written as the article (only *the* for Greek and Hebrew) before the noun followed by the article before the adjective. Keeping in mind that the definite article in Hebrew occurs as a prefix before the noun or adjective but is a separate word in Greek, here are examples for both Hebrew and Greek:

- Hebrew Example: *hā-ʾāreṣ* *ha-ṭṭôbâ*
the-land the-good
"the good land"

- Greek Example: *ho poimēn* *ho kalos*
the shepherd the good
"the good shepherd"

Greek also has the possibility of a structure very similar to English (*ton kalon agōna,* "the good fight"), but in Hebrew the adjective never comes before the noun in these phrases.

An English noun phrase must have a noun and may also have a number of other words, such as determiners *(a, the, this),* numerals, and adjectives. These words appear in a standard order as illustrated by the following phrases:

Determiner	**Numerals**	**Adjective**	**Noun**
the	*two*	*intelligent*	*students*
my	*three*	*favorite*	*idioms*

English noun phrases can, of course, be much more complex. They can include clauses and other large units as in the following examples:

- *two of the books that she enjoyed reading*
- *the teacher whom he appreciated the most*

A standard rule of thumb for the Hebrew noun phrase is that adjectives and determiners (words like *this* or *that*) will group next to the head noun in exactly the opposite direction as for English.

Noun	**Adjective**	**Determiner**
hā-ʾōt-ôt	*ha-ggedōl-ôt*	*hā-ʾēlleh*
the-sign-s	the-great-(plural)	the-these

"these great signs" (Joshua 24:17)

Noun	**Adjective**	**Determiner**
ha-ssaʿar	*ha-ggādôl*	*ha-zzeh*
the-storm	the-great	the-this

"this great storm" (Jonah 1:12)

Unlike English and Hebrew, Greek noun phrases can have several different word orders. If we compare the gospel of Mark to Paul's epistles, we can see that Mark uses the noun-adjective order as the primary order and Paul uses the adjective-noun order in over half of his noun phrases.[2] Thus, Paul writes:

> *monō sophō theō*
> only wise God
> "(to the) only wise God" (Rom. 16:27)

while Mark writes:

> *phōban megan*
> fear great
> "(with a) great fear" (Mark 4:41)

2. See Stanley Porter, *Idioms of the Greek New Testament,* 2d ed. (Sheffield: Sheffield Academic Press, 1995), 288–97, for a detailed comparison of Greek word order.

The Greek noun phrase also is tied together by concord. The noun determiner and adjectives all must have the same gender, case, and number. These grammatical features are indicated by inflectional suffixes as shown above.

Another topic within the noun phrase is the genitive, or "possessive," construction. English again differs from Hebrew and Greek, although "Bible English" introduced a new English pattern as early as William Tyndale's translation in the sixteenth century. The primary way possession is shown in English is as follows:

Noun+'s	**Noun**
child's	*book*
book's	*cover*

We can, of course, also say *the book of the child* or *the cover of the book*. This form can be traced back to Hebrew and Greek word order that was copied by early Bible translators. Thus, it became familiar in Bible English and church language. This is how we came to have phrases such as *Son of Man, Bread of Life,* and *love of God.*

We already have seen the Hebrew construct state pattern in chapter 3. The interesting difference between English and Hebrew is that in Hebrew the changes indicating possession (or other relationship) occur on the noun that is the possessee, rather than the possessor.

Hebrew Form		**Primary English Form**
dĕbar	*ha-mmelek*	the king's word
word-of	the-king	
the word of the king		

Greek also uses the pattern noun + possessor:

hē	*agapē*	*tou*	*theou*
the	love (of)	the	God
"God's love" or "the love of God"			

to	*phōs*	*tōn*	*anthrōpōn*
the	light (of)	the	men
"the light of men"			

These genitive constructions can have many different meanings. Your textbook may call them "genitives of possession," "genitives of source," or "subjective genitives." These terms are a blend of grammatical (genitive) form and semantic meaning.

Verb Phrases

As the head of the verb phrase, a verb determines or controls the various parts of the verb phrase. Many of the additional parts of a verb phrase are determined by the characteristics of the verb. Information about verb types or classes is often put in the dictionary. For example, some verbs must occur with an object; others never take an object. We refer to verbs that have a subject but no object as **intransitive** *(they fell, she slept)*. Verbs that have a subject and a direct object are called **transitive** *(he saw the book, we study Hebrew)*. Verbs that have a subject, a direct object, and an indirect object are called **ditransitive** *(we gave the money to the orphanage)*. When a verb is transitive or ditransitive, the direct object and indirect object are necessary parts of the verb phrase. We refer to such necessary objects as *complements* of the verb. Some of the typical complement structures of English verbs are listed in table 4.2 (PP stands for *prepositional phrase*).

Note that the verbs *put* and *place* require a location phrase.

Table 4.3 presents some typical complement structures of Hebrew verbs. Sometimes a pronoun complement can be attached to the end of a verb to make a single word. This will be shown below by the plus sign (+). Also, a particle, *ʾet,* is sometimes used before a noun to mark it as an object complement.

Table 4.2: Typical Complement Structures of English Verbs

Verbs	Complements	Examples
sleep	NONE	*they slept*
hit	NP	*they hit the ball*
give	NP PP to	*give a book to the child*
send		*send a book to the child*
give	NP NP	*give the child a book*
send		*send the child a book*
put	NP PP loc	*put a book on the table* (but not *put a book)*
place		*place a book on the table* (but not *place a book*)

Table 4.3: Typical Complement Structures of Hebrew Verbs

Hebrew Verbs	Complements	Examples
ntn (give)	PP *l-* (to) NP	*ten l-î ha-nnepeš* (Gen. 14:21) give to-me the-people "Give the people to me." *wĕ-yaʿăqōb nātan lĕ-ʿēśāw leḥem* (Gen. 25:34) and-Jacob gave to-Esau bread "Then Jacob gave Esau bread."
šlḥ (send)	+ PP *ʾel-* (to)	*šĕlāḥ-anî ʾălê-kem* (Exod. 3:13) (God) sent-me to-you "God sent me to you."
ntn (give)	PP *ʾet* PP *l-* (to)	*tᵉnā ʾet bit-kā li-bn-î* (2 Kings 14:9) give daughter-your to-son-my "Give your daughter to my son." *nātan ʾet- Mîkal . . . lĕ-Palṭî* (1 Sam. 25:44) (Saul) gave Michal . . . to-Palti "(Saul) gave Michal to Palti."
ntn (give)	NP PP *l-* (to)	*tᵉnā ʿuzz-ĕkā lᵉ-ʿabd-ĕkā* (Ps. 86:16) give strength-your to-servant-your "Give your strength to your servant."
śym (place)	NP PP *ʿal* (loc)	*śîm yᵉmîn-ĕkā ʿal rōʾš-ô* (Gen. 48:18) place right-hand-your on head-his "Place your right hand on his head."
śym (place)	PP *(ʾet)* PP *ʿal* (loc)	*wᵉ-śîm ʾōt-ô ʿal nēs* (Num. 21:8) and-place it on standard "and place it on a standard"

These six different patterns for Hebrew verb phrases have some general similarities. First, the direct object phrase is either unmarked (shown by NP in the table), attached as a pronoun to the end of the verb (+ in the table), or marked with the particle *ʾet.* Since the only function of *ʾet* is to mark the object of a verb, there is no English equivalent for it (English marks the object by position in the sentence, not by a particle). Second, the indirect object is always marked by a preposition, either *l-* (to), *ʾel* (to), or *ʿal* (on). Third, the relative order of object and indirect object varies, but usually the indirect object will occur first if it is a pronoun and second if it is a noun.

Greek verbs also can be divided into various classes depending on whether they can have an object or other complement.

Table 4.4: Typical Complement Structures of Greek Verbs

Greek Verbs	Complements	Examples
dipsō "thirst"	NONE	*dipsō* "I thirst"
eimi "be"	NP in Nominative	*theos ēn ho logos* God was the word "the Word was God" *ho theos agapē estin* the God love is "God is love"
agapaō "love"	NP in Accusative	*ēgapēsen ho theos ton kosmon* loved the God the world "God loved the world" *ēgapēsen me ho patēr* loved me the Father "the Father loved me"

Adjective Phrases

English adjectives can be grouped in different subclasses by how they function in noun phrases. See Dixon for more discussion about adjective classes in a variety of languages.[3] Figure 4.5 shows the relative ordering of adjectives in English according to type.

Figure 4.5: The Relative Ordering of Adjectives in English

	Value	Dimension	Physical Property	Speed	Human Propensity	Age	Color
Examples:	*good*	*big*	*hard*	*fast*	*happy*	*new*	*black*
	bad	*large*	*soft*	*slow*	*kind*	*young*	*white*
	excellent	*long*	*heavy*	*quick*	*clever*	*old*	*red*
	poor	*thick*	*light*		*rude*		
			hot		*proud*		

These categories must be ordered from left to right. Thus, an English speaker might say "a nice, big, new red wagon," but not "a red new big nice wagon."

Adjective phrases in English also can have other modifiers such as *very* or *really* as in the following phrases:

- *very intelligent*
- *really clever*
- *extremely smart*

Thus, an adjective phrase in English can have an adverb in front of the adjective.

In Hebrew the intensifier (adverb) comes after the adjective:

makk-â	*gĕdôl-â*	*mĕʾōd*
slaughter-(feminine)	great-(feminine)	very

"very great slaughter" (Joshua 10:20)

3. R. M. W. Dixon, "Where Have All the Adjectives Gone?" *Studies in Language* 1, no. 1 (1977): 19–80.

Prepositional Phrases

The English prepositional phrase consists of a preposition followed by a noun phrase. Some examples of English prepositional phrases include:

- *in the classroom*
- *under the large old oak tree*
- *with the several clever Hebrew students who excelled in every way*
- *with them*
- *for us*

Note that when a pronoun comes after a preposition in English it is in the accusative case (*them, us, me,* etc.) This is called the **object of the preposition.**

Hebrew has some prepositions that are independent words and others that become attached to the following noun. The preposition *ʾel* ("to") is a separate word.

ʾel	*māqôm*	*ʾeḥād*
to	place	one

"to one place"

The preposition *b-* ("in") is an example of a preposition that attaches directly to its object.

bi-rqîaʿ	*ha-ššāmayim*
in-expanse-of	the-sky

"in the expanse of the sky"

Greek also has prepositional phrases, but it is more complex in regard to how it marks the case of the noun or noun phrase that follows a preposition. Some prepositions in Greek are followed by the accusative case and others by the dative case. There are also some prepositions that can be followed by more than one case. Here are some examples from John 1:1–3:

en archē
in beginning (dative)
"in (the) beginning"

pros ton theon
with the God (accusative)
"with God"

di' autou
through Him (genitive)
"through Him"

Textbooks and grammars often use special terms to talk about the meaning of these prepositional phrases. For example, there is the *locational dative* and the *instrumental dative.* This terminology blends the morphological marker of dative with the meaning of the phrase. You should be able to understand these meanings from the context and from the meaning of the individual words.

Combining Phrases

As we noted in the beginning of this chapter, clauses are groups of phrases, not just groups of words. Each language combines noun phrases, verb phrases, and other types of phrases in particular ways. As we conclude this section, we will look briefly at some common terminology related to clauses.

Clauses often are grouped by the type of verb that serves as the main verb: stative, intransitive, transitive, or ditransitive. We already have looked at the subcategories of verbs and have seen that the verb determines what other phrases are needed to complete a clause.

Clauses can also be classified in regard to whether they express a complete thought or not. **Independent clauses** can occur by themselves; **dependent clauses** cannot. In the sentence *I studied Greek after I entered seminary,* the first clause *(I studied Greek)* is an independent clause and *after I entered seminary* is a dependent clause.

It is helpful that each language has only a relatively small set of phrase and clause patterns. Although they may be different from English or your native language, they are still limited in number.

Classifying Languages by Word Order

There are general truths about all human languages and general tendencies in language patterns. Often, these tendencies are called universals. They help a linguist make preliminary hypotheses about the grammatical patterns in a language.

Types of Universals

The study of the world's languages has led to a number of statements about the features they have in common. *Absolute* universals discuss traits that have been found in every language studied thus far. If there are exceptions to the common traits or if a feature depends on other patterns in the language, it is called an *implicational* universal. A *tendency* is a generalization that has many exceptions.

Absolute Universals

Absolute universals deal with the patterns found in all languages, such as word order. On Greenberg's list of universals, statement 42 says:

> All languages have pronominal categories involving at least three persons and two numbers (e.g., speaker, addressee and other; singular and non-singular).[4]

This and other universals about the existence of certain elements in every language are absolute universals. Others include the existence of categories such as noun and verb, vowels and consonants, and so forth.

Implicational Universals (if X then Y)

On Greenberg's list of universals, statement 40 says:

> When the adjective follows the noun, the adjective expresses all the inflectional categories of the noun.[5]

---

4. Joseph Greenberg, ed., *Universals of Human Language* (Cambridge, Mass.: MIT University Press, 1966), 96.
5. Ibid., 95.

Spanish illustrates this universal:

• *maestr-o*	*viej-o*	"teacher-(masc.)"	"old-(masc.)"
• *maestr-a*	*viej-a*	"teacher-(fem.)"	"old-(fem.)"
• *maestr-o-s*	*viej-o-s*	"teacher-(masc.-pl.)"	"old-(masc.-pl.)"
• *maestr-a-s*	*viej-a-s*	"teacher-(fem.-pl.)"	"old-(fem.-pl.)"

These words show that Spanish nouns and adjectives are both marked for gender and number.

Hebrew and Greek also illustrate this general pattern. Here is an example from Hebrew of both nouns and adjectives marked for gender:

• *ʾîš ṭōb*	man good	"(a) good man"
• *ʾiššâ ṭōbâ*	woman good	"(a) good woman"

Greek shows this same pattern:

• *anthrōpos*	*agathos*	man good	"(a) good man"
• *gunē*	*agathē*	woman good	"(a) good woman"

Absolute Universals Versus Tendencies

Statement 4 on Greenberg's list of universals is a tendency, not an absolute:

> With overwhelmingly greater than chance frequency, languages with normal SOV order are postpositional.[6]

There are six logically possible combinations of the three elements of a transitive clause (subject, verb, object). All six orders occur, although object-initial languages are very uncommon.

Types of Languages

Linguists are interested in several types of relationships between languages. In the chapter on language change, we will see that some languages are *genetically* related; that is, they share a common ancestor. Typically such languages

6. Ibid., 79.

Table 4.5: Word Order Tendencies Among Languages of the World[7]

Verb before Object 35%	SVO	**English** French Hausa Vietnamese Thai
Verb before Object 19%	VSO	**Hebrew** (Classical) Arabic (Classical) **Greek**[8] Welsh Tongan Tagalog
Verb before Object 2%	VOS	Malagasy Tzotzil (Mexico) Cakchiquel (Guate- mala)
Object before Verb 44%	SOV	Japanese Korean Amharic Tibetan Turkish Georgian
Object before Verb less than 1%	OVS	Hixkaryana (Brazil) Barasano (Colombia)
Object before Verb less than 1%	OSV	Xavante (Brazil) Apurina (Brazil)

7. The percentages listed here are taken from Thomas W. Stewart Jr. and Nathan Vaillette, eds., *Language Files*, 8th ed. (Columbus: Ohio State University Press, 2001), 191.
8. As with many topics, scholars disagree about the basic word order pattern of Koine Greek. Here we follow Timothy Friberg, *New Testament Greek Word Order in Light of Discourse Considerations* (Ph.D. dissertation, University of Minnesota, 1982).

share many words, have similar sound systems, and have many grammatical features in common.

Sometimes languages that are not genetically related also exhibit similar grammatical patterns. Linguists are interested in these non-genetically inherited features because they may indicate how human language is structured at a deeper level. The study of these features is called *language typology.*

Some universals have to do with word order. Languages that have a basic clause order in which the object follows the verb (VO) tend to have similar patterns elsewhere in the language. Typically, in VO languages the adjective follows the noun it modifies, the adverb follows the verb it modifies, and so on, as seen below, and the pattern is reversed in OV languages. These two categories of language are referred to as *head-initial* and *head-final,* based on

Table 4.6: Head-Initial Language Patterns—VO

Verb	Object	Koine Greek	Classical Hebrew
Verb	Adverb	*poieson taxion* "do quickly"	*wa-yyirbû mĕʾōd* "they increased greatly"
Noun	Adjective	*zoe aionios* "life eternal"	*ʾeres ṭôbâ* "land good"
Noun	Possessive	*huios theou* "son of God"	*ʾebed ha-mmelek* "servant-of the king"
Noun	Relative		*hāʾîš ʾăšer* "the man *who*"
Preposition	Noun	*en theou* "in God"	*b-a-bbayit* "in the house"

whether the main element of the phrase appears at the beginning or end of the phrase. Tables 4.6 and 4.7 give an overview of these patterns.

Koine Greek is said to have relatively free word order. This is made possible by the systematic case marking system that indicates the grammatical function of each word (e.g., subject, direct object). Nevertheless, Koine Greek follows many of the characteristics of the VO pattern above:

Noun	**Adjective**
zoē	*aionios*
life	eternal
"eternal life"	

Noun	**Possessor**
huios	*theou*
son	God-of
"God's Son"	

Preposition	**Noun**
en	*theou*
in	God
"in God"	

Classical Hebrew has an order that is more fixed than Koine Greek but more flexible than English. One thing that helps is that Hebrew often uses a particle to mark the object of a verb *(ʾet).* The following sentence shows the standard Hebrew order of VSO.

wa-yyiben	*Šĕlōmōh*	*ʾet ha-bbayit*
and-built	Solomon	obj the-house
"And Solomon built the house" (1 Kings 6:14)		

Because Hebrew does not have to rely on word order to show the object relationship, as English does, it is possible to put the object before the verb for special reasons.

wĕ-ʾet	*bêt-ô*	*bānâ*	*Šĕlōmōh*
and-obj	house-his	built	Solomon

"And Solomon built his house" (1 Kings 7:1)

Table 4.7: Head-Final Language Patterns—OV

Object	Verb
Verb	Auxiliary
Adverb	Verb
Adjective	Noun
Possessor	Noun
Relative	Noun
Noun	Postposition

Other languages place the object before the verb. These languages typically have postpositions; they place the adjective before the noun, and so on, as summarized in table 4.7.

Japanese, Korean, Turkish, and many other languages are OV languages.

Summary and Preview

In this chapter we have looked at how words are put together into phrases and clauses. Again we saw that English, Hebrew, and Greek have particular patterns that they use on a regular basis. This limited set of patterns is further simplified by the fact that Hebrew and Greek are both head-initial languages and share many predictable patterns in common.

Many linguistic studies stop at the clause level and never move on to larger units of language. In the next chapter we will introduce you to this larger world of discourse. We will (again) see that there are patterns at this level of language.

For Further Study

Comrie, Bernard. *Language Universals and Linguistic Typology.* 2d ed. Chicago: University of Chicago Press, 1989.

Dixon, R. M. W. "Where Have All the Adjectives Gone?" *Studies in Language* 1, no. 1 (1977): 19–80.

Greenberg, Joseph, ed. *Universals of Human Language.* Cambridge, Mass.: MIT University Press, 1966.

O'Grady, William, Michael Dobrovolosky, and Mark Aronoff. *Contemporary Linguistics: An Introduction.* 2d ed. New York: St. Martin's, 1993.

Payne, Thomas A. *Describing Morphosyntax: A Guide for Field Linguists.* Cambridge: Cambridge University Press, 1997.

Porter, Stanley E. *Idioms of the Greek New Testament.* 2d ed. Sheffield: Sheffield Academic Press, 1994.

Stewart, Thomas W., Jr., and Nathan Vailette, eds. *Language Files: Materials for an Introduction to Language and Linguistics.* 8th ed. Columbus: Ohio State University Press, 2001.

Exercises

1. Describe the syntax of ordering coffee at coffee specialty stores. Note the order that is used for the size, type, flavor, and so forth.
2. Make a chart of at least five technobabble phrases of at least three elements (for example, "integrated multitasking freeware"). Note which words (and types of words) can occur in each position. Make a phrase-structure tree of one example.
3. From the following Hebrew sentences, see if you can figure out what is the verb, the subject, and the object.

    - *ʿāśâ Yahweh ʾet haššāmayim*
    - *wa-yĕbārek ʾĕlōhîm ʾet Nōaḥ* (*Wa* at the beginning of a word always means something like "and.")
    - *bānû štêhem ʾet bêt yiśrāʾēl*
    - *wĕ-ʾābîw šāmar ʾet haddābār*
    - *wa-yyirʾû bĕnê-ʾĕlōhîm ʾet bĕnôt-hāʾādām*

5

Telling Stories and Writing Letters

Understanding Discourse

It seemed fitting for me . . . to write it out for you in consecutive order.

—Luke 1:3 NASB

In previous chapters we have seen how Hebrew and Greek put words together to make clauses and sentences. Many textbooks stop at this level of complexity and neglect to look at the structures larger than a sentence. In this chapter we will look at these larger patterns and consider how they can help us understand the biblical languages better.

Discourse Patterns

Once upon a time and *Dear sir* are well-known discourse patterns. So are *and they lived happily ever after* and *in conclusion.* Such phrases are more than just a group of words and more than just a certain type of phrase; they tell us something about the larger unit of which phrases, clauses, and sentences are a part. Languages have patterns that encompass more than a single clause or sentence. There are ways to introduce stories and ways to end them. There are also ways to help the reader/listener discern the thread of thought from topic to topic throughout an entire unit of discourse. Letters and sermons have their own unique patterns, just like other specific types or genres of discourse. These larger patterns are discourse patterns, and they vary from language to language.

Discourse influences how phrases and clauses are formed. In our earlier look at syntax, we mentioned that Hebrew and Greek have certain "normal" word-order patterns. Discourse considerations affect which patterns are used. In English, for example, we can say:

- *The children gave the teacher flowers.*
- *The children gave flowers to the teacher.*
- *The teacher was given flowers by the children.*
- *The flowers were given to the teacher by the students.*
- *The flowers were given by the students to the teacher.*

We can even express the same action in phrases such as:

- *the children who gave the flowers to the teacher*
- *the children who gave the teacher flowers*
- *the flowers (that) the children gave the teacher*
- *the flowers (that) the teacher was given by the children*

The larger discourse influences which of these patterns we use. In a paragraph about a teacher, for example, we might use *The teacher was given flowers by the students.* This passive sentence keeps the teacher as the main topic in the story. Passive is not merely a grammatical pattern; it serves a function in the larger context of discourse.

Discourse Patterns in Hebrew

A common discourse pattern in biblical Hebrew has the verb *wayĕhî* (usually translated "and it came to pass" in the KJV or "and/now it came about" in the NASB) followed by a time reference. Thus,

> And it came to pass *[wayĕhî]*, as they journeyed from the east, that they found a plain in the land of Shinar; and they dwelt there. (Gen. 11:2 KJV)

This pattern gives the setting in past time for a narrated event, and it usually occurs as well at major breaks or transition points in a biblical book. For example, in Genesis 6:1 it marks the beginning of a new narrative after the genealogies of chapter 5 have come to an end. Even though *wayĕhî* itself is technically a verb, it really says only that what follows is something that happened in the past at the time indicated. Some modern English versions have rendered Genesis 11:2 without any formal equivalent for *wayĕhî*. It is not really necessary because the structure of the English pattern makes the same discourse pattern clear.

> As men moved eastward, they found a plain in Shinar and settled there. (NIV)

> And as they migrated from the east, they came upon a plain in the land of Shinar and settled there. (NRSV)

> As the people migrated eastward, they found a plain in the land of Babylonia and settled there. (NLT)

For another example of a discourse issue in Hebrew, we will consider how the language refers to the (grammatical) subject of a sentence. The Hebrew verb has distinct forms that agree with the person, gender, and number of the subject. It is not necessary, then, to include a separate pronoun when the identity of the subject is already known from the context. Even so, when the subject is clear from the context, there are three choices.

1. No pronoun is added; the subject marker on the verb is adequate:

   wayyiben *šām* *mizbēaḥ* *lĕYHWH*
   and-he-built there altar to-YHWH
   "So he built there an altar to the LORD" (Gen. 12:7 NIV)[1]

2. A pronoun is added even though it is also marked by the form of the verb:

   wĕhûʾ *ʿābar* *lipnêhem*
   and-he he-passed-on in-front-of-them
   "But he himself passed on ahead of them" (Gen. 33:3 NASB)

---

1. We will follow the conventional English equivalent of using "the LORD" for the divine name Yahweh, represented in transliteration as YHWH.

3. The subject noun may be repeated even though it has already been mentioned in the context:

wayebārek	*ʾōtām*	*ʾĕlōhîm*	*wayyōʾmer*	*lāhem*	*ʾĕlōhîm*
and-he-blessed	them	God	and-he-said	to-them	God

"God blessed them, and God said to them . . ." (Gen. 1:28)

The choice among the three is determined by discourse considerations. Example number 1 above might be considered the default method. Once a subject noun has been mentioned in the context, it is not necessary for the writer to repeat it with a new verb or even to refer to it with a pronoun. The verb itself normally carries all the information that is needed because of the agreement rules.

In the second example, Jacob's position in relation to Esau is shown over against the position of the women and children. He will meet Esau first, and they will follow behind him. This kind of contrast is often shown by placing the contrasting word or phrase in front of the verb.

The third sentence is an example of **topicalization.** In Genesis 1:1–2:3, the word *God* is mentioned thirty-five times, even though no other person takes any active role in the creation of the world. The writer stresses that *ʾElōhîm,* "God," is the one who created heaven and earth. Such constant repetition is not always pleasing to speakers of English. While the NASB, the NRSV, and the KJV all translate the sentence as indicated above, the NIV and the NLT conform the sentence to normal English style:

- God blessed them and said to them . . . (NIV)
- God blessed them and told them . . . (NLT)

These versions do not change the essential meaning of the verse; they still refer to the one God acting as subject of both verbs. The more literal translations preserve the topicalization found in the Hebrew, but they also make the text sound awkward to English ears.

Can you find another example of topicalization in the KJV of Genesis 37:28?

> Then there passed by Midianites merchantmen; and they drew and lifted up Joseph out of the pit, and sold Joseph to the Ishmeelites for twenty pieces of silver: and they brought Joseph into Egypt.

Be sure to compare some modern versions as well.

Discourse Patterns in Greek

The Greek verb *egeneto* sometimes means "he/she/it became" and is completed by a noun or adjective that tells what the subject of the verb became. The adjective or noun is called a complement and typically occurs after the verb. The verb-adjective order is seen in John 5:9:

kai eutheōs	*egeneto hugiēs*	*ho anthropos*
and immediately	became well	the man

"And immediately the man became well"

John 11:25 illustrates the verb-noun pattern:

egō	*eimi*	*hē*	*anastasis*
I	am	the	resurrection

"I am the resurrection."

In John 1:14 the complement is placed before the verb:

Kai	*ho*	*logos*	*sarx egeneto*
And	the	Word	flesh became

"And the Word became flesh"

By putting the word *flesh* before *became,* the writer highlights a theme of John 1: the Word (Jesus Christ) became a real human being and lived among the disciples.

The passive in New Testament Greek is used to make an object (patient) the grammatical subject. One reason this happens is to bring the object to the forefront when it is the topic of a paragraph.

Egeneto	*anthrōpos*	*apestalmenos*	*para theou*
was	a-man	sent	from God

"There was a man sent from God" (John 1:6 KJV)

The verb *apestalmenos* describes who this man was, and the passive form keeps him as the topic of the paragraph. The paragraph goes on to describe John the Baptist and his unique role in relation to "the true light" (John 1:9).

Discourse Types

One important objective of discourse study is recognition of the various discourse types in a particular language. As in other areas of syntax, we do not just make up names for patterns; we look for patterns in the language and then identify them. In English, for example, we have predictable patterns for telling stories and patterns for explaining how to make a cake. A story starts with such phrases as:

- *Once there was a man . . .*
- *One day a new girl appeared at school . . .*

These *narrative* discourses begin by identifying a character. After the character has been introduced, the narrative can continue:

- *. . . the man*
- *. . . her name was Sandy. She . . .*

The use of *a* versus *the* relates to the position of the phrase in the larger discourse.

Recipes have standard patterns, such as:

- *Take two eggs*
- *Mix the dry ingredients*

These imperative sentences are typical of *instructional* or *procedural* discourse in English.

Explanatory discourses in English sometimes sound like recipes, but they use such phrases as:

- *First, you take two eggs.*
- *Then you mix the dry ingredients.*

They also can sound like this:

- *The chef takes two eggs.*
- *Then the chef mixes the dry ingredients.*

Hortatory discourses in English also can sound like recipes, but they use phrases such as:

- *You must/should take two eggs.*
- *You must/should mix the dry ingredients.*

They can also use the first person plural *we:*

- *We must take two eggs.*
- *We must mix the dry ingredients.*

A primary use of *hortatory* discourse is preaching.

English also has discourse patterns that are typical for letters *(epistolary).* There are often standard greetings:

- *Dear sir . . .*
- *To whom it may concern . . .*

There are also typical clauses at the beginning of a letter, such as:

- *I am writing this letter to tell you about . . .*
- *It has been a long time since I last wrote . . .*

These English discourse types have different grammatical patterns and, sometimes, unique vocabulary. The biblical languages also have such patterns, and we will look at the major features of each discourse type. Here we will give a few examples from the Hebrew of the Old Testament to illustrate the discussion.

When ancient scribes copied Hebrew poetic lines, they did not normally set them apart line by line. As a result, poetry does not stand out from the rest of the passage by its physical appearance. It is possible to distinguish poetic lines, though, on the basis of certain discourse characteristics, even when they occur embedded within a different type of discourse.

1. A poetic line is normally short and consists of two or sometimes three parts.

šōpēk	*dam*	*hāʾādām*	*bāʾādām*	*dāmô*	*yiššāpēk*
shedder-of	blood-of	the-man	by-the-man	his-blood	will-be shed

"Whoever sheds the blood of man, by man shall his blood be shed."
(Gen. 9:6a NIV)

2. Poetic lines normally occur in pairs or, occasionally, triplets. Here is the second half of Genesis 9:6.

kî	*bĕṣelem*	*ʾĕlōhîm*	*ʿāsāh*	*ʾet*	*hāʾādām*
for	in-image-of	God	he-made	obj.	the-man

"For in the image of God he made man."
(Gen. 9:6b NIV)

3. Parallelism of various kinds often occurs between lines or half lines.

ʾārûr	*ʾappām*	*kî*	*ʾāz*	*wĕ ʿebrātām*	*kî*	*qāshātâ*
cursed	their-anger	for	fierce	and-their-fury	for	cruel

"Cursed be their anger, so fierce, and their fury, so cruel!"
(Gen. 49:7 NIV)

4. Sometimes there can be a kind of "stair-step" effect, with the second part building on the first.

hābû	*lĕ YHWH*	*bĕnê*	*ʾēlîm*	*hābû*	*lĕ YWHY*	*kābôd*	*wāʿōz*
ascribe	to-YHWH	sons-of	mighty/gods	ascribe	to-YHWH	glory	and-strength

"Ascribe to the LORD, O mighty ones, ascribe to the LORD glory and strength."
(Ps. 29:1 NIV)

5. Other features may include repetition, high concentration of figurative language, unusual or archaic grammar, and rare words.

The Hebrew verb system is quite different from the English system, and the choice of forms appears to have a lot to do with discourse considerations. There are two basic forms that are marked for person, gender, and number (PGN):

1. A form where the PGN markers occur at the end of the base, and so it is called the suffix conjugation (SC).[2] Thus: *kātab-tî* (*wrote-I,* "I wrote.")
2. A form where the PGN markers are prefixed to the base, the prefix conjugation (PC).[3] Thus: *ʾe-ktōb* (*I-write,* "I will write.")

No helping verbs are used (verbs like *will, did, have,* etc.), but there is a peculiarity when the word *and* is prefixed to either the suffix conjugation or the prefix conjugation. Sometimes when *and* is prefixed to the prefix conjugation, it makes what could be considered a third form, which is often called "*waw*-consecutive with imperfect" ("*waw*-consecutive" or WCI for a shorter form). This form is virtually always confined to telling about an event that happened in the past (a narration). Some grammars refer to it as a *preterite.*

Two conditions must apply in order to use the WCI. First, the verb must refer to events that are a part of the main storyline, not to a background event (with some exceptions). Examine the following from Genesis 24:1–5, for which the *waw*-consecutive verbs are underlined and the suffix conjugation verbs are put in italics. When a verb has to be supplied in the English, it is put in parentheses.

> Now Abraham (was) old, advanced in age; and the Lord *had blessed* Abraham in every way. Abraham <u>said</u> to his servant, the oldest of his household, who had charge of all that he owned, "Please place your hand under my thigh, and I will make you swear by the Lord, the God of heaven and the God of earth, that you shall not take a wife for my son from the daughters of the Canaanites, among whom I live, but you will go to my country and to my relatives, and take a wife for my son Isaac." The servant <u>said</u> to him, "Suppose the woman is not willing to follow me to this land; should I take your son back to the land from where you came?" (NASB)

The first sentence gives background to the narration that follows. It does not mention any events that bring the narrative forward, and thus no *waw*-consecutive is used. Actually, there are only two narrative statements: "Abraham <u>said</u> to his servant" and "the servant <u>said</u> to him." Both of these verbs have the *waw*-consecutive form. The two quotations of direct speech give instructions

2. Many Hebrew grammars call this form the **perfect.**
3. Many Hebrew grammars call this form the **imperfect.**

and raise a hypothetical possibility, respectively. Therefore they do not have any *waw*-consecutive forms either. The narrator used the suffix conjugation for the Lord's blessing of Abraham. It was a past event but serves only to give background to the story. That is, it helps the reader to understand how Abraham was able to send such an extravagant gift with his servant. Of course, it is a very significant statement for the Abraham narratives as a whole, but within this particular chunk of narration it forms background to the actual story.

A second condition for using the *waw*-consecutive is that it must be the first word in its sentence. If something else comes before it (e.g., a negative), then it is replaced by a suffix conjugation verb. This happens, for example, in Genesis 8:12:

wayyîyāḥel	*ʿôd*	*šibʿat*	*yāmîm*	*ʾăḥērîm*	*wayešallaḥ*	*ʾet*	*hayyônâ*
and-he-waited	again	seven	days	another	and-he-sent-out	obj.	the-dove
(*waw*-consecutive)					(*waw*-consecutive)		

"He waited seven more days and sent the dove out again,

wĕlōʾ	*yāsépâ*	*šûb*	*ʾēlāw*	*ʿôd*
and-not	she-added	to-return	to-him	again
	(suffix conjugation)			

but this time it did not return to him." (NIV)

While the *waw*-consecutive has a very narrowly defined function, there is an additional verb form with the word *and* prefixed to the suffix conjugation that has a much looser function. It can be abbreviated as w+SC. Some grammars call it the "*waw*-consecutive with the perfect" (WCP), although there are some problems with that terminology. In one of its uses, it joins together the mainline predictions in a prophetic discourse. In the following selection from Joel 3:1–2, the verbs are italicized and identified by the abbreviations given above.

> In those days and at that time, when *I restore* [PC] the fortunes of Judah and Jerusalem, *I will gather* [w+SC] all nations *and bring them down* [w+SC] to the Valley of Jehoshaphat. There *I will enter into judgment* [w+SC] against them concerning my inheritance, my people Israel, for *they scattered* [SC] my people among the nations and *divided up* [SC] my land. (NIV)

"When I restore" gives the future time frame for the prophecy and has a PC (prefix conjugation) for its verb. Then each of the predictions has the form w+SC. The last two verbs give the reasons for the stated judgments in terms of the past behavior of the nations. The prophecy focuses on "my inheritance, my people Israel" and "my land" in placing the verbs after the object, hence requiring the suffix conjugation form.

Discourse Tools

To study discourse we need special tools. We will examine two of those tools here: breaking a larger unit into smaller units such as paragraphs and keeping track of the various participants.

Discovering Paragraphs and Other Units

For a written text, the writer or scribe may have some graphic way to show the boundaries of units like paragraphs or larger or smaller units. Some manuscripts of both the Old Testament and the New Testament did have such devices, but here we want to examine some linguistic means of marking off units. We might expect that linguistic devices that structure a text would occur at the beginning of a unit and at its end, thus marking the boundaries of the unit. So we will examine how paragraphs look different at their boundaries than in their middle sections in order to isolate characteristic features.

As an example, consider the paragraphs of Genesis 1, a chapter that is clearly structured by the six days of creation.[4] Each new day receives its own paragraph in the Hebrew text because of the change of topic. What are some other organizing features of this chapter?

Formulaic Expressions

Each day closes with the expression: "There was evening and there was morning, day X." This formula clearly marks the end of each of the paragraphs for the various days.

Other than the first day (for which see below), each paragraph begins with "and God said" (literally, "and said God," vv. 6, 9, 14, 20, 24). The third and

4. Some of the ideas given here were informed by an unpublished seminal paper by Ernst R. Wendland, "Biblical Hebrew Narrative Structure."

sixth days include two creative events each, and the second event in each case is also introduced with "and God said" (vv. 11, 26). These two days apparently consist of two subparagraphs apiece, and the end of the first subparagraph for each is marked with the formula, "and God saw that (it was) good." The sixth day actually appears to include a third subparagraph, where God apportions food for both things that he has created, land animals and man. This subparagraph is also marked at its beginning by "and God said" (v. 29). The previous subparagraph concludes with a lengthy summary of all the realms over which man will have ruling authority.

We note that the one occurrence in the English of "and God said" that is not at the beginning of a paragraph or subparagraph (v. 28) has the structure in Hebrew, "and said to them God." That is, inserting "to them" between the verb and the subject signals here that rather than starting a new paragraph, the current paragraph is continuing.

Other verbs also are used with God as the subject to show the sequence of events within a paragraph. For example, for the fourth day we are told that God *made* the sun, moon, and stars and *put them* in the sky (vv. 16–17).

Backgrounding

Information that helps to understand a passage but that does not carry the argument forward directly will usually occur at the beginning of the first paragraph in the section. If such background information is lengthy, it can itself be taken as the first paragraph of the passage. This appears to be the case with Genesis 1:1–2, although the example is controversial. The first verse pinpoints the time for creation as the "beginning" and establishes that God created everything ("the heavens and the earth"). Verse two shows how the primitive earth needed to undergo some organization ("formless and void") and have some light ("darkness was on the surface of the deep"). It also makes us expect that God will act soon when it speaks of the movement of God's Spirit "over the surface of the waters." The expression "and God said" in verse three occurs with the narrative *waw*-consecutive form, thereby signaling the beginning of the main actions of the chapter, namely God's organizing and filling activities. Significantly, this first instance of divine speech results in the creation of light in direct response to the problem of darkness introduced in the previous verse. It seems likely, then, that Genesis 1:1–2 should be taken as a separate background paragraph for the entire chapter. The sentences in these verses contain either a verb in the suffix conjugation ("God created," "and the earth was"), a participle ("the Spirit of God was moving/hovering"), or even no verb at all ("darkness [was] over the surface of the deep"). Sentences like these are typical of how background information is introduced into a Hebrew narrative.

X+Verb Word Order

In chapter 4 we pointed out that a Hebrew verb will usually occur first in its clause or sentence. Sometimes a paragraph will begin with a clause or sentence that has the verb in second position. This is especially the case if the sentence contains background information. Genesis 1:1 has the structure "in-beginning created God." The verb *created* is in second position. The essential background information is that God's creative activity occurred at the beginning. For another example see Genesis 3:1, "and-the-serpent was craftier than . . ." The verb *was* is in second position, and the sentence introduces us to a new character in the scene: the serpent.

Keeping Track of Participants

Each individual participant in a discourse can be "tracked" through a discourse in terms of how the language refers to the participant at each mention. A rather literal translation, such as the KJV or the NASB, enables us to do this in a rough way. Once you can use Greek and Hebrew as a tool, it will be possible to do a more exact study of participant reference. Of course, English discourse patterns are different from Hebrew or Greek, and a more idiomatic translation will translate the underlying Hebrew or Greek patterns into more natural English patterns.

Old Testament Example from the KJV—Genesis 22:1–6

The following example taken from the KJV of Genesis 22:1–6 will help us to see how participants can be tracked.

> [1]And it came to pass after these things, that God did tempt Abraham,
> and said unto him, Abraham: and he said, Behold, *here* I *am.* [2]And he
> said, Take now thy son, thine only *son* Isaac, whom thou lovest, and
> get thee into the land of Moriah; and offer him there for a burnt offering

upon one of the mountains which I will tell thee of. [3]And Abraham
rose up early in the morning, and saddled his ass, and took two of his
young men with him, and Isaac his son, and clave the wood for the
burnt offering, and rose up, and went unto the place of which God
had told him. [4]Then on the third day Abraham lifted up his eyes, and
saw the place afar off. [5]And Abraham said unto his young men, Abide
ye here with the ass; and I and the lad will go yonder and worship, and
come again to you. [6]And Abraham took the wood of the burnt offering,
and laid *it* upon Isaac his son; and he took the fire in his hand, and a
knife; and they went both of them together.[5]

How is Abraham "tracked" in this passage? See if you can answer this question for yourself by listing each place that Abraham either does something or has something happen to him in this passage. What is it that lets you know in each instance that the story is referring to Abraham (his name, a pronoun, etc.)? Then see how Isaac is tracked. Are there some differences in this tracking if you compare the KJV with the NIV or the NLT?

New Testament Example from the NASB—Matthew 4:1–11

Now let's look at a New Testament example from the NASB of Matthew 4:1–11.

[1]Then Jesus was led up by the Spirit into the wilderness to be tempted
by the devil. [2]And after He had fasted forty days and forty nights, He
then became hungry. [3]And the tempter came and said to Him, "If You
are the Son of God, command that these stones become bread." [4]But
He answered and said, "It is written, 'MAN SHALL NOT LIVE ON BREAD ALONE,
BUT ON EVERY WORD THAT PROCEEDS OUT OF THE MOUTH OF GOD.'" [5]Then the
devil took Him into the holy city and had Him stand on the pinnacle
of the temple, [6]and said to Him, "If You are the Son of God, throw
Yourself down; for it is written, 'HE WILL COMMAND HIS ANGELS CONCERNING YOU'; and 'ON *their* HANDS THEY WILL BEAR YOU UP, SO THAT YOU WILL NOT
STRIKE YOUR FOOT AGAINST A STONE.'" [7]Jesus said to him, "On the other

5. The italicized words were supplied by the KJV translators to make the English more natural.

> hand, it is written, 'YOU SHALL NOT PUT THE LORD YOUR GOD TO THE TEST.'"
> [8]Again, the devil took Him to a very high mountain and showed Him
> all the kingdoms of the world and their glory; [9]and he said to Him,
> "All these things I will give You, if You fall down and worship me."
> [10]Then Jesus said to him, "Go, Satan! For it is written, 'YOU SHALL WOR-
> SHIP THE LORD YOUR GOD, AND SERVE HIM ONLY.'" [11]Then the devil left Him;
> and behold, angels came and *began* to minister to Him.[6]

How is Jesus tracked through this passage? How is the devil tracked? For this passage also compare a more idiomatic translation such as the NIV or the NLT to see if you can detect some differences.

Summary and Preview

The syntax of a language does not stop at the clause level. Larger units such as paragraphs and even whole stories and letters also have structure. This chapter has reminded us to look for patterns in these larger units.

This chapter concludes our discussion of morphology and syntax (chaps. 3–5). We now turn our attention to meaning as we study semantics. We will see once again that English, Hebrew, and Greek share some common traits. We will also see that we need to think about how syntax interacts with meaning.

For Further Study

Bodine, Walter R., ed. *Discourse Analysis of Biblical Literature: What It Is and What It Offers.* Atlanta: Scholars Press, 1995.

Dooley, Robert A., and Stephen H. Levinsohn. *Analyzing Discourse: A Manual of Basic Concepts.* Dallas: SIL International, 2001.

Levinsohn, Stephen H. *Discourse Features of New Testament Greek.* 2d ed. Dallas: SIL International, 2000.

6. The NASB uses capitalized words to indicate a quotation from the Scripture and italicized words to indicate words the translators supplied to make the English text more natural.

Exercises

1. Write down the results of the participant tracking you did for the above passages from the Old and New Testaments. What conclusions can you make from those results?
2. Here are some statistics regarding Hebrew verb forms in certain biblical books. On the basis of what was said above, why are some forms more common in certain books than in others?

Table 5.1: Hebrew Verb Forms in Biblical Books

Form	Book	Number of Occurrences
waw-consecutive (WCI)	Genesis and Exodus	2,993
	Leviticus	189
	Ezra	86
	Esther	159
	Job	260
	Psalms	333
	Proverbs	32
	Ecclesiastes	3
	Song of Songs	2
	Lamentations	29
	Ezekiel	513
	Obadiah	0
	Joel	7
	Jonah	84
wayĕhî, "and it came to pass" in the KJV (a special case of *WCI*)	Genesis and Exodus	87
	Leviticus	1
	Ezra, Esther, Job, Psalms, Proverbs, Ecclesiastes, Song of Songs, Lamentations, Ezekiel, Hosea, Obadiah, Micah, Nahum, Habakkuk, Zephaniah, Haggai, Malachi	0
w+SC	Genesis and Exodus	780
	Leviticus	719
	Esther	14
	Job	61
	Psalms	78
	Proverbs	51
	Ecclesiastes	50
	Song of Songs	4
	Ezekiel	833
	Obadiah	15
	Joel	29
	Jonah	2

6

What Do You Mean?

It's Just Semantics

Let the use of words teach you their meaning.[1]

—Ludwig Wittgenstein
Austrian philosopher (1889–1951)

When we learn a language like Hebrew or Greek, we need to consider more than just the sounds and the structures of words and phrases. We also need to study how these forms convey meaning. We need to be able to look at the forms of the language and understand the message they contain. In this chapter we will look at meaning and its role in the larger study of language. This study of meaning is called **semantics.**

Although English, Hebrew, and Greek are similar in many ways, there are differences in the ways that they communicate meaning. Semantics will give us tools, however, that we can apply in similar ways to all three languages. There are certain principles for determining meaning that are universal. Much of what people call exegesis is, in fact, semantics.

WHAT DO WE MEAN BY SEMANTICS?

Semantics is the study of linguistic meaning. Semantics emphasizes how

1. Ludwig Wittgenstein, *Philosophical Investigations,* 3d ed., trans. G. E. M. Anscombe (New York: Macmillan, 1958), 220.

people use words to convey meaning. How do we know what a word or a phrase means? In English we use the verb *mean* in many ways:

- *Sandy means to write.* (*means* = "intends")
- *A green light means go.* (symbolic meaning; "green color = go")
- *"Bilabial" means produced with both lips.* (linguistic meaning)

A native English speaker understands that the word *mean* is used in different ways (has different meanings) in different contexts. As we study Hebrew or Greek, we need to learn how to determine the meaning of words and phrases so that we can understand the message that was originally conveyed.

The meaning of a word can be considered from several angles. First, we need to consider what the word **denotes.** Each word refers to something in the real world or in an imaginary world. The English word *book,* for example, refers to a wide variety of objects that share some common traits that all denote a booklike object. The objects may be large or small, thick or thin. They can be of different colors and have different kinds of paper. A dictionary definition of *book* would refer to the types of objects that can be described by the word. A Hebrew or Greek word also denotes a concept or refers to an object, a person, an action, or a relationship.

Some denotations are complex. The word *assassin,* for example, conveys more than the notion of "killer." It also contains information about the type of person that is killed. If we say, "Mr. Jones was assassinated," an English speaker knows that Mr. Jones is a politically important person. It is interesting that English has a number of words that describe the act of killing *(kill, murder, assassinate).* To understand the meaning of these English words, a student of English would need to compare and contrast how these words are used in context. In a similar way we will need to study Hebrew and Greek words to know how they "package" the world.

Second, words have **connotations;** they convey a particular value or attitude. *Book* may have a positive connotation to a professor and a negative connotation to students. The word *tome,* while it may refer to the same object as *book,* may convey a rather different attitude or value judgment. Likewise, the English words *slender* and *skinny* may both denote a certain physical characteristic, but *skinny* also carries a more negative connotation.

As we look at words in English, and other languages, we will see that the denotation and connotation of a word can be very specific. This makes it difficult to translate from one language into another. English, for example, has various specific words to talk about cooking, including: *bake, barbeque, boil, broil, grill, roast, sauté.* Semantic studies can help us understand what these words mean and how they are related to each other.

Hebrew has a variety of terms for destructive speech, and it is hard for English speakers to distinguish them. A detailed semantic study could perhaps give more precision to English translations. Table 6.1 gives the Hebrew terms and how they have been translated in three different English versions.

Table 6.1: Hebrew Terms for Destructive Speech

Hebrew Word	Reference	NASB	NIV	NLT
rākîl	Prov. 11:13	*a talebearer*	*a gossip*	*a gossip*
nirgān	Prov. 16:28	*a slanderer*	*a gossip*	*gossip*
dibbâ	Ps. 31:13	*slander*	*slander*	*rumors*
ʾāwen	Ps. 41:6	*falsehood*	*falsely*	*gossip*

Greek also has sets of closely related words. Around the time of the New Testament, there were several Greek words that could mean "servant." Note how difficult it is to give a concise definition of the words in English.

Table 6.2: Greek Terms for Servant

Greek Word	Reference	NASB	niv	nlt
doulos	Matt. 10:24	*a slave*	*a servant*	*a servant*
diakonos	Rom. 13:4	*minister*	*servant*	*to help*
pais	Matt. 8:6	*servant*	*servant*	*servant*
oikonomos	Luke 12:42	*steward*	*manager*	*servant*

It is important to note that the meaning of Hebrew and Greek words are not limited to one English word or to one concept. We must always look at the context to understand what a word means. For example, while Hebrew *ʾāwen* can signify false speech, it may sometimes have the more concrete sense of an idol, which the Bible considers something false (see Isa. 66:3). Likewise, the Greek noun *pais* can refer to a boy (Matt. 17:18) or a child (Luke 8:54). These words have multiple meanings or senses as do most words.

How Can a Word Have More Than One Meaning?

Words normally have more than one meaning. The specific meaning of the word depends on its context. We usually think of words as having a primary meaning and some secondary or figurative meanings. Dictionaries typically give what they consider to be the primary meaning of a word first. The word *head,* for example, has a primary meaning that refers to the part of the body above the neck. This would be the first thing we would think of if we were asked to define *head.* In English, however, we can also say things such as:

- *the head of the line*
- *the head of the office*
- *the head of lettuce*

In each case *head* has a slightly different, but obviously related, meaning. We can refer to these meanings as secondary or figurative. The word *head* is said to be **polysemous;** it has more than one meaning. We realize that these meanings are based on the primary meaning of *head,* but we do not necessarily imagine a physical head each time we talk about the front of a line, the leader of an office, or lettuce.

Another English example is the word *run.* The primary meaning refers to a particular way of moving one's legs that is faster than *walk* and different from *skip* or *hop.* Stop a minute and try to define this basic meaning of *run.* You may find that you need to think about how *run* is different from the other words mentioned above. For one thing, *run* is based on a pattern of right-left-right-left that is different from *skip* and *hop.* This primary meaning probably also includes the fact that people and animals are the normal ones who run. But English also uses *run* to refer to things rather than to people or animals:

- *the clock runs*
- *the river runs*
- *the vine runs*
- *my nose runs*

These secondary and figurative meanings of *run* do not involve moving legs, but they do include movement of some kind, though in *my nose runs,* of course, the nose itself does not move. When we compare English to other languages, we often find that the various meanings of *run* cannot be expressed by a single word in the other language. As we study Hebrew and Greek, we need to remember that words will typically have a number of meanings. While there will be a primary meaning, there also will probably be a number of secondary or figurative meanings.

Hebrew *nepeš* is a good example of the wide range of meanings that a word can have. Note that when we discuss these meanings in English, we need to use many different words, while in Hebrew they are all the same word (much as the many meanings of *run* cannot be discussed in Hebrew or Greek without using a variety of words in those languages).

The primary meaning of *nepeš* is "breath," but *nepeš* also can refer to "life," "soul," "desire," and other concepts. The KJV translators felt that they needed to use a number of English words to convey the secondary meanings of *nepeš* in different contexts:[2]

- *nepeš* = "life" (Gen. 9:4)
- *nepeš* = "souls" (Gen. 12:5)
- *nepeš* = "persons" (Gen. 14:21)
- *nepeš* = "mind" (Gen. 23:8)
- *nepeš* = "soul" (Gen. 27:4; Prov. 24:14)
- *nepeš* = "appetite" (Prov. 23:2)
- *nepeš* = "hearty" (Prov. 27:9)
- *nepeš* = "heart" (Prov. 28:25; 31:6)

In the same way, Greek words have primary and secondary meanings that may be difficult for us to express in English without using a variety of words. The Greek word *sarx* is a good example of this difficulty. The primary meaning of *sarx* is "meat," as in "the meat of a person or animal." The KJV used *flesh,*

2. Many people think that the King James Version (KJV) is a "literal" translation and that it normally uses one English word for each Hebrew or Greek word. In fact, in the preface to the KJV the translators state clearly that they frequently had to use different words for a single Hebrew or Greek word because there was no single English word that could express the various meanings of the original-language word. If you think about why you use a concordance, you will realize it is because there are so many English words used for the same Hebrew or Greek word, even in a rather literal translation such as the KJV.

because in the seventeenth century *flesh* was the typical word corresponding to modern English *meat*. Many of the uses of *sarx* in the New Testament, however, are secondary or figurative senses of the word. Consider the following examples:

- all *sarx* will see the salvation of God (Luke 3:6)
- not by the will of the *sarx* (*sarkos*, John 1:13)
- the *sarx* is weak (Matt. 26:41)
- the *sarx* lusts against the Spirit (Gal. 5:17)

We certainly would not like to hear the word *meat* in each of these verses, even though that can be considered the primary or "literal" meaning of *sarx*. Many people, however, use the KJV word *flesh* as though it adequately translates the original word. To some degree English-speaking Christians have become used to the way *nepeš* and *sarx* have been expressed in English translations and feel that they understand the original Greek words, even though the translations do not recognize secondary and figurative senses of the word.

We must remember that the context of a word helps us to understand which meaning or sense is being used; the appropriate English word that will express that meaning will be based on the context. In much the same way that the English word *run* has different meanings and must be expressed by different words in other languages, Hebrew and Greek words also have multiple meanings and must be expressed by different words in English. As you study Hebrew or Greek, you will probably start by learning the primary meaning of a word, but you need to remember that most words also have secondary meanings.

Before we conclude this section, we need to reflect on some bad habits that people have when they study Hebrew and Greek words. James Barr, in his pioneering work on biblical semantics, referred to the error of "illegitimate totality transfer."[3] Many word studies appear to promote the view that words "mean" every part of their meaning in all contexts. Thus, *the head of the office* would in some way still have a literal "head" meaning as well as the secondary sense of being in charge. A typical example of this practice in New Testament studies is the understanding that the word *ekklēsia* ("congregation") always includes the sense of being "called out" since the word is based on a prefix *ek-* meaning "out of" and a root that refers to being called.

---

3. James Barr, *The Semantics of Biblical Language* (Oxford: Oxford University Press, 1961), 218.

The habit of thinking that every sense of a word will occur in all of its contexts or even the habit of seeking some presumed root or primary meaning in all of a word's contexts actually works against the principle of context. The meaning of a word has to be deduced from the context in which it is used. To try to derive a meaning from it that does not fit its context runs the risk of importing meaning into the context, which is known as **eisegesis.**

How Are Words Related?

Words can be related in various ways. Some words, such as a *bow* on a boat and a *bow* to an audience sound and look alike but have different meanings. Words such as *hair* and *hare* sound alike but have different spellings. In *I feel the wind* and *I wind the clock,* we see words that are spelled the same way but that have different pronunciations. Other words, such as *furniture* and *chair,* represent sets of generic-specific items. Some words, such as *large* and *big,* look and sound different but have very similar meanings. Words such as *friend* and *foe* or *large* and *small* are related by being opposites in some way. In the following sections we will look at homonyms, homophones, homographs, hyponyms, synonyms, and antonyms. As you study Hebrew or Greek, you will benefit from seeing how words relate to each other.

Words That Are Related Through Their Sounds or Spelling

Due to the overabundance of words in any language, some words with separate meanings end up sharing the same phonetic shape (they sound alike). These overlapping words are called homonyms or homophones.

Homonyms have the same pronunciation and the same spelling but different meanings. In English there are two different words that have the shape *b-a-t* and two that are spelled *b-e-a-r:*

- *bat* "a winged animal"
- *bat* "a wooden object used in baseball"

- *bear* "to carry"
- *bear* "a large ursine animal"

These pairs of homonyms are not at all related. They are not like the primary and secondary meanings of the examples in the previous section. Speakers of English, of course, have no problem knowing which word is meant in most contexts. If we are talking about baseball, *b-a-t* will probably refer to a wooden stick rather than a flying rodent. As nonnative speakers of Hebrew and Greek, however, we have more difficulties recognizing which word is being used in a particular context. Indeed, it is the context that we need to study to know which word is being used.

In Hebrew, the following two pairs of words are homonyms. They sound alike when spoken and they look alike when written, but they are not at all related. They merely share the same sound and spelling:

- *bar* "grain"
- *bar* "pure"

- *rôʾš* "head"
- *rôʾš* "poison"

Greek also has homonyms. The following two words sound alike and look alike but are not related:

- *ei* "you (sing.) are"
- *ei* "if"

It is often difficult to determine whether two forms are actually two separate words (homonyms) or if they are separate meanings or senses of the same word (polysemy). Homonyms are not related in meaning:

- *bat* "a winged animal"
- *bat* "a wooden object used in baseball"

Polysemous forms, however, share some component of meaning:

- *bat* "a wooden object used in baseball"
- *bat* "to hit a ball with a stick [bat]" (secondary sense)

In most dictionaries homonyms are listed as two separate words; polysemous pairs are listed under the same main entry.

How do we know what a word means? Our primary tool is the context. The word *bank* in *I sat down by the river* *bank* obviously refers to the edge of the river, but in *I keep my money in the* *bank* it refers to a financial institution.

A very similar group of words are called **homophones.** Homophones have the same pronunciation, like homonyms, but have different spellings as well as different meanings. Homophones are common in English, partly because our writing system allows words that are spelled differently to be pronounced the same. The following English words are homophones:

- *to* *too* *two*
- *rode* *rowed*
- *bare* ("without clothing") *bear* ("to carry")

Hebrew and Greek have fewer homophones because the writing systems had a clearer relationship between the letters and the pronunciation. An example of Hebrew homophones is:

- *bēn* ("son"), spelled consistently with the letters *bn*
- *bên* ("between"), spelled consistently with the letters *byn*

Although your instructor will probably teach you to pronounce Greek words in such a way that words that are spelled differently are pronounced differently, New Testament Greek actually had many homophones. Due to changes in pronunciation from the Classical Greek period to Koine Greek, some words that were written differently were pronounced the same way; that is, they were homophones. These homophones frequently led scribes to misspell a word in the Greek manuscripts because it sounded the same as another word. In a similar way, English speakers might write "bare skin" when they meant to write "bear skin."

The following pairs of words are examples of Greek homophones at the time of the New Testament:

- *hēmeis* "we" versus *humeis* "you (plural)" in 1 John 1:4
- *hēmōn* "to us" versus *humōn* "to you (plural)" in 2 John 1:12

There are textual variants in these passages. Because these pairs of words sounded alike some scribes wrote the text one way and others wrote the other homophonous word.

A third group of words related to spelling and sound are called **homographs.** Homographs have the same spelling but different pronunciations and different meanings. English has many of these types of words because of the fact that words that are spelled the same way may be pronounced differently. For example:

- *wind* (a noun, as in *I hear the wind.*)
- *wind* (a verb, as in *I will wind the clock.*)

- *content* (a noun, as in *I know the content of the book.*)
- *content* (an adjective, as in *I am content.*)

- *minute* (a noun, as in *That will take one minute.*)
- *minute* (an adjective, as in *The molecule is very minute.*)

Hebrew has many examples of homographs in texts that use only consonants (i.e., when the Masoretic vowels are not included):

- *dbr* (*dābār,* "word") and *dbr* (*dibber,* "he spoke")
- *ʾm* (*ʾēm,* "mother") and *ʾm* (*ʾim,* "if")

The preface to the NIV indicates that a textual variant which involves only a change in the vowels of a Hebrew word and not in its consonants normally will not be noted in the margin. A case in point is found at Isaiah 7:11. The literal Hebrew for the second half of the verse reads as follows:

make-deep a-question or make-high to heaven

The KJV renders the Hebrew text as "ask it either in the depth, or in the height above."

The Hebrew term meaning "a-question" is *šĕʾēlâ,* with the consonants *šʾl* and the letter *h* at the end to show the final vowel. These also happen to be the same letters that could be rendered "to Sheol" if the vowel between the first and second consonants is read as *ō (šĕʾōlâ).* Jerome used the Latin word *inferni* to translate it, a form of Latin *infernum,* the usual term he chose for "Sheol." Jerome translated the Latin Vulgate in the fifth century, a time before the

Masoretes added the vowels to the text. The NIV has "in its deepest depths" as its equivalent for "to Sheol."[4]

Hebrew also has a few forms in which word stress (according to the Masoretic system) changes the meaning:

- *qā-**mâ*** second syllable stressed "one (feminine) getting up"
- ***qā**-mâ* first syllable stressed "she got up"

- *šā-**râ*** second syllable stressed "a (female) singer"
- ***šā**-râ* first syllable stressed "she sang"

Reading Hebrew texts that do not have the Masoretic vowel letters is similar to reading words in some versions of shorthand or speed writing. We could write many English words the same way if we left out the vowels. For example, the letters *b-t-r* might refer to any of the following words:

- *beater*
- *better*
- *butter*
- *batter*

Can you think of more words like these?

The context of this hypothetical English word would help us decide which word was meant, but there could still be potential misunderstanding when more than one word would fit the context. Thus, *the b-t-r lemon* would most likely be *the bitter lemon,* but it could also be *the better lemon.*

Words That Are Related Through Their Meanings

Some words refer to specific types of a more generic idea. For example, the words *chair, table, desk,* and *divan* are all types of *furniture.* Words like this are called **hyponyms;** the specific types of furniture are hyponyms of the word *furniture.* It is important that you understand these sets of generic-specific words in Hebrew and Greek because they help you see how the original speakers talked about the world around them.

4. One word of caution, the Masoretes based their pronunciation on ancient tradition, so a change in the vowels of a word should not be accepted without strong supporting evidence.

Hebrew has a variety of terms for different types of motion. The most general term is *hālak*, "go." Table 6.3 shows different hyponyms of *hālak*, or more specific types of going.

Table 6.3: Hebrew Verbs of Motion

Hebrew Verb	English Meaning
hālak	"to go" (the most general term)
bāʾ	"to go in, enter"
yārad	"to go down, descend"
ʿālâ	"to go up, ascend"
yāṣāʾ	"to go out, leave"

In Greek there are many words dealing with speaking. The most generic word is *laleō* "to speak." Greek also has hyponyms of this generic word that are more specific ways of speaking, such as the following:

- *kērussō* "to proclaim"
- *kaleō* "to call"
- *aiteō* "to ask"
- *martyreō* "to testify"

Louw and Nida's Greek lexicon is a good resource for seeing how groups of Greek words relate to each other.[5]

Synonyms are words that have different phonetic shapes, but the same meaning in *some* contexts. Crystal says, "Items are synonyms if they are close enough in meaning to allow a choice to be made between them in some contexts, without this affecting the meaning of the sentence as a whole."[6] In English, for example, we can say:

- *The book is big.*
- *The book is large.*

5. Johannes P. Louw and Eugene A. Nida, eds., *Greek-English Lexicon of the New Testament Based on Semantic Domains* (New York: United Bible Societies, 1988).
6. *An Encyclopedic Dictionary of Language and Languages,* ed. David Crystal (Oxford: Blackwell, 1992), s.v. "synomym."

The meaning of each sentence is the same, because *big* and *large* are synonyms.

Although synonyms share a common meaning in most contexts, they may have different connotations, some more positive than others. In the following sets of words, many English speakers would say that the last word definitely has a negative value:

- *slender, skinny, gaunt*
- *chubby, fat, obese*

These words cannot be substituted freely in all circumstances even though they are somewhat synonymous.

As we approach the biblical languages, we need to understand how words are related to each other within the Hebrew or Greek languages. Too often we forget that these languages also have synonyms that are interchangeable. We do not always have to find detailed differences between biblical synonyms, much as we do not need to distinguish *big* and *large* in English. For example, Hebrew has a word *bārāʾ* ("to create") and the word *ʿāśâ* ("to make" or "to do"). From the following verses, does it seem that *bārāʾ* and *ʿāśâ* are synonymous or refer to different actions in Genesis 1:1–2:3?

> *In the beginning God created [bārāʾ] the heavens and the earth.* (Gen. 1:1 NIV)
>
> *Let us make [ʿāśâ] man in our image, in our likeness.* (Gen. 1:26 NIV)
>
> *So God created [bārāʾ] man in his own image.* (Gen. 1:27 NIV)
>
> *He rested from all the work of creating [bārāʾ] that he had done [ʿāśâ].* (Gen. 2:3 NIV)

One way to distinguish synonyms or closely related words is to look for the *semantic features* of the words that show the similarities and the differences. These features are like parts of the overall meaning of a word, but they do not show up as separate morphemes or grammatical parts like prefixes and affixes. If the words share all of the various parts of meaning, they are synonymous. If there are some parts of the meaning that are different, the words are related in some other way. The following words, for example, all have the semantic feature "young" but differ in regard to the type of animal:

- *kitten*
- *colt*
- *baby*
- *foal*
- *chick*
- *infant*

We can use semantic features to distinguish and to define words that are closely related.

One way to distinguish the particular meanings of a set of related words is to construct a matrix of semantic components such as in the following table. Note that all of the terms listed in table 6.4 are "human." We can mark them with a "+" symbol to show that they are all included in the class or set of humans (and thus are hyponyms of "human"). The next line shows whether the word also has the aspect of "young" in it. *Boy* and *girl* are [+ young]. *Girl* and *woman* are [- male].

Table 6.4: Matrix of Semantic Components

	boy	man	girl	woman
human	+	+	+	+
young	+	-	+	-
male	+	+	-	-

It is, of course, not necessary to make a complex chart to compare related words, but it does help to sort out the significant differences in closely related words.

Antonyms are typically said to be words with opposite meanings. While this is a helpful idea, there are actually several types of antonyms. Some pairs, such as *here/there* express mutually exclusive states. You can be one or the other but not both: A person is either *here* or *there.* But words such as *large/small* present information that is on a relative scale. A person can be *rather small* or *rather large* but not *rather there.* The third type of antonyms show a relationship between two words. For example, *employee* relates to the antonym *employer.* Notice the differences among the three subtypes of antonyms in the following examples:

1. *Complementary* or mutually exclusive antonyms express ideas that are either one thing or the other (either x or y) but not both:

   - *alive/dead*
   - *present/absent*
   - *visible/invisible*
   - *married/single*

   One can be either *married* or *single* but not both.

2. *Gradable/scalar* antonyms are relative to each other (x as compared to y on a scale):

   - *large/small*
   - *hot/cold*

   Something can be *rather hot* or *rather cold.*

3. *Relational/converse* antonyms are related to each other (x as related to y)

   - *give/receive*
   - *under/over*
   - *employer/employee*
   - *parent/child*
   - *buy/sell*

An unusual set of antonyms are words that are actually spelled the same way, even though they have opposite meanings. In English, for example, we have the following such pairs of words:

- *cleave* "to separate"
- *cleave* "to adhere firmly"

- *buckle* "to fasten together"
- *buckle* "to fall apart, collapse"

- *oversight* "supervision"
- *oversight* "neglect"

Such words are sometimes called *antagonyms, contronyms,* or *"Janus words,"* based on the Greek myth of Janus, a two-faced god.

The Hebrew verb *bērēk* normally means "to bless," but when its object is either God or the king, it is sometimes translated "to curse." This appears to be an issue of euphemism, which of course relies on the usual sense of "bless" (1 Kings 21:10, 13; Job 1:5; 2:9).

Also the Hebrew verb *yārad* usually means "go down," but occasionally it apparently means "go up" (Judg. 1:9; 11:37; 15:8; 2 Kings 2:2; 1 Chron. 11:15). The Hebrew noun *nepeš* is associated with concepts that relate to life. However, a specialized use of *nepeš* by priests occurs in the book of Numbers, where the term sometimes refers to a dead body (Num. 5:2; 6:11).

Hyponyms, synonyms, and antonyms need to be understood in context, as do all other words. As you study Hebrew or Greek, you should think through the various ways that the meaning of a word is determined by how it relates to other words.

What About Figurative Language?

Language has more than literal meaning. To say that a line is "straight" may not be literally accurate when we are referring to a specific line. If we could examine almost any line with a laser beam, we would find many parts of it that are not literally straight. They are, however, straight enough for most purposes. In this section we also will consider the nonliteral aspects of meaning, such as the figurative and metaphorical meanings of words and phrases.

Human languages are full of nonliteral meaning. In one sense, we use very few literal meanings. We frequently rely on metaphors and idioms to express our opinions and our feelings. Even the biblical languages talk about "hard hearts" and "stiff-necked" people. Lakoff and Johnson, in their book on the metaphorical nature of human language, note that "our ordinary conceptual system, in terms of which we both think and act, is fundamentally metaphorical in nature."[7] The meaning of a sentence is not always obvious from the meaning of the individual words; sometimes the meaning is conveyed in some figurative way. Think of the difference in meaning between the following sentences:

---

7. George Lakoff and Mark Johnson, *Metaphors We Live By* (Chicago: University of Chicago Press, 1980), 3.

- *The people have ears.*
- *She has an ear for music.*
- *The walls have ears.*

Note that *ears* in the first sentence is used in the primary sense of the word. We might think of this as the literal meaning. There also are secondary senses of the word *ear* as seen in the second sentence, *She has an ear for music,* where there is a thread of meaning between the literal or primary sense and the secondary sense of being able to hear. But in the third example there are neither literal ears nor a reference to some extended meaning of *ears.* Rather, the sentence has an idiom that uses *ear* in a **figurative** way. You will need to think about figurative meaning frequently as you study the biblical languages, just as you would if you studied other languages. An enormous number of biblical texts involve figurative meanings, and we need to be able to recognize when they are being used and what they mean.

There are two main types of figurative meaning: metaphors and idioms. We will take a look at those types here.

Metaphors Are Pictures

In a **metaphor** a word that usually refers to (denotes) a particular object or concept is compared to another object or concept. For example, we talk about a person being "a bear to work with" or "wise as an owl." In English we distinguish between metaphors and similes, but they are basically the same thing. The only difference is that a simile uses a word such as *like* or *as.* We will use the term *metaphor* to discuss both types of words in this section.

Each metaphor has three parts: a topic, an image, and a point of similarity. The *topic* is the item being discussed. The *image* is the new word or concept to which the main idea is being compared. The *point of similarity* refers to some feature that the two things have in common. The key to understanding a metaphor is determining the point of similarity. Often the comparison is implicit; the reader must figure out the puzzle. We might ask, "How is a person like a bear?" In the typical use of this English phrase, the focus of comparison is not on physical characteristics such as fur and eating habits but on characteristics of the personality. In fact, many metaphors present cultural beliefs and values that are not related to scientific truth. Owls are considered to be wise in English similes, but other cultures consider owls to be foolish because they sit around making strange noises.

Consider the following metaphor using these three parameters: *The children were* <u>*angels*</u> *at lunch.* We recognize that the children were not literally angelic beings. Thus, we are considering a metaphor. What is the point of similarity? While children could be compared to many aspects of angels (e.g., their appearance, their power), English speakers have been taught to think about angels as having good behavior. This cultural understanding of the metaphor can be broken down like this:

- Topic: *the children*
- Image: *angel*
- Point of similarity: *behave well*

When we approach the biblical languages, we are not, of course, native speakers; neither are we cultural insiders. Metaphors often will prove to be very difficult to understand, especially if we only use our English language understandings and our own cultural patterns in our study. Let's consider two biblical metaphors and determine the topic, image, and point of similarity.

In Psalm 119:105, God's Word is compared to a lamp. We recognize that this is not a literal statement because God's Word is not made of clay or bronze; it does not have a wick or oil. The topic, of course, is God's Word, and the image is a lamp. Our task is to understand the point of similarity between God's Word and a lamp. One way to do this is to consider the *form* of a lamp in Old Testament times and the *function* a lamp had for the writer. In other words, we need to know more than just what the Hebrew word means; we also need to understand the metaphorical use of lamp. The main idea of a lamp, of course, is to illuminate the area around the lamp. If this is the point of similarity between God's Word and a lamp, we then have to ask, "What does God's Word illuminate?" A model of the metaphor might look like the following:

- Topic: *God's Word*
- Image: *lamp*
- Point of similarity: *illuminates*

To understand the metaphor we also might want to consider the physical nature of a lamp in Old Testament times. It was obviously not a modern searchlight or even an overhead light bulb. Rather, it was most likely a small oil-burning lamp that someone might carry by hand to shine light on the path being followed. If we consider these cultural factors and the way Hebrew speakers thought of a lamp, we will gain a better understanding of the metaphor than if we use only our contemporary English ideas of lights.

A second biblical example is when Jesus refers to Herod as "that fox" (Luke 13:32). Here only the image is expressed, but we can determine the topic from the nearby context. We still need to think through the point of similarity because it is not expressed in the text. We can assume that Jesus and his disciples knew the standardized metaphorical meaning of the word *fox* and that they shared a common cultural understanding of the ways Herod could be talked about as a fox. Unfortunately, our modern metaphors about foxes are not the same as the New Testament usage. We cannot merely look at the word *fox* and assume Jesus meant that Herod was "sly as a fox" as in our English simile nor that Herod was good-looking as in more contemporary English use. Commentaries and other books about biblical times may help us understand the metaphor more accurately. The nearby and larger context of the metaphor also may shed light on the figurative meaning. We will leave the solution to this puzzle for you to study.[8]

- Topic: *Herod*
- Image: *fox*
- Point of Similarity: *?*

Idioms Are Hard Nuts to Crack

A second type of figurative language is the **idiom.** Again, the meaning of the words of an idiom is obviously not literal; they are used in a figurative way that speakers of the language understand. The meaning of an idiom is not clear from the usual meaning of the words themselves. That is, even if we know the meaning of each word in an idiom, we still do not know the meaning of the idiom as a whole unless we understand that it is a figure of speech, a figurative use of the words. Compare the following examples:

---

8. To help you solve it see Geoffrey W. Bromiley, ed., *The International Standard Bible Encyclopedia,* rev. ed. (Grand Rapids: Eerdmans, 1979), s.v. "fox"; Clinton E. Arnold, ed., *Zondervan Illustrated Bible Backgrounds Commentary,* vol. 1 (Grand Rapids: Zondervan, 2002), s.v. "Luke 13:32"; and Norval Geldenhuys, *Commentary on the Gospel of Luke,* New International Commentary on the Old Testament (Grand Rapids: Eerdmans, 1968), s.v. "Luke 13:32."

- *The driver stepped on the oil.*
- *The driver stepped on the gas.*

- *The old cowboy kicked the pail.*
- *The old cowboy kicked the bucket.*

Note that the first sentence in each pair is normally understood literally, while the second sentence has taken on an idiomatic meaning (i.e., its meaning is not the same as the literal combination of the words in the sentence). The phrase *stepped on the oil* is literal; *stepped on the gas* refers to accelerating a car. Likewise, *kicked the pail* is literal; *kicked the bucket* refers to dying.

In many languages emotions are referred to by idioms involving body parts. English refers to such things as *a hot head, a big heart.* As we compare English with other languages, however, we see that *a hot head* may refer to anger, but not necessarily so. *A big heart* may refer to someone who is generous or to someone who is proud. The meaning is idiomatic and culturally determined. The meaning of an idiom has nothing to do with the literal hardness of a head or the physical size of a heart.

When we look at the biblical languages, we see many idioms that appear to be similar to English, such as "stiff-necked people" and references to Pharaoh's "hard heart." To some degree our familiarity with Hebrew and Greek biblical idioms comes through the fact that English Bible translations often translated the idioms literally, and the idioms were conveyed down through the years as a part of the English language. It is a mark of biblical literacy in the Western world that so many Hebrew and Greek idioms can be understood by people who do not even read the Bible. Unfortunately, this familiarity with certain biblical idioms may make us think that we understand them, when in fact we do not. We need to be careful to think through biblical idioms so that we understand them as they were originally used.

Hebrew has an idiom that translates literally as "uncover the ear." An example is found in Ruth 4:4, "I thought *I should bring the matter to your attention . . .*" (NIV). The italicized words are literally, "I should uncover your ear." Someone who has a message to convey to another "uncovers the ear" of the listener. In this case, Boaz wanted to "uncover the ear" of the relative who had more of a right to redeem Naomi's property than he had. Perhaps we could guess the meaning of the idiom, but translators have rightly recognized an idiom and translated something like "inform" or "tell about" something to the listener. Some other passages where the idiom is used are 1 Samuel 9:15 (the Lord's revelation to Samuel); Job 33:16; and Isaiah 22:14. The last two passages are translated more literally by some of the English versions.

When Is Language Ambiguous?

A further difficulty in learning a language is that some words and phrases can have more than one meaning; they are **ambiguous.** Such ambiguity can derive from the meaning of a word itself or from the way a phrase or sentence is made. A word may be unclear because the context allows for several meanings, or the structure of a phrase or sentence may allow for more than one understanding. We will look at these two types of ambiguity and note some examples from Hebrew and Greek.

Sometimes Words Are Ambiguous

Some phrases or sentences are ambiguous because a particular word or particular words have more than one potential meaning. In the sentence *Chris walked past the bank,* the *bank* could refer to the edge of a river or to a financial institution. The larger context of the sentence might clarify which meaning is intended, but sometimes there is not enough information to decide. Sometimes it helps to know who the original author or writer is. If you heard or read the sentence *Chris was mad about the flat,* you might at first think that Chris was upset or angry about having a flat tire. That is, you might think that if you are American and assume that the person who said this was also American. If you are British or know British English, you might understand the sentence to mean that Chris really liked the apartment. The near and distant context, as well as the cultural setting, can help us understand many ambiguous words.

When we look at the biblical languages, we also need to consider the linguistic context and the cultural setting to understand ambiguous expressions. Look at the following Hebrew examples:

yāmay	*qallû*	*minnî*	*ʾāreg*	*wayyiklû*	*bĕʾepes*	*tiqwâ*
days-my	swift	from	weaver's-bobbin	and-end	in-absence-of	*hope*

"My days are swifter than a weaver's bobbin and come to an end without hope." (Job 7:6)

Robert Gordis suggested that since *tiqwâ,* translated here "hope," can also mean "cord" or "thread," there is a play on words. The sentence could be rendered, "My days are swifter than a weaver's bobbin and come to an end without thread." That is, the "thread of life" runs out swiftly. This would be an example of deliberate ambiguity for the sake of a play on words.[9]

taʿan	*lĕšônî*	*ʾimrāteka*	*kî*	*kol*	*miṣwōteykā*	*ṣedeq*
let-sing	tongue-my	word-your	for	all	commandments-your	righteous

"May my tongue sing of your word, for all your commands are righteous."
(Psalm 119:172 NIV)

The KJV has, "My tongue shall speak of thy word." The Hebrew verb root *ʿnh* (*taʿan* is a form of it) can mean either "answer, reply" or "sing." Perhaps the parallel with verse 171 led the translators to choose the meaning that refers more to speaking than singing. At first glance it might appear that these are two meanings that come from the same root, but there is evidence that these are two unrelated meanings. The situation would be similar to English *ball,* which has the unrelated meanings of "a round object" and "a fancy party," or *date,* which can refer to a sweet food or an appointment.

A Greek example of this kind of ambiguity is in Mark 1:10, in which the Spirit is described as "descending *like* a dove" *(hōs peristeran).* It is ambiguous as to whether the movement of the Spirit was like the descent of a dove or whether the Spirit took the shape of a dove. Artists, of course, have taken the latter view and have embedded that meaning in our minds, but the words are ambiguous.

Another example in Greek is the word *anōthen* in John 3:7 when Jesus is speaking to Nicodemus. The word can mean either "from above" or "again." Thus, some English translations say "born from above" *(New Jerusalem Bible)* and others say "born again" (NASB, NIV, NLT).

Sometimes Clauses Are Ambiguous

Some phrases or clauses are ambiguous because of their structure; they can be understood in different ways depending on how the structure of the sentence is interpreted. Consider the following sentence: *The young men and women*

9. Robert Gordis, *The Book of God and Man: A Study of Job* (Chicago: University of Chicago Press, 1965), 168.

went first. Are just the men young, or does *young* refer to both the men and women? Your decision is based on how you interpret the grammatical structure of the sentence; it is ambiguous. Another example is the sentence *The teacher saw the child with the telescope.* Who had the telescope, the teacher or the child? (Can you see both of these potential meanings? If not, read the sentence again, and try to see the one you overlooked.) A final English example: *Visiting relatives can be a nuisance.*

The biblical languages, of course, also have ambiguous structures. This is a normal phenomenon of language. As students of Hebrew and Greek, we need to study the way sentences are put together (as we did in chap. 4) so that we can find the best understanding of ambiguous forms.

How Is a Sentence Like a Play?

When we watch a play, we need to understand the different roles of the various actors. In a similar way the various parts of a sentence have a semantic role to play in that sentence. These roles are connected with some of the grammatical terms we saw in chapter 4, like subject, object, or verb, yet we use different terms for semantic roles to help us see the connection between the grammatical terms and the meaning of the sentence.

One of the major semantic roles in a sentence is the **agent,** which may be described as something that initiates the event described in the clause. Often the agent will be the same as the grammatical subject of the sentence, but not always. Examine the following pair of sentences:

- *Chris gave the flowers to Jan.*
- *The flowers were given to Jan by Chris.*

In the first sentence *Chris* is the grammatical subject, while in the second sentence the subject is *the flowers.* In both sentences, though, Chris is the semantic agent; he took the initiative to give the flowers.

What about the role of *the flowers* in the above sentences? In semantic terms we would say they have the role of the **patient.** Much as a patient does not do anything when the doctor treats him or her, the semantic patient does not actively do anything in the sentence. However, the patient does receive in some way the action of the agent. The agent acts on the patient, whether it is the grammatical object as in the first sentence or the grammatical subject as in the second.

Finally we come to Jan's role in these sentences. Semantically we define her role as the **goal** or **recipient.** Chris, the agent, acts on the flowers, the patient, and gets them to Jan, the goal. These three **semantic** or **thematic roles** relate to the real-world experience of "who did what to whom" rather than on the surface level of grammatical structure. Here are two more ways to express this same scenario and these same roles:

- *Chris gave Jan the flowers.*
- *Jan was given the flowers by Chris.*

Table 6.5 lists six basic semantic roles; some scholars identify many others.

Table 6.5: Six Semantic Roles in a Sentence

Role	Explanation	Typical Grammatical Role in English	Example
Agent	Deliberate initiator of events	subject	*Chris ran.*
Patient or theme	Entity undergoing a change of state or transfer	object	*Chris kicked the chair.* *Chris died.*[10]
Location	Place at which an entity or action is located	prepositional phrase	. . . *in the yard.*
Goal	End point of a motion or of a transfer	prepositional phrase	. . . *to the house.* . . . *to Chris.*
Source	Starting point of a transfer	prepositional phrase	. . . *from the city.*
Instrument	Entity used to carry out an action	prepositional phrase	. . . *with a shovel.*

10. *"Someone or something killed Chris."*

The way these real-world roles are expressed in the grammar of a particular sentence may change, but the semantic roles remain constant. The semantic agent is often the grammatical subject, as in:

Subject	**Verb**	**Object**
X	receives	Y
Agent		Patient

In English, however, we can express the sentence in other ways, including making the patient the subject of a passive sentence. In fact, a passive sentence in English can be defined as a sentence in which the patient is the grammatical subject.

Subject	**Verb**	**Prepositional Phrase**
Y	*was received*	*by X*
Patient		Agent

"Paul and Barnabas were received by the church."

English also can express the agent, patient, and goal relationships in more than one way:

Subject	**Verb**	**Object**	**Indirect Object**
X	*gave*	*Y*	*to Z*
Agent		Patient	Goal

"Solomon gave the child to its mother."

Subject	**Verb**	**Object**	**Object**
X	*gave*	*Z*	*Y*
Agent		Goal	Patient

"Solomon gave the mother her child."

Subject	**Verb**	**Object**	**Prepositional Phrase**
Z	*was given*	*Y*	*by X*
Goal		Patient	Agent

"The mother was given her child by Solomon."

Hebrew has patterns that resemble English but with some important differences. In the passive construction it is rare for the agent to be mentioned in the sentence. However, the agent is sometimes explicit:

- Agent expressed with a preposition

nittĕnû	*mē-rōʿeh*	*ʾeḥād*
they-are-given	by-shepherd	one

"They [the words of the wise] are given by one Shepherd [Agent]." (Eccles. 12:11 NASB)

- Agent expressed in a separate clause

ûlĕYôsēp	*yûlad*	*šnê*	*bānîm*	*ʾăsher*	*yālĕdâ*	*lô*	*ʾasĕnat*
and-to-Joseph	was-born	two	sons	whom	bore-she	to-him	Asenath

"Two sons [Patient] were born to Joseph [Goal] by Asenath [Agent]." (Gen. 41:50 NIV)

It is clear that the woman who bore Joseph's sons was his wife Asenath, but she is specified only in the relative clause ("by Asenath") that gives more information about the sons.

- Agent omitted because it is unknown

hûšab	*kaspî*
has-been-returned	money-my

"My money [Patient] has been returned." (Gen. 42:28 NASB; Joseph's brother is shocked to find the money in his sack and has no idea how it got there.)

- Agent omitted because it is irrelevant (most common use of the passive in Hebrew)

wayyuggad	*lĕʾAbrāhām*	*lēʾmōr . . .*
it-was-told	to-Abraham	(saying)

"Abraham was told . . ." (Gen. 22:20 NIV)

The news that Abraham heard is the patient, while Abraham is the goal. There is no concern in the context for how Abraham got this news, only that he got it. This is also the case in the following example:

šāmmâ	*qubbar*	*ʾAbrāhām*	*wĕŚārâ*	*ʾištô*
there	was-buried	Abraham	and-Sarah	wife-his

"There Abraham [Patient] was buried along with Sarah his wife." (Gen. 25:10 NASB)

Presumably a family member buried Abraham, but the narrator is not concerned with it.

It is possible (though rare) for the patient in a passive sentence to be marked in the same way as in an active sentence (i.e., with the object marker *ʾet*). Waltke and O'Connor mention this, along with a couple of other rare situations where *ʾet* is used other than to mark the patient of a transitive verb.[11]

How Does Context Relate to Language?

Meaning is related not only to the sounds and forms of words, but also to the situation or context in which the words are used. **Pragmatics** is the study of how language is used in particular contexts and the ways language is used to make things happen. Both of these factors inform us that we need to know more than just the words and the structures of the biblical languages; we need to understand how they relate to their larger cultural contexts.

To understand an utterance we need to understand the context in which it was spoken (or written). Anyone who has ever worked a crossword puzzle can understand how important context is. There may be several ways to respond to a single clue, but once intersecting words are taken into account only one answer is possible. The context can be viewed in terms of the linguistic, the social, and the physical context.

The Linguistic Context

Words normally occur in a larger context, not in isolation. One part of understanding a word or an utterance is knowing what has preceded it. If we hear the sentence <u>*The*</u> *child was happy,* we know that the child has already been

11. Bruce K. Waltke and M. O'Connor, *An Introduction to Biblical Hebrew Syntax* (Winona Lake, Ind.: Eisenbrauns, 1990), 182–83, par. 10.3.2.

mentioned earlier in the context. And due to polysemy, the word *chair* means something different in *Chris sat on the chair* than in *Chris is the chair.*

The Social Context

Language cannot be separated from its setting within society and the social forces and trends within a particular culture. For example, languages often indicate gender distinctions. In English there has been a recent tendency to reduce the number of gender-specific forms such as *waiter/waitress* or *actor/actress.* Also, there is the increasingly frequent *guys* used as a generic for both men and women. When studying a term like *waiter* or *guys,* we need to consider the social and cultural issues involved. Likewise, when studying terms in Greek or Hebrew we will need to ask about issues from the social context that influence how the original authors meant their words to be understood.

An example from Greek is the term *peirazō,* which can mean either "test" or "tempt" (to do evil). The Devil, or Satan, was viewed as someone who leads people to sin against God (cf. 1 Peter 5:8). So when the Devil is the agent for the action of *peirazō,* it makes sense to translate it as "tempt" (e.g., Matt. 4:1; 1 Cor. 7:5). Unlike Satan, God does not tempt people to do evil (James 1:13). So if God (or Jesus) is the agent of *peirazō,* the verb must be translated "test" (e.g., John 6:5–6; Heb. 11:17). The social context that the New Testament and the Old Testament present about the way people believed makes the proper sense clear.[12]

The Physical Context

The physical context of an utterance or a discourse also influences what is said and how it is expressed. In English the words *come* and *go* relate to the speaker and the hearer and their normal spatial relationships. For example, on the telephone we might say, "I will come to your house" or "Can you come to my house?" even though in the first example we are moving away from our own location. When both the speaker and the hearer are moving away from

12. Some might complain that theology is dictating the translation here, but the issue is not so much theology as the entire social context in which the terms are used. Of course, theology itself is always within a social context, because communities of faith express their theology as a community.

their present location or from their normal location, we might say, "Shall we go to a movie?"

Words such as *this* and *that* also refer to the physical context of what we say. For example: *Please sit in this chair, not that one.*

Since Jerusalem is located in the Judean mountains, the verb used for going to Jerusalem is often "go up" (Hebrew *ʿālâ*). One "goes up" to Jerusalem (cf. 2 Sam. 19:34; Ezra 7:7). Another example of the importance of physical context for Hebrew concerns the references in the prophets to an enemy "from the north." Sometimes this refers to the Babylonian army, which could be better described as east of Israel (Jer. 25:9) or east of Tyre (Ezek. 26:7). However, people did not travel from Babylonia to Israel by a direct route because of the hostile desert. Rather, they traveled in a northwest direction up the Euphrates River and then turned south from a point roughly due north of Damascus. So the invading army would indeed come from the north, even though the location of Babylon from Jerusalem was not north on the compass.

How Do We Get Things Done with Language?

Another aspect of pragmatics is that of speech acts. Sometimes language is viewed as merely telling some information (asserting), asking a question, or giving a command. In fact, language is often less straightforward. Speech act theory looks at the ways in which syntactic forms are used to "get things done."

Making an Assertion

When we say "I am here" or "You are correct," we are asserting or stating that information. We might think of the words "I assert that" as being implied in such statements.

Asking a Question

We frequently use questions to ask for information, but not all questions are, in fact, requests for information. Note the following examples:

- *How far is it to San Jose?*
- *Aren't you ever going to stop whining?*

The second question is best understood as a command that the other person stop whining; it is not a request for information. We call such examples *rhetorical* questions. The Scriptures include hundreds of rhetorical questions. It is important to look beyond the grammatical shape of the questions and to consider the meaning that was being conveyed. For example, consider the following rhetorical questions from the New Testament:

> To what shall I compare the kingdom of God? (Luke 13:20 NASB)

> Shall we continue in sin? (Rom. 6:1 KJV)

Neither of these questions are seeking information; they are a rhetorical device that makes a statement. In the first, Jesus uses a rhetorical question to introduce a parable (he was not expecting the listeners to suggest answers). In the second, Paul uses a rhetorical question to make a strong command: "We should not keep on sinning!"

Giving a Command

Imperative forms are often commands, but sometimes they might have some different functions.

> Leave your country, your people and your father's household. (Gen. 12:1 NIV)

> Please listen to this dream which I have had. (Gen. 37:6 NASB)

> Create in me a clean heart, O God. (Ps. 51:10 NASB)

> Pray to the Lord for me. (Acts 8:24 NIV)

Only the first of these four quotations is a true command. Authority is a key issue in interpreting whether an imperative form actually commands something. The Lord obviously had the authority to command Abraham, so in the first quotation the underlying Hebrew imperative form is really a command. In the other three examples, the person stating the imperative does not have authority over the person or persons addressed (Joseph to his brothers, David to God, Simon Magus to Peter). Even though the imperative form was used, each of the other three cases represents a request or even an entreaty. This is made explicit in the Hebrew of Genesis 37:6, where a word is placed after the imperative that means something like "please."

Looking at commands another way, we see that they are not always expressed in an imperative form. You might, in various contexts, have heard all the following ways people try to get someone else to close a door:

- Imperative: *(Please) close the door.*
- Question: *Could you (please) close the door?*
- Statement: *I would like it if you closed the door.*

These issues of context and of the practical use of language are important in understanding the biblical languages, just as they are in our day-to-day communication in English.

Summary and Preview

In this chapter we have looked at the connection between linguistic forms and meaning. We have seen that words normally have multiple senses and that this makes it difficult to translate a word in one language by just one word in another. We have also seen that some meaning is related to whole phrases, rather than only to individual words. Even linguistic forms such as the genitive can have more than one meaning.

In the next chapter we will see that variety and change are normal in every language. We will also trace some of the history of Hebrew and Greek.

For Further Study

Barnwell, Katharine. *Introduction to Semantics and Translation.* 2d ed. Dallas: SIL, 1980.

Barr, James. *The Semantics of Biblical Language.* London: Oxford University Press, 1961.

Caird, G. B. *The Language and Imagery of the Bible.* Philadelphia: Westminster, 1980.

Eastman, Carol M. *Aspects of Language and Culture.* 2d ed. Novato, Calif.: Chandler and Sharp, 1990.

Goddard, Cliff. *Semantic Analysis: A Practical Introduction.* Oxford: Oxford University Press, 1998.

Katz, Eliezer. *A Classified Concordance to the Bible in Four Volumes.* Jerusalem: Central Press, 1964–74.

Lakoff, George. *Women, Fire and Dangerous Things: What Categories Reveal About the Mind.* Chicago: University of Chicago Press, 1987.

Lakoff, George, and Mark Johnson. *Metaphors We Live By.* Chicago: University of Chicago Press, 1980.

Louw, Johannes P. *The Semantics of New Testament Greek.* Philadelphia: Scholars Press, 1982.

Louw, Johannes P., and Eugene A. Nida, eds. *Greek-English Lexicon of the New Testament Based on Semantic Domains.* 2 vols. 2d ed. New York: United Bible Societies, 1989.

Rheingold, Howard. *They Have a Word for It: A Lighthearted Lexicon of Untranslatable Words and Phrases.* Los Angeles: Jeremy P. Tarcher, 1988.

Silva, Moisés. *Biblical Words and Their Meaning: An Introduction to Lexical Semantics.* Grand Rapids: Zondervan, 1983.

———. *God, Language and Scripture: Reading the Bible in the Light of General Linguistics.* Grand Rapids: Zondervan, 1990.

Internet Resources

There are numerous dictionaries on-line. These can be used as a resource to find homonyms, synonyms, antonyms, et cetera.

The Homonym Page: www.taupecat.com/personal/homophones.

Alan Cooper's Homonyms page: www. cooper.com/alan/homonym.html.

Exercises

1. Identify which of the following sets of English words are homonyms (unrelated words that happen to share the same pronunciation) and which are related meanings of the same word (polysemous).

    - *deep* (water)
    - *deep* (thoughts)

- *two*
- *to*

- *bear* (the animal)
- *bare* (skin)

- *bear* (the animal)
- *bear* ("to tolerate")

- *head* (of body)
- *head* (of an office)

- *foot* (of body)
- *foot* (of mountain)

2. Metaphors and similes compare two items that are normally considered to be related. List the image, topic, and point of similarity for each of the following metaphors.

    - *The mouth of the righteous is a fountain of life.* (Prov. 10:11a)
    - I am the good shepherd. (John 10:11a)
    - You are the light of the world. (Matt. 5:14)

3. Make a semantic feature chart that distinguishes the following words: *bless, praise, thank.* Use only enough categories to show how the words are distinct. Use plus (+) or minus (-) to indicate whether a category is important to define a particular word.
4. Idioms have a meaning that is not merely the sum of the meanings of the words in the idiom. Give an example of a common idiom and some non-idiomatic phrases that have the same form but different words.

    - Example: *step on the gas* ("accelerate") and *step on the oil*

5. The following Hebrew words can sometimes have the same English translation. See if you can decide on the basis of the biblical references whether or not they are really synonyms in Hebrew and how they

should be distinguished. You may need to check more than one modern version in some cases.

- *ḥāyâ* "to live" (Gen. 3:22; 5:3; 9:28; 17:18)
- *yāšab* "to live" (Gen. 14:7, 12; 16:3; 19:29)

- *lammâ* "why?" (Gen. 4:6; 12:18–19; 18:13; 24:31) [hint, check the context!]
- *maddûaʿ* "why?" (Gen. 26:27; 40:7; Exod. 1:18; 2:18)

- *kî* "that" (Gen. 1:4; 3:5, 6, 7; 6:2)
- *ʾăsher* "that" (Gen. 1:31; 5:5; 6:17, 22; 7:2)
- *hahûʾ* "that" (Gen. 2:12; 10:11; 15:18; 19:35)

- *nātan* "to put, place, set" (Gen. 1:17; 9:13; 18:8; 38:28)
- *śîm* "to put, place, set" (Gen. 2:8; 6:16; 21:14; 24:2)

7

Variety Is the Spice of Life

Dialects and Change

The Gileadites captured the fords of the Jordan leading to Ephraim, and whenever a survivor of Ephraim said, "Let me cross over," the men of Gilead asked him, "Are you an Ephraimite?" If he replied, "No," they said, "All right, say 'Shibboleth.'" If he said, "Sibboleth," because he could not pronounce the word correctly, they seized him and killed him at the fords of the Jordan.

—Judges 12:5–6

A language is more than a collection of words and grammatical structures. The ways we adjust our speech in different situations also is important. A language is not a static, uniform thing; it is dynamic and varied. Jawaharlal Nehru (1889–1964), a former prime minister of India, noted:

> A living language is a throbbing, vital thing, ever changing, ever growing and mirroring the people who speak it and write it. It has its roots in the masses, though its superstructure may represent the culture of a few.[1]

In this chapter we will look at some of the key elements of the variation in language and the normal changes that have occurred in Hebrew and Greek.

---

1. Cited in Peter H. Burgess, *Selected Quotations from the East and West* (Singapore: Graham Brash, 1983), 117.

Why Do People Speak Differently?

It is extremely difficult to pin down a language. In one sense, a language is only a collection of all the ways that people use it, and people change their speech in many ways. Each individual speaks in a variety of ways, even within the same language or dialect. These variations may be due to a number of factors, including:

- Age: old terms versus new terms (e.g., slang)
- Geographical Region: for example, Texas, New York City, Chicago
- Occupation: insider talk (jargon)
- Social Situation: formal versus informal
- Social Status: talking with peers versus talking with superiors

When we speak to people older than ourselves, we may not use the same words and style that we use when we talk to younger people. Most of us also have a different way of talking in formal situations compared to the way we talk to our close friends. To describe the speech patterns of even one person would be a daunting task, much less an entire language.

Accents and Dialects

Dialects can be defined in terms of geography or various social parameters. Thus, geographic regions may differ in how words are pronounced (an **accent**) or in the meaning of words. An American example is the different words used to talk about carbonated beverages. Some people say *pop,* others say *soda.*

Regional dialect differences also can be identified in the Hebrew Bible. There is evidence of a southern, or Judean, dialect that differed from a northern, or Israelite, dialect. Gary Rendsburg claims to have found evidence for a northern dialect, which he calls "Israelian Hebrew." For example, some psalms have features that Rendsburg finds characteristic of Israelian Hebrew.[2]

Some scholars call Israelian Hebrew forms "Aramaisms." An Aramaism shows

---

2. See Gary A. Rendsburg, *Linguistic Evidence for the Northern Origin of Selected Psalms,* Society of Biblical Literature Monograph Series 43 (Atlanta: Scholars Press, 1990), 83–86, 91–93. See also by Rendsburg, *Israelian Hebrew in the Book of Kings,* Occasional Publications of the Department of Near Eastern Studies and the Program of Jewish Studies Cornell University 5 (Bethesda, Md.: CDL Press, 2002).

the influence of Aramaic on Hebrew. Since northern Israel had direct contact with ancient Aram (Syria) whereas southern Judah did not, it is not surprising that Israelian Hebrew would share some features with Aramaic.

Social differences also can exhibit dialect differences. Whether an American speaker says *doing* or *doin'* is sometimes related to social class distinctions. The biblical languages also had dialect differences based on geography (e.g., people knew Peter was from Galilee by the way he talked). We can also see differences in how biblical writers used words. That is why it is important to study, for instance, how James used the term *faith* in his epistle as compared to how it is used in the Gospels or the Pauline Epistles.

Social Attitudes

In addition to regional and social distinctions, we can also consider types of language that people consider offensive or impolite. Some of the ways we use language exclude other people.

Jargon (or **argot**) refers to specialized words and phrases that help a small group of people communicate. Jargon is more for ease of communication than for excluding others, although insiders need to remember that they are using specialized words when they attempt to communicate with people from other professions. People often complain about doctors who cannot communicate in simple terms. Perhaps you have felt excluded by the many technical terms in your Hebrew or Greek textbooks. Our hope is that we can help you understand what some of these specialist words mean.

The closest thing to jargon in the Hebrew Bible undoubtedly would be the many specialized terms used for describing what happened during Israelite worship. They tend to be confined to Exodus through Deuteronomy, and often they are very hard to translate. For example, *šelem* is translated in modern versions variously as "peace offering" (NASB), "fellowship offering" (NIV), or "offering of well-being" (NRSV).

Another way that language can exclude some people is through the use of gender-related grammatical markers. Many languages have grammatical distinctions of gender (e.g., *he* vs. *she*). Sometimes the masculine word is used as a generic, and an affix must be attached to indicate that the noun is feminine (e.g., *waiter/waitress, actor/actress*). As you learn Hebrew or Greek, you will encounter gender-specific words and gender markers that differ from English use. For example, the morphological gender of the little girl in Mark 5:41 is neuter, and the normal word for the Spirit of God in the Old Testament is marked as a feminine word by its agreement with the verb (e.g., Gen. 1:2; Num. 24:2). Also, "Holy Spirit" in the New Testament, despite the fact that the term refers to a person of the Trinity, is sometimes treated as neuter because of the grammatical gender of *pneuma* ("wind" or "spirit"; cf. Mark 13:11; Luke 2:25; Eph. 4:30). Recent discussions about Bible translation have centered on whether these morphological markers should be translated literally into English, especially when the Greek form is masculine.

People have strong attitudes about language and the way others speak. When an American hears someone speak with a "proper" British accent, he or she may think the person speaking is well educated, snobbish, or just "different." Our reaction to other dialects is often very prejudiced. George Bernard Shaw, the English playwright, said, "It is impossible for an Englishman to open his mouth, without making some other Englishman despise him."[3]

In Judges 12:5–6 we see the dialectal difference in pronunciation between the Gileadites and the Ephraimites. The prophet Isaiah referred to a time when the Lord would speak to the people in a "foreign language," which he also dubbed "stammering lips" (Isa. 28:11). In the New Testament we see Peter stigmatized by the people of Jerusalem because of his Galilean accent (Matt. 26:73).

Why Do Languages Change?

Languages are constantly changing. In fact, at any given moment in time, a language exhibits wide diversity. If English, for example, were written phonetically, the dialect differences between Sydney, Australia, and Dallas, Texas, would be very obvious. There are differences in pronunciation, in morphology, in syntax, and in semantics. Such present-day, or **synchronic,** differences can help us understand changes through time (**diachronic** changes). In this section we will look at some of the major topics about language change and apply them to Hebrew and Greek.

Language is a vital, ever-changing element of human culture. Pronunciations change from generation to generation. Words shift in meaning. Even grammatical structures change through time (although they are normally more stable than words).

3. George Bernard Shaw, preface to *Pygmalion* (n.p., 1913).

Richard Bentley (1662–1742), in his *Dissertation upon the Epistles of Phalaris,* noted:

> Every living language, like the perspiring bodies of living creatures, is in perpetual motion and lateration; some words go off, and become obsolete; others are taken in, and by degrees grow into common use; or the same word is inverted to a new sense and notion, which in tract of time makes as observable a change in the air and features of a language as age makes in the lines and mien of a face.[4]

The study of how languages change through time is called *historical linguistics.* Linguists can reconstruct, or "predict backward" from current language information to earlier forms by following general principles of how language changes. They can study changes in pronunciation, phonology, morphology, syntax, and so forth.

If there are written records of a language, linguists can observe change occurring through time. Thus, we can compare the writings of Chaucer, Shakespeare, and modern writers and see the numerous ways that English has changed over the years. If there are no written records, linguists still can make educated guesses on what changes have taken place.

Linguistic differences based on language change should be expected for biblical Hebrew, since the writing of the Hebrew Bible covered a period of roughly a thousand years (ca. 1400–400 B.C.).[5] There has been a growing recognition in recent years of a "late" Biblical Hebrew as opposed to an earlier form. The details are controversial, but it does seem possible to distinguish some late (i.e., after ca. 600 B.C.) characteristics from earlier material. Many writers also have viewed the "Song of Deborah" (Judg. 5) and some other poetic material as among the earliest examples of written Hebrew.[6]

Different generations and regional groups speak in ways that are not shared

---

4. Richard Bentley, *Dissertation upon the Epistles of Phalaris* (n.p., n.d.); cited in Henry Louis Mencken, ed., *A New Dictionary of Quotations* (New York: Alfred A. Knopf, 1946), 648.
5. When the biblical books were written turns out to be a very controversial subject. Some would prefer a range of about 1200–200 B.C., and still others prefer to think of oral transmission during the earliest periods, with the bulk of the Old Testament written down somewhere between 500–200 B.C. Even the narrowest range allows sufficient time for linguistic changes to have occurred.
6. See David A. Robertson, *Linguistic Evidence in Dating Early Hebrew Poetry* (Missoula, Mont.: Scholars, 1972).

by other segments of the society. At some point a particular way of speaking may become more or less accepted and be the standard for a period of time. These changes can relate to how words are pronounced (phonetics and phonology), how words are formed (morphology), how words combine into phrases and clauses (syntax), and what words mean (semantics.)

Pronunciation Changes

Changes in pronunciation can take any of several forms. Many of these pronunciation changes tend to make words easier to say.

Clusters of consonants frequently change from a more difficult sequence to one that is easier to pronounce. English words such as *indestructible, impossible,* and *irregular* used to all start with *in-*. Since it is easier to pronounce *<u>im</u>possible* than *<u>in</u>-possible,* English speakers changed the way the word was pronounced. The same thing happened with *<u>ir</u>regular.*

In Hebrew, the pattern *yi-šmōr* ("he will watch"), applied to the root *npl* does not become *yi-npōl* but changes to *yi-ppōl* ("he will fall"). The preposition *min* ("from") can attach directly to its object noun, but it does not become *min-bĕśārî;* it is pronounced *mib-bĕśārî* ("from/of my flesh").

Difficult sequences of sounds are frequently broken up by the insertion of an additional letter (**epenthesis**). In Hebrew when a vowel other than *a* occurs immediately prior to a laryngeal in final position in a word, an epenthetic *a* vowel is inserted between the non-*a* vowel and the laryngeal. The participle pattern *śōmēr* applied to a root that ends with the laryngeal *chet* requires the epenthetic *a* to be inserted just prior to the laryngeal sound (e.g., *šlḥ: šōlēaḥ*). The epenthetic *a* is always unstressed.

Morphology Changes

Since Chaucer's time, English has switched from a regular system of case marking on nouns and pronouns to only a residue of case marking on pronouns (*he/him/his; she/her/hers,* etc.) and the possessive suffix *–'s* on nouns *(Pat's).* It appears that the case-marking distinction between *who* and *whom* also will be dropped if the current trend continues. Greek, of course, had a rich system of case marking, as we saw in chapter 3. Between Classical Greek and Koine Greek, however, several case endings were "lost," as there were in earlier forms of English.

Word Order Changes

Languages also change in their syntactic patterns. In English, the basic word order has changed to SVO (i.e., subject—verb—object) from a freer mix of SOV and SVO in Old English, when the nouns were marked for case. Once the case markers were gone, it became important to use fixed word order to keep track of which noun was the actor or grammatical subject. That is, word order determines the difference between subject and object in the following:

- *The prophet met the king.*
- *The king met the prophet.*

Without a fixed pattern of SVO, one could not tell the difference that in earlier times was marked by different case endings for the subject and the object.

Semantic Changes

Words not only change in their pronunciation or morphology; sometimes their meaning shifts slightly or even completely. In English, *square* once meant "nutritious" but now also means "nerdlike." *Gay* has shifted in very recent history from "happy" to "homosexual."

Samuel Johnson, the great lexicographer of English, noted:

> As any custom is disused, the words that expressed it must perish with it; as any opinion grows popular, it will innovate speech in the same proportion as it alters practice.[7]

In the biblical languages, words also underwent shifts in meaning from one era to the next. The Old Testament was written over a period of more than one thousand years. At one point the biblical author explained that people used to call certain people "seers," although the appropriate term at the time he was writing was "prophet" (1 Sam. 9:9). Between the time of Classical Greek and Koine Greek, many words shifted in meaning. The word *laleō,* for example, meant "I babble" in Classical Greek, but this shifted to a more neutral "I speak" in Koine Greek. We need to look at the current use of a word (e.g., the New

---

7. Samuel Johnson, preface to *Dictionary of the English Language* (n.p., 1755).

Testament writings) to know what the word meant at the time. The meaning of a word in context does not necessarily include the past history of the word.

Language groups frequently borrow words from other languages when they encounter new materials or concepts. English has received hundreds of words from interaction with other languages. In English, for example, we have borrowed the following words from other languages:

- French: *beef, pork, judge, jail, fashion, ruby*
- Hindi: *thug, punch, shampoo*
- Amerindian languages: *toboggan, wigwam, chipmunk*

Ancient Hebrew tended to borrow a lot from the neighboring Aramaic language. This borrowing occurred in all time periods but accelerated rapidly after the Babylonian exile.

- *bĕrôt* ("cypress, fir tree," Song 1:17)
- *šallîṭ* ("ruler, governor," Gen. 42:6; Eccl. 8:8)
- *ṭaʿam* ("decision, decree," Jonah 3:7)

How Do We Know When Languages Are Related?

By studying sets of words that sound alike and have similar or related meanings, linguists can reconstruct earlier forms of a given word (e.g., English *father* and Latin *pater* come from an earlier form in a language that preceded them both). Such a reconstruction is, of course, only a hypothesis, but when dozens of similar patterns have been found, it is unlikely that these similarities are merely coincidental.

The discovery that English, Latin, Greek, and many other European languages were related created an interest in the older forms of this group of languages. By comparing written records and present-day forms, linguists can reconstruct what the language of Europe might have been like before the "daughter" languages became mutually unintelligible.

Greek and English Are Related

Greek and English are members of a larger "family" of languages, the Indo-European language family. As the name indicates, it includes some of the languages of India and many of the languages of Europe, although not all the languages in these areas belong to the group. If we look at the present-day languages in this family, we would notice some similarities, especially in basic vocabulary. English and German, for example, share hundreds of basic words, as do Spanish and Portuguese. Table 7.1 summarizes some of the subgroups within this greater Indo-European family of languages. Note the position of Greek and English.[8]

These relationships are based on the way languages have changed through the years. When we compare Greek and English words, we can see regular, systematic differences. The first consonant of the Greek word *kardia,* for example, occurs as an *h* sound in English *heart,* and the *d* in the middle of the Greek word is a *t* sound in English. We can find many other examples of these same two differences where Greek voiceless stops *(p, t, k)* occur as English voiceless fricatives *(f, th, h),* and Greek voiced stops *(b, d, g)* occur as English voiceless stops *(p, t, k).*[9] This pattern was discovered by Jacob Grimm in the 1800s and is called *Grimm's Law.*

Hebrew and Aramaic Are Related

Hebrew and Aramaic are members of the Semitic language family, which in turn is part of the Afro-Asiatic family. The broader group includes ancient Egyptian and some other African languages. Extinct languages are in *italics* in table 7.2. Note the position of Hebrew and Aramaic.

Hebrew and Aramaic are closely related languages. Aramaic was the language of the area east of Israel, and some people were bilingual before the Israelites were taken into captivity. An interesting passage in 2 Kings 18 describes a time in which the leaders of Jerusalem were bilingual in Aramaic while the common people understood only Hebrew:

> Then Eliakim son of Hilkiah, and Shebna and Joah said to the field commander, "Please speak to your servants in Aramaic, since we understand it. Don't speak to us in Hebrew in the hearing of the people

---

8. The chart only indicates the general groupings within the Indo-European language family. The relationship between groups (e.g., Germanic and Slavic) is not shown.
9. See chapter 2 for a discussion of how these consonants are classified. Seeing the close relationship between the sounds helps us to understand the reason for the change.

Table 7.1: Indo-European Languages

Major Group	Subgroup	Related Languages
GERMANIC	Western Germanic	Dutch **English** German
	Northern Germanic	Danish Norwegian Swedish
ITALIC	ROMANCE (Latin)	French Italian Portuguese Romanian Spanish
HELLENIC		**Greek**
CELTIC		Irish Scots Gaelic Welsh
BALTIC		Latvian Lithuanian
SLAVIC	Northern Slavic	Russian Ukranian
	Western Slavic	Polish Slovak Czech
	Southern Slavic	Croatian Serbian Bulgarian
ALBANIAN		Albanian
ARMENIAN		Armenian
INDO-IRANIAN	Iranic	Persian/Farsi
	Indic	Bengali Hindi Punjabi Urdu

Table 7.2: The Semitic Languages

Major Groups of Semitic Languages	**Subgroup**	**Related Languages**
NORTHWEST SEMITIC	Early Northwest	*Ugaritic* *Amorite* *Eblaite*
	Canaanite	*Phoenician* **Hebrew** *Moabite* Edomite *Ammonite*
	Aramaic	**Old Aramaic** (biblical Aramaic) Nabatean Palmyrene Jewish-Palestinian Aramaic Samaritan Aramaic *Christian-Palestinian Aramaic* Syriac *Mandaic* Modern Aramaic
SOUTHWEST SEMITIC	North Arabic	Arabic (classical and modern dialects)
	South Arabic	*South Arabic Inscriptions*
	Ethiopic	Geez Tigre Tigrina Amharic
EAST SEMITIC (Old Akkadian)	Assyrian	*Old Assyrian* *Middle Assyrian* Neo-Assyrian
	Babylonian	*Old Babylonian* Middle Babylonian *Neo-Babylonian*

> on the wall." But the commander replied, "Was it only to your master and you that my master sent me to say these things, and not to the men sitting on the wall—who, like you, will have to eat their own filth and drink their own urine?" Then the commander stood and called out in Hebrew: "Hear the word of the great king, the king of Assyria! This is what the king says: Do not let Hezekiah deceive you. He cannot deliver you from my hand." (2 Kings 18:26–29 NASB)

The invading forces spoke enough Hebrew to shout their demands up to the people of Jerusalem who had gathered on the city wall. The leaders of Jerusalem, bilingual in the invaders' Aramaic language, requested that the enemy forces not use Hebrew, lest the common people be disturbed by their news. Bilingualism was not, and normally is not, equally spread throughout a society. In this case, only the leaders were bilingual.

After the people of Jerusalem were taken captive into the Aramaic-speaking land of Assyria, they gradually shifted to using Aramaic as their primary language. The Aramaic sections of the Old Testament (Jer. 10:11; Dan. 2:4b–7:28; Ezra 4:8–6:18; 7:12–26) show the widespread importance of Aramaic during and after the Exile.

During the time of Jesus and the disciples, Greek was a language of commerce, and Aramaic was the language used in Jewish homes. Hebrew was known as the language of the Old Testament, but Jesus and the disciples also knew of the Greek translation, the Septuagint. Jesus was multilingual, using Aramaic predominantly in his ministry in Israel (e.g., *talitha kum,* Mark 5:41). There is good reason to believe that Jesus spoke Aramaic and Greek and also knew Hebrew. Paul also was probably multilingual and used these same three languages, although his primary language appears to have been Greek rather than Aramaic.

When we compare Hebrew and Aramaic words, we can see regular changes in pronunciation.

The Hebrew words *zāhāb* and *zābaḥ* both have the consonant *z* as their first letter. The corresponding Aramaic words have a *d* instead; otherwise the Aramaic word has the same consonants and similar vowels. Linguists assume that there was a parent language (proto-Semitic) that had a sound that became a *z* in Hebrew but a *d* in Aramaic. A candidate for that sound in the parent language has to have characteristics that can explain this fact. In this case

Table 7.3: Hebrew and Aramaic Words Compared

Hebrew Word	Aramaic Word	Meaning
zāhāb	*dĕhab*	"gold"
zābaḥ	*dĕbaḥ*	"he sacrificed"
šôr	*tôr*	"bull, ox"
šûb	*tûb*	"to return"
ṣûr	*ṭûr*	"rock, cliff, mountain"
ʿēṣâ	*ʿēṭâ*	"counsel, advice"

linguists have posited that the sound in the parent language was an *interdental fricative* that was *voiced.* The sound would have shifted to the *voiced alveolar fricative* in Hebrew and to the *voiced alveolar stop* in Aramaic. Remember that to form an interdental the tongue is placed between the teeth, whereas for the alveolar the tip of the tongue touches the alveolar ridge just behind the teeth (cf. chap. 2).

Also for the set of words where the Hebrew word has a *š* but the Aramaic word has a *t,* we can posit that the parent language had a *voiceless interdental fricative.* Here the Hebrew sound shifted to a *palatal fricative.* This is a bit farther back in the mouth than the alveolar ridge, but it is still a possible shift from a phonetic point of view. The Aramaic sound shifted to the *voiceless alveolar stop,* a sound that is closer to the parent sound than the Hebrew sound.

Finally, the last set of words shows that the parent language had a sound that shifted to the *velarized alveolar fricative* in Hebrew and to the *velarized alveolar stop* in Aramaic. The sound in both languages is voiceless. A velarized sound is made with the tip of the tongue touching some part of the mouth forward of the velum but with the back part of the tongue touching the velum simultaneously. Linguists have suggested that the parent sound might have been a *velarized interdental fricative* that was *voiceless.*

Sets of words like those listed in table 7.3 show that we can consider Hebrew and Aramaic to be languages that are related through a common parent language. There are a number of other similar correspondences for both consonants and vowels that support this conclusion.

Summary and Preview

A language is hard to pin down. Different speakers and different groups of speakers have their favorite pronunciations and terms. Hebrew and Greek are no different from other languages in this. As changes continue through time, words can change meaning and even syntactic patterns can change. As students of the biblical languages we need to recognize this variation and understand the way context influences meaning.

This concludes our overview of the basic features of language and the basic patterns of Hebrew and Greek. Our final chapter will focus on how you can best apply your personality and personal learning preferences to learning the biblical languages.

For Further Study

Aitchinson, Jean. *Language Change: Progress or Decay?* New York: Universe Books, 1985.

Crowley, Terry. *An Introduction to Historical Linguistics.* Oxford: Oxford University Press, 1992.

Grimes, Barbara, ed. *Ethnologue.* 14th ed. Dallas: SIL International, 2000.

Malmkjaer, Kirsten, ed. *The Linguistics Encyclopedia.* London: Routledge, 1991.

Nida, Eugene A. "Sociolinguistics and Translating." In *Sociolinguistics and Communication,* edited by Johannes P. Louw, 1–49. UBS Monograph Series, no. 1. London: United Bible Societies, 1986.

Sáenz-Badillos, Angel. *A History of the Hebrew Language.* Trans. John Elwode. New York: Cambridge University Press, 1993.

Trudgill, Peter. *Sociolinguistics: An Introduction to Language and Society.* New York: Viking Penguin, 1983.

Webb, V. N. "Some Aspects of the Sociolinguistics of Bible Translation and Exegesis, and of Religious Language." In *Sociolinguistics and Communication,* edited by Johannes P. Louw, 50–82. UBS Monograph Series, no. 1. London: United Bible Societies, 1986.

Internet Resources

The premier web site for learning about the world's languages is, of course, the Ethnologue: www.ethnologue.com/web.asp.

Exercises

1. Write a one-page reflection paper on your reactions to other accents (e.g., British, Southern, "foreign").
2. Compare the following words in English, German, Spanish, and Latin.

    - English *father* *mother* *foot*
    - German *vater* *mutter* *fuss*
    - Spanish *padre* *madre* *pie*
    - Latin *pater* *mater* *ped*

    Note the similarities and the differences.

8

Practical Ways to Study (and Learn) the Biblical Languages

To subdue [the promptings of sin] I put myself in the hands of one of the brethren who had been a Hebrew before his conversion, and asked him to teach me his language. Thus . . . I now began to learn the alphabet again and practice hard and guttural words. . . . I thank the Lord that from a bitter seed of learning I am now plucking sweet fruits.[1]

—Jerome (c. 342–420)
early church father and
translator of the Latin Vulgate

Most adults in North America find it hard to learn another language. Meanwhile, the vast majority of the world's population, even those without formal education, are bilingual. As far as we can tell, Jesus knew Aramaic, Hebrew, and Greek, as did Paul. What is it about the way we try to learn other languages that makes us think it is so difficult? Remember your high school French class or your college Spanish? Did you learn as much as you wanted to? Perhaps you did not really have a desire to learn. But now you are starting to study Hebrew or Greek. Is your motivation different? Are you now more mature in your study skills? Do you know more about language now than when you were a teenager in a high school language class? Reflection on the answers to

1. F. A. Wright, trans., "Letter 125, 'To Rusticus,'" in *Select Letters of St. Jerome* (Cambridge, Mass.: Harvard University Press, 1933), 419–20.

these and other questions should help you succeed in your new efforts to study the biblical languages. This chapter will guide you through some of the major issues in adult language learning and give you tools to help you learn in the most effective way.

Separating the Children from the Adults

Your maturity and adult learning skills are significantly different from the skills you used unconsciously as an infant when you learned (or, more properly, acquired) your first language. Let's look at some of these differences. How does an infant start learning a language? Do you have children or nieces and nephews? Perhaps you have noticed certain patterns and developed your own hypotheses about this. Some of our famous Christian ancestors felt compelled to talk about this. For example, Augustine (354–430) himself came up with the following view of his personal experience:

> . . . I turned my attention to the way in which I learned to speak. It was not that older people taught me by offering me words by way of formal instruction, as was the case soon afterward with reading. No, I taught myself, using the mind you gave me, O my God, because I was unable to express the thoughts of my heart by cries and inarticulate sounds and gestures as to gain what I wanted to make my entire meaning clear to everyone as I wished.[2]

Martin Luther, famous for many other things besides watching his children learn to speak, noted:

> By imitating speech a subject is more easily learned than by study and books. You can see this in my little daughter. Although she is not four years old, she knows how to speak well and, indeed, clearly, about household matters.[3]

While these are not scientific statements about how children begin to speak, they do make sense. Children just seem to start speaking. They do not go to

---

2. Augustine, *Confessions* 1.8, cited in Maria Boulding, trans., *The Confessions* (Hyde Park, N.Y.: New City Press, 1997), 47.
3. Ewald M. Plass, comp., *What Luther Says* (St. Louis: Concordia, 1959), 727.

classes. They do not take notes. They do not know how to talk about nouns and verbs. Their major progress as a speaker of their first language all comes before they can read or write and happens in some natural way. Should you imitate these childlike behaviors to learn Hebrew or Greek?

Let's consider some of the ways we are different from the way we were as infants, at least in regard to learning languages. How do you think you have changed since you were a child in the following areas?

- language patterns
- willingness to make mistakes
- time availability
- responsibilities

The general wisdom of our culture is that after a certain age we can no longer learn another language. This is often called the "critical age hypothesis," because there appears to be an age limit to successful language learning. Fortunately, this popular notion is not true. Many adults do learn another (and another) language. You too can succeed in learning most any language you choose. Right now, we want to help you successfully learn one or more of the biblical languages.

So what about these differences? Yes, you do start your current study with a lot of English "ruts" in your thinking. Those of you who have learned Spanish may have said to yourself, "Spanish puts the words together backward." Instead of *grande casa* ("big house") Spanish says *casa grande* ("house big"). A young child learning Spanish would not think about this being either backward or forward. But you can use these English "ruts" to help you understand the new patterns of Hebrew and Greek. You can apply your organizing and reasoning skills to compare and contrast what you know with what you are learning.

Infants are blissfully unaware that they are making "mistakes." In fact, when they say "widdle wabbit" instead of "little rabbit," adults laugh and think it is cute. Meanwhile, the child does not feel embarrassed (at least not for a few years) and keeps saying words in "odd" ways and making up forms such as *I go-ed* and *I swimmed* without emotional trauma. This childlike boldness about making mistakes is something you will want to rekindle. It is indeed embarrassing as an adult to say the wrong word or to mangle the syntax of a foreign language. But if you wait until you can speak and write without mistakes, you may well not speak or write at all. As we consider personality types, we will note that some of us have a harder time with making mistakes than others. All we can say is: be willing to try, and work on being more childlike in your response to laughter as you learn language.

What about your time and responsibilities? Have they changed since you were a two-year-old? Of course. For some reason people now expect you to attend meetings, to earn money for tuition, to go to prayer meetings and Bible studies, to go to other classes, to clean your room, and on and on. Society gave you freedom to explore and use language for several whole years when you were small. Now you have to consciously budget your time and focus your energy to learn another language. That means you are now in charge of your own success as a language learner. It will indeed take time, and you will indeed need to think through the best ways to study. We will talk about various learning styles and approaches to learning in a little bit.

Can non-infants learn another language? Of course. Think of Daniel and his three friends. They were most likely at least in their teenage years when they were taken to Babylon. Scripture tells us:

> Then the king ordered Ashpenaz . . . to bring in some of the . . . young men without any physical defect, handsome, showing aptitude for every kind of learning, well informed, quick to understand, and qualified to serve in the king's palace. He was to teach them the language and literature of the Babylonians. (Dan. 1:3–4)

How did Daniel do in learning the language? Apparently quite well. He was appointed to a senior government post and was a close confidant of the king. How did Daniel's age help him learn? We believe adults have a number of helpful characteristics that can make them successful language learners:

- ability to collect data
- ability to analyze data
- ability to organize data
- motivation
- awareness of personal strengths and weaknesses
- awareness of how they learn

The same skills you use to learn other subjects can help you learn another language. An infant is more like a stationary sponge, waiting to take in what comes near. You can move yourself to different situations to hear (or see) more examples of language. The baby, through a God-given ability to absorb the patterns of language, eventually comes out speaking like an adult. You too can merely absorb language, but you also can make charts of the patterns and use your adult ability to see how things work to your advantage.

The final three characteristics in the list above will form the bulk of the remainder of this chapter: your motivation to succeed, awareness of your personality, and awareness of your learning preferences.

Are You Motivated? Yes!

Motivation plays an important part in adult language learning. Some people learn Japanese to get a job overseas. Others study English to be able to read the great literary works of Shakespeare. Why are you studying the biblical languages? Your answer to this question will have an impact on your success.

Martin Luther, not normally considered a missionary strategist, encouraged Christians to learn foreign languages in order to share the gospel:

> I am not at all in sympathy with those who cling to one language and despise all others. I would rather train youth and people to be the kind that could also be of service to Christ in foreign countries and could converse with natives there.[4]

Luther's quote reminds us of a significant purpose of language learning: service to speakers of other languages. A recent book, *The Gift of the Stranger,* discusses in detail the role of language learning and language teaching in the Christian tradition.[5] Throughout the history of the church, believers have chosen to learn other languages in order to share the gospel message. Comenius and other church leaders established language schools to prepare people for outreach. Learning other languages puts us in a position of learning and serving other people (cf. Phil. 2).

You, of course, are entering the land of the Bible. You are motivated to get to know the original languages and to understand the original message. This motivation will help you as you organize your time and choose your study

4. Ibid., 728.
5. David I. Smith and Barbara Carvill, *The Gift of the Stranger: Faith, Hospitality, and Foreign Language Learning* (Grand Rapids: Eerdmans, 2000).

methods. We too want you to succeed. We know from experience that the effort you put into your studies will bear fruit. As Jerome was quoted at the beginning of this chapter as saying: "I thank the Lord that from a bitter seed of learning I am now plucking sweet fruits."

How Your Personality Type Affects Learning

Your basic temperament has a great influence on how you relate to other people and how you learn. It is important to understand your temperament and how it either helps or hinders you as you learn another language. Awareness of these personality strengths and weaknesses will help you choose appropriate learning activities.

There are two well-known tests of temperament: the Myers-Briggs Type Indicator and the Keirsey Temperament Sorter II. Both use a set of dichotomies to define your particular personality traits (e.g., introvert versus extrovert). You may have already taken one of these tests. If so, you can go on to the next section. If you have not yet taken one of these personality inventories, we recommend that you do so soon so that you can apply our recommendations appropriately. The tests may be available through a school. The Keirsey Temperament Sorter II is also available on the Internet at www.Keirsey.com.

The basic way you see the world and interact with other people also affects your language learning. If you like cold, hard facts (sensing) rather than warm, fuzzy concepts (intuitive), you will approach language in a different way. Each of the eight aspects of personality has both assets and liabilities when it comes to language learning. Table 8.1 gives a brief overview of these differences. You can find more details in the books and web sites listed at the end of this chapter.

Which personality type is the best for language learning? In one sense, all types of people can successfully learn another language. Are there certain personality traits that hinder language learning? Yes. This is where your own self-awareness is important. Notice in table 8.1 that each trait has strengths and weaknesses that can affect language learning. People who are on the introvert side of things are less willing to step out and try new things. They can still learn a language, but they will need to overcome their hesitancy to some degree, or they will not get the practice they need to feel confident. Extroverts, on the other hand, need to learn to focus and study even when other people are not around to encourage them. Since all kinds of people speak a language, we are confident that all kinds of people can learn a language. It just takes more effort for some types to catch on to some aspects of language. For example, the "fuzzy" nature of meaning is easy for an intuitive type but more difficult for a sensing type to understand. Since words normally have a wide range of meanings (see chap. 6), both types of people will need to learn the meanings of words in context.

Table 8.1: Personality Type and Language Learning

Personality Preference	Strengths	Weaknesses
Extroversion	Willing to take risks	Needs stimulation from other people; cannot study alone
Introversion	Able to focus; can study on one's own	Unwilling to take risks or to make mistakes
Sensing	Attentive to detail; works hard	Has a hard time when the language is irregular and with "fuzzy" meanings
Intuitive	Can make inferences from context; can organize groups of concepts	Inattentive to details
Thinking	Good at analyzing patterns; self-disciplined	Anxious about achievement; needs to control the learning process
Feeling	Relates well with speakers of the language	Gets discouraged by interpersonal problems
Judging	Works systematically; gets the job done	Rigid; intolerant of ambiguity
Perceiving	Open; flexible; adaptable	Lazy; inconsistent

Seeing, Hearing, and Doing

Each of us learns in a variety of ways. Some of us can read a book and understand new ideas. Other people "just don't get it" when they read; they learn best by listening and talking about new ideas. Still others need to act out or interact physically with new ideas to truly understand them. These strategies are called *learning style preferences* and are based on the way we prefer to receive information. We can each learn in more than one way, and we often learn better using more than one of these strategies. As with personality traits, there is a test you can take that measures your preferred learning styles. The Sensory Preferences Inventory evaluates your learning in terms of the three primary senses you use for processing information:

- Visual (you prefer to see objects, pictures, or written forms to learn)
- Auditory (you prefer to hear and to speak to learn)
- Tactile (you prefer to touch, to handle, or to do things to learn)

Knowing the learning style that best helps you learn will help you plan your language learning strategy. Some learning activities your teacher assigns (e.g., translate a passage, identify past-tense verb forms) may match your learning style preferences, and you will be motivated to do them. Other assignments may not match your preferences, and you may become frustrated if you cannot learn well that way. You will need to modify the activities to take advantage of your learning skills. In the end, if you want to master Hebrew or Greek, you will need to use whatever learning activities you can to help you learn. There are many ways you can adapt your language learning to fit your best learning patterns. In the next three sections, we will give you some useful hints. Start with these and add your own successful strategies.

Tips for Visual Learners

If you learn best by seeing information, you are probably doing pretty well in school already. Most of our Western educational system has been based on processing information through reading. When you study the biblical language in a classroom, you will again find yourself with a textbook and other reading materials. You can use the written form of the language, or you can draw pictures to help you in language learning. Here are some other ideas to get you started:

- Make your own charts, graphs, or mind maps.
- When hearing a new word you want to remember, visualize the spelling.
- Make your own vocabulary cards. (Purchased ones are usually not as effective.)
- When you try to learn a word, look at it as you try to connect it with its

meaning. Try going the other direction by taking the English equivalent and visualizing the Hebrew word connected with it.

- Make crude drawings to represent a vocabulary word. For example, the word for "town" or "city" in Hebrew sounds like the English word *ear*. Draw or visualize someone surrounded by buildings with a hand cupped over his or her ear.
- Use your computer to review, rework, and organize your data.
- Read as much as you can.
- Take your Hebrew or Greek Bible to church and try to follow along with the Scripture reading. Take notes about any comments made from the Greek or Hebrew.

Tips for Auditory Learners

If you learn best by listening and discussing new information, you probably enjoy classes that include a lot of small-group discussions. Unfortunately, the large amounts of reading required for some courses is not easy for you, and you do not totally understand new information if it is presented only in written form. You would have a great advantage in language learning if you were studying a spoken language. While the visual learners would be frustrated if they could not see the words they were trying to learn, you could actually learn by hearing the word in context and using it in conversation. For practical reasons, most classes in the biblical languages use only limited oral and hearing strategies. You will need to augment what is presented in class and what is assigned in written form so that you can master the language material. Here are some ideas to get you started:

- Always pronounce vocabulary or exercise sentences out loud. If tapes or CDs are available, use them.
- Have a partner read words or text out loud, and try to determine the sense only from what you hear.
- When you read, discuss what you read with others. If you are alone, talk to yourself out loud about what you read.
- Listen to tapes or CDs of portions of the Hebrew or Greek Bible being read aloud. Listen while you read the text.
- Sing Scripture songs. There are many tapes or CDs available of Hebrew songs.

- Attend some Hanukkah celebrations or Passover Seders and try to pick up as much as you can through listening to Hebrew as it is recited, read, or spoken.
- Attend services in a Greek Orthodox church and listen to the readings and the liturgy.

Tips for Tactile or Action Learners

You may be one of those people who learn best by hands-on experience. If someone told you to read the repair manual or talked you through the process, you would still need to try things for yourself. Language, of course, is primarily visual and auditory. At some point you will need to read and write, listen and speak in your new language. You can, however, use your tactile preference for hands-on learning as a bridge to language skills. One of the better-known methods of getting involved in learning languages is the Total Physical Response (TPR) technique. You may have used this in other language classrooms. The general idea is to respond to oral cues or commands such as "Stand up" and "Open your book." If your teacher does not include these kinds of learning activities, you can make your own, either with a partner or by recording the cues yourself.

Here are some more ideas to help you use your tactile learning style:

- When you learn vocabulary, try doing an action or touching something while you listen to the word.
- Study vocabulary by typing words on your computer or writing them by hand.
- Use interactive, computer-assisted language learning if available.
- Take your Hebrew or Greek Bible to church and follow along with the Scripture reading.
- Have a meal where you emphasize Middle Eastern foods and practice reading your Bible with other students.
- Read the Hebrew or Greek Bible with classmates in a dramatic fashion, with different ones taking turns at being the narrator or different characters in the story.
- Attend a synagogue (Jewish or messianic) and find some activities you might participate in.
- Write out all of your vocabulary words or exercise sentences.
- Make your own flash cards.

- If you have a vocabulary word that represents something concrete, like *table,* then feel a table as you try to memorize it. Think about how the surface of the object represented by the word might feel (rough, smooth, uneven, etc.).
- If you are working with abstract words, try to connect them with certain textures or objects that you can feel. For example, the word for "wisdom" could be connected with the tassel on a graduation cap, or the word for "love" could be associated with a stuffed animal. Try to imagine the textures of such words.

Setting Goals in Language Learning

How can we measure success in learning a language? This question has been addressed by many scholars and agencies. A common guideline is called the ACTFL Proficiency Guidelines. These have been created by the American Council for the Teaching of Foreign Languages (1985) and are based on common skills (how well one communicates, pronunciation, knowledge of vocabulary, ability to use a variety of grammatical forms). They divide language into four sets of skills: listening, speaking, reading, and writing. The Foreign Service Institute (FSI) of the United States government also has a scale to measure language skills in these four areas.

Table 8.2: The Four Skills of Language

	Passive	**Active**
Oral	Listening	Speaking
Visual	Reading	Writing

When we study the biblical languages, we might not immediately think about all four of these areas of language. In fact, courses in the biblical languages might restrict the goals and activities of the course to only the reading and writing skills. For our purposes we will look only at reading skills. We will also present a set of exegetical skills as a measuring device to evaluate your learning. You can use these skills to set language learning goals, to plan learning activities, and to evaluate your proficiency.

The ACTFL and FSI guidelines refer to stages of proficiency, not to passing tests or completing courses. This makes them useful as a measuring rod to provide comparative evaluations of people who have similar ability regardless of where they studied, how long they studied, or what book they used to study a language. The ACTFL guidelines describe a particular range of ability in each of the four language skills. You are a novice when you start your studies of a new language. As an educated speaker of your native language, you are either superior or distinguished. Between these extremes are intermediate and advanced levels. The FSI system starts with level 0 and goes through level 5, the ability of an educated native speaker.

Measuring Your Reading Ability

How can you measure your progress in reading Hebrew or Greek? Certainly you need to recognize the letters and other symbols such as accents and punctuation. This is one of the first goals your teacher no doubt will set for you. A more advanced ability in reading includes being able to read a variety of styles of writing beyond the neat examples in your textbook, including your instructor's handwritten notes on the board!

Another aspect of reading is being able to understand the meaning of a text by seeing it. Here you can measure your vocabulary skills. As a novice you recognize only a few words. As you learn more words and understand their meaning in different contexts, you progress to higher levels of ability. Your instructor no doubt will set standards for you in terms of how many vocabulary words you need to recognize.

A third aspect of reading ability is being able to interpret all the morphology and syntax of a text. To understand what a text means, you need to be able to find the root meaning of the word and determine what all the affixes mean. Again, your teacher will have goals for you. In Greek class you may need to know all the forms of the verb *luō,* "I loose," by a certain date.

Measuring Your Ability to Understand the Biblical Languages

Let's consider how you can set goals for your overall knowledge of the biblical languages. You will, of course, be trying to pass a class. We encourage you also to remember your motivation to use Hebrew or Greek and to consider whether you are meeting your internal goals. At first you are a relative novice.

Your goal is to be able to remember what words mean and to read the biblical text with some ease. Here are our suggestions for goals in understanding the biblical texts:[6]

Table 8.3: Exegetical Skills Checklist

Novice-Low	Able occasionally to identify simple parts of clauses, such as the subject and object when these are clearly marked by case endings, word order, or some other overt marker. Able to find words in a lexical work which has a dictionary lookup form that is easy to discern.
Novice-Mid	Able to identify the verb in a clause. Able to read with some understanding the discussion in a specialized lexical work (theological dictionary, advanced lexicon) concerning a word read in a particular passage. The word in context still must have a fairly obvious relationship to its lookup form.
Novice-High	Able to determine clause boundaries and discern simple phrases (prepositional phrases, nouns modified by adjectives, etc.). Able to apply the discussion about a term in a specialized lexical work to the particular context being studied. This assumes that the passage is simple prose and that the word studied still has a fairly obvious relationship to its lookup form.
Intermed-Low	Able to recognize more complicated or difficult constructions, such as the construct state in Hebrew or various types of infinitive constructions in Greek. Able to read noncomplex prose with understanding, though still needs to look up many of the words. Now able to look up words with a less obvious relationship to the lookup forms. Able to glean simple insights from exegetical commentaries that apply to the passage read.

6. These are meant to be only suggestive; we have not conducted a formal study to test their validity. Still, we believe these can be useful benchmarks to measure your progress toward the goal of doing exegesis from the biblical text.

Intermed-Mid	Beginning to formulate questions about the relationship between clauses and sentences, thereby gaining some sense of the flow of a passage (still simple prose). Starting to think about synonyms in the passage and their relationship to each other. Able to use some basic tools such as concordances and lexicons to gain further insights about key terms. Beginning to recognize which terms are most significant for further exegetical study.
Intermed-High	Able to understand and apply exegetical insights from reference works to the passage studied. Reading skills increasing to encompass more complex prose texts.
Advanced	Starting to formulate exegetical questions before consulting reference works. Reading skills expanding to simple poetic texts and complex prose.
Advanced Plus	Able to formulate and answer exegetical questions before consulting reference works. Reading skills expanding to more complex poetic texts and virtually any prose text. Able to do thoughtful word studies based on sound linguistic theory.
Superior	Able to research in an expert way complex and difficult exegetical questions. Able to thoroughly evaluate various reference works from the standpoint of sound linguistic theory and sound exegetical methodology.

How Can I Learn All Those Words?

How many words do you think are in the Bible? Well, that's an ambiguous question isn't it? One way to look at the number of words in the Bible is to count them one by one. That, of course, would yield one or more answers in English depending on the translation and other answers in Hebrew and Greek. In any case, it would soon become obvious that we really want to know how many *different* words or roots there are in Hebrew and Greek that we might need to learn. The fact of the matter is that we are dealing with a rather limited set of words in each language and that a relatively small group of words in each language constitute a majority of the biblical text. This is much different than trying to learn "all" the words in Spanish, because the biblical text has been recorded and transmitted already, and no new words are going to show up to add to the list.

New Testament Greek, for example, has "only" about 5,500 different words. (University-educated English speakers may, in contrast, have a vocabulary of over 20,000 words.) Of these, about 20 percent (1,000) are used more than ten times and represent more than their fair share of all the words in the New Testament text. Another 65 percent (3,600) occur less than four times each and are thus only a small portion of the New Testament text.

Open All the Gates

We all learn in a variety of ways, and we can each benefit from a number of different approaches to learning. Seeing a word and then saying it may help you more than just seeing it. Seeing a word and then writing it may help other learners more than it helps you. The important thing is to use many different "gates" to let information in. Some people talk about the "eye gate" and the "ear gate." We can also think of our hands (writing) and even our whole body (acting out a verb) as gates to learning.

"We all learn in a variety of ways." Some of us learn best using actions, others using sight and writing. "In a variety of ways we all learn." By using a range of activities, we can all learn. Use as many avenues of sense as possible:

- Tactile: practice writing out the words in Hebrew and Greek.
- Auditory: practice reading the words aloud. Precision in pronunciation is less important than the practice you get in speaking and hearing the words.
- Visual: be sure to look at the Hebrew of Greek every time you read the words out loud. If the word has a concrete sense, try to visualize the actual object (foot, chair, etc.) as you say it.

The Literal Truth

Compare a verse in your English Bible with the Hebrew or Greek, and try to figure out which words go with which part of the translation. This will work best with a more literal type of translation such as the NASB or the KJV.

Flashy Card Tricks

Jot down new words or idioms when you see them. Make flash cards for vocabulary or short phrases or idioms. You can buy flash cards, but it is more helpful to make your own. Put only Hebrew or Greek on one side and the English meaning on the other side. You can include grammatical information, such as gender. Separate cards can be made for words with irregular plurals or unusual verb forms. Flash cards can be reviewed while standing in line, waiting at the doctor's office, or in any number of other places.

Birds of a Feather Get Caught Together

As an adult you can use your organizational skills to your advantage as you learn Hebrew or Greek. You are able to organize groups of words and see the patterns and relationships they have with other words. Use this strength to help yourself catch on to new words. You can sort your written vocabulary cards into different sets. The following are just a few suggestions:

- lists of body parts
- kinship terms *(mother, father)*
- geographical terms
- types of actions (movement, states of being)
- noun-verb sets (*eye* and *see*, *ear* and *hear*)
- grammatical categories (nouns, verbs, adjectives, pronouns, etc.)
- synonyms (*small* and *tiny*, *bad* and *evil*)
- antonyms (*good* and *evil*, *here* and *there*)

Draw Yourself a Map

Words are related to each other in many ways, as we have seen in chapter 6. You can use semantics to help you "see" these relationships. Here are some suggestions:

- Make a map using basic geographical terms such as *mountain, river, house,* etc.
- Draw family trees showing the various words used for "father," "mother," "son," and "daughter."

- Make your own picture of how the language expresses "on," "in," "through," etc.
- Draw a person and write all the body parts you know.
- Make a series of pictures that show a sequence of events (e.g., waking up, eating, leaving the house), and talk about the pictures with a friend.

Hints for Learning Hebrew Vocabulary

One of the more difficult aspects of Hebrew is the vocabulary, because there are few obvious associations with English. Yet there are some things that you know in English that do relate to learning Hebrew. Here are a few ways to make associations.

You Already Know a Little Hebrew

When you learn the alphabet, try putting it to music. Observe how the alphabet is an organizing principle for Psalm 119 (made explicit in most modern translations).

Memorize common phrases or words, such as the Shema in Deuteronomy 6:4 (*šĕmaʿ Yiśrāʾēl ʾădōnāy ʾĕlōhēnû ʾădōnāy ʾeḥād* ["Hear, O Israel: The Lord our God, the Lord is one"]) or phrases from songs you might have heard, such as *ʾēl šadday* ("God Almighty") or *šaʾlû šĕlôm yĕrûšālayim* ("Pray for the peace of Jerusalem," from Ps. 122:6).

Focus on the rare Hebrew loanwords in English or analyze Hebrew names as they are explained in the Bible: *hallelujah* ("Praise *Yah!*" = "praise the Lord!"), *amen, Joseph* ("may he add"), *Abraham* ("father of a multitude"), and so on.

Popularity Contest

Use a word frequency list to concentrate on the words that occur most often in the Hebrew Bible. For example, there is Larry A. Mitchel's *A Student's Vocabulary for Biblical Hebrew and Aramaic*[7] or George M. Landes's *Building Your Biblical Hebrew Vocabulary: Learning Words by Frequency and Cognate.*[8]

7. Larry A. Mitchel, *A Student's Vocabulary for Biblical Hebrew and Aramaic* (Grand Rapids: Zondervan, 1984).
8. George M. Landes, *Building Your Biblical Hebrew Vocabulary: Learning Words by Frequency and Cognate,* Society of Biblical Literature Resources for Biblical Study 41 (Atlanta: Society of Biblical Literature, 2001).

Produce Large Crops from a Single Root

Most Hebrew words can be related to a root consisting of three letters (triliteral). All of the following are derived from the root *yšb: yāšab* ("he sat, he lived [in a location]"); *yōšēb* ("inhabitant"); *šebet* ("seat, dwelling place"); *môšāb* ("seat, assembly"); *tôšāb* ("sojourner").

Think of Something Memorable

Try to make "nonsense" associations between the sound of the Hebrew word and some word in your native tongue. For example, the word for "land" *(ʿereṣ)* sounds like "air-its." Picture a scene in the open country where you get more of "its air" and add a way to remind yourself to reverse the words.

Hints for Learning Greek Vocabulary

Greek vocabulary for most people is not as difficult a challenge as Hebrew vocabulary, because so many of the words can be related more directly to English words. Even so, you will still need to devote a lot of time to learning Greek words.

You Already Know a Little Greek

Greek is in many ways a major source of English vocabulary. We can use this background to our advantage when we learn Greek words. Since English and Greek are both Indo-European languages, many Greek words have gone through a series of historical changes to become English words. Many Greek roots have been "grabbed" from the past and incorporated into English medical and legal vocabulary. Thus, the same *kardia* ("heart") has the shape *cardia* in English, as in *cardiac* and *cardiovascular.* Likewise, Greek *phobos* ("fear") appears in English *phobia* and *hydrophobia* ("water-fear").[9] The latter words, of course, are easier to recognize because they sound more like the Greek words. You may, in fact, have had a vocabulary course in high school or seen

9. Several books on Greek vocabulary list such related words as memory aids, including Robert E. Van Voorst, *Building Your New Testament Greek Vocabulary* (Grand Rapids: Eerdmans, 1990); and Thomas A. Robinson, *Mastering Greek Vocabulary* (Peabody, Mass.: Hendrickson, 1990).

books that use these borrowed Greek roots to "increase your vocabulary in thirty days."

Popularity Contest

Several books gives lists of New Testament Greek words in order of their frequency. Bruce Metzger's book *Lexical Aids for Students of New Testament Greek* has been in print since 1946 and has helped many people before you.[10] Wilson and Oden provide a helpful system for learning Greek vocabulary in their book *Mastering New Testament Greek Vocabulary Through Semantic Domains.*[11]

Produce Large Crops from a Single Root

Many Greek words are formed from a single root by adding derivational prefixes or suffixes. This is especially true for verbs, which often receive a prefix that has the same form as a preposition. The verb *erchomai* ("to come"), for example, serves as the basis for *exerchomai* ("to come out of"), *aperchomai* ("to go away"), and *proserchomai* ("to come to, approach"). The preposition *ek* (*ex* before a vowel) means "out of," *apo* means "away from," and *pros* means "to" or "toward."

Think of Something Memorable

Nonsense associations can work with any language, and Greek is no exception. It is best for you to make up your own, but here is one example. The Greek verb *trechō* means "to run." It sounds similar to "trek-o." A trek is a long hike; so draw some hikers with a runner overtaking them. They are exhausted from this long trek, but here comes someone who is actually running over the same course. This makes them exclaim "Oh!"

Summary and Preview

This chapter has provided some practical steps you can take to master the biblical languages. We have seen that adult learners like yourself have many

10. Bruce M. Metzger, *Lexical Aids for Students of New Testament Greek,* 3d ed. (Grand Rapids: Baker, 1998).
11. Mark Wilson with Jason Oden, *Mastering New Testament Greek Vocabulary Through Semantic Domains* (Grand Rapids: Kregel, 2003).

skills that can help you learn another language. The key idea is that you have to take control of your learning and use your best techniques to learn.

We have worked and prayed many years to make this book a helpful tool for students of the biblical languages. It is our prayer that you will have a better understanding of the languages and will become an active user of these languages as you seek to know God personally and as you teach others God's Word.

For Further Study

Brewster, Thomas, and Elizabeth E. Brewster. *Language Acquisition Made Practical.* Pasadena, Calif.: William Carey Library, 1984.

Brown, H. Douglas. *Breaking the Language Barrier.* Yarmouth, Me.: Intercultural Press, 1991.

———. *Principles of Language Learning and Teaching.* 3d ed. Englewood Cliffs, N.J.: Prentice Hall Regents, 1994.

Fuller, Graham E. *How to Learn a Foreign Language.* Friday Harbor, Wash.: Storm King Press, 1987.

Landes, George M. *Building Your Biblical Hebrew Vocabulary: Learning Words by Frequency and Cognate.* Society of Biblical Literature Resources for Biblical Study 41. Atlanta: Society of Biblical Literature, 2001.

Larson, Donald N., and William A. Smalley. *Becoming Bilingual: A Guide to Language Learning.* New York: University Press of America, 1984.

Lawrence, Gordon. *People Types and Tiger Stripes: A Practical Guide to Learning Styles.* 2d ed. Gainesville, Fla.: Center for Application of Psychological Types, 1982.

Marshall, Terry. *The Whole World Guide to Language Learning.* Yarmouth, Me.: Intercultural Press, 1989.

Metzger, Bruce M. *Lexical Aids for Students of New Testament Greek.* 3d ed. Grand Rapids: Baker, 1998.

Mitchel, Larry A. *A Student's Vocabulary for Biblical Hebrew and Aramaic.* Grand Rapids: Zondervan, 1984.

Rubin, Joan, and Irene Thompson. *How to be a More Successful Language Learner.* 2d ed. Boston: Heinle & Heinle Publishers, 1994.

Wilson, Mark, with Jason Oden. *Mastering New Testament Greek Vocabulary Through Semantic Domains.* Grand Rapids: Kregel, 2003.

Internet Resources

There is a wide range of material about language learning on-line and through software that can be personalized to your needs. Here are a few initial links to get you started:

- SIL's web site includes many articles and additional references to language learning: www.sil.org/lglearning/.
- A personality test can be taken on-line at http://keirsey.com/.
- The *Language Impact* web site has articles on how to learn a language and also provides a free newsletter: www.languageimpact.com.
- The *Resources for Learning New Testament Greek* site offers suggestions and materials to help you in the early stages: http://www.ntgreek.org/.
- The *Little Greek* site may also be helpful. It is meant to lead students through the basics of New Testament Greek: www.ibiblio.org/koine/.

Exercises

1. Take the Myers-Briggs type Indicator. Comment on the results and how your personality type can help you learn Hebrew or Greek.
2. Take a learning style inventory. Comment on the results and how your learning style preference(s) can help you learn Hebrew or Greek.
3. Write a one-page reflection paper on a past experience learning a foreign language. In what ways do you plan to change your own approach to studying the biblical languages based on this experience?

Appendix

Glossary of Linguistic Terms

Whenever we learn a new subject, we are faced with new terminology. This glossary is meant to help you understand key terms used in this book and in many standard textbooks on Hebrew and Greek. We have attempted to give a concise definition of each term and some examples of how these new concepts work in various languages, primarily in English, Hebrew, and Greek.

One word of advice: learn these key concepts well. Many of them will be used repeatedly in your classes. If you understand these main ideas, you will be better able to put the bits and pieces of your biblical language studies together in a more orderly way.

One word of warning: your textbook and your instructor may use some of these terms differently. All we can say is that we have sought out the clearest way to talk about these terms and have combined our knowledge of the field of general linguistics with our experience in Hebrew and Greek.

Definitions

ablative (case). A morphological marker on a noun or its modifiers indicating the locational **source** of a verb of motion. Ablative is not used in biblical Hebrew or Greek, although some textbooks may refer to the idea of ablative in discussing Koine Greek, based on the fact that Latin has a distinct ablative case.

absolute state. In Hebrew grammar the standard or normal form of a noun, especially that form that is found in the dictionary or lexicon. It is to be distinguished from the **construct state,** which is a special form of the noun used in a **construct phrase.** Hebrew *dābār* "a word" (absolute) versus *dĕbar* "word of" (construct); *tôrâ* "law" (absolute) versus *tôrat* "law of" (construct); *ʾĕlōhîm* "God" (absolute) versus *ʾĕlōhê* "God of" (construct).

accent. *See* **stress.**

accidence. *See* **inflection.**

accusative (case). A morphological marker on a noun or its modifiers or a pronoun typically indicating the **object** of a verb. Greek *tē̲n̲ kefalē̲n̲* "the head."

active (voice). A syntactic construction in which the grammatical **subject** is (typically) the **agent/actor** of a **transitive** verb: The student helped the teacher. *Contrast* **passive** and **middle.**

adjective. A **lexical category** of words that specify characteristics of nouns. An adjective can be either a descriptive, or **attributive adjective** *(The wonderful book)* or a **predicate adjective** *(The book is wonderful.).*

adverb. A **lexical category** of words that specify characteristics of verbs and other non-noun words: *They left quickly. She is very capable. They will come soon.* Adverbs are used to express time *(now, soon),* place *(here, there),* and manner *(quickly, well).*

affix. A **bound morpheme** attached to a **root:** *They deiced the plane. The students wanted to learn.* Hebrew: *šāmartî* "I watched," *šĕmûrâ* "she was/is watched," *tišmĕrî* "you (fem. sg.) will watch." *See also* **prefix, suffix, infix, circumfix.**

affricate. A sound that is a combination of a **stop** followed by a **fricative** that is in the same **place of articulation.** The sounds *ch* and *j* in the English words *chair* and *juice* are affricates.

agent. A **semantic role.** The person or people who deliberately perform an action: *Chris ate dinner. Chris jumped. Contrast* **patient.**

agreement. The way a language indicates grammatical relations between certain words. In English, for example, the **subject** of a clause and the **verb** show agreement in **number:** *He walks. They walk.*

allomorph. Alternate forms of a **morpheme;** can be caused by phonetic or lexical factors. In English the sound of the plural marker *-s* varies when the noun ends in a voiceless sound *(cat-s),* a voiced sound *(dog-s),* or a sibilant *(rose-s).*

allophone. Predictable alternate form of a **phoneme.** In English the *p* sound at the beginning of the word *pot* is different from the *p* sound in *spot* (the former is aspirated, the latter is unaspirated), but English speakers consider it to be the same sound.

alveolar. Sound made when the tongue tip is on or near the alveolar ridge. The sounds *t, d, n, s, z,* for example.

anaphora. The relationship of a word or phrase (the **anaphor**) that refers to a previous word or phrase (its **antecedent**): *The two students* (**antecedent**) *studied, and then they* (**anaphora**) *ate dinner.*

antecedent. A word or phrase to which a later word or phrase (its **anaphor**) refers: *The two students studied, and then they ate dinner. See also* **referent.**

antepenult. The third **syllable** from the end of a word. Normally regarding **stress** patterns: Jerusalem, Bethlehem, theology.

antonym. A word that is considered the semantic opposite of another word: *hot/cold, dead/alive, parent/child.*

aorist (aspect). In Greek studies aorist refers to an event in the past that is not specifically **progressive** or **perfective.** The term is technically an **aspect** indicator, but is commonly referred to as a **tense.**

apocope. The deletion or **elision** of a **vowel** from the end of a word.

apodosis. The conclusion or result that follows when a condition or circumstance is met (the **protasis**): *If they go to a good seminary, they will study Hebrew.*

apparatus. Notes in the margins of a printed text that normally deal with issues of transmission by scribes. The *Biblia Hebraica Stuttgartensia* and the Nestle-Aland edition of the Greek New Testament both have an apparatus at the bottom of each page that refers to text critical issues.

apposition. The placing together of two words with essentially the same **referent:** *King Solomon, the Lord God, Jesus the Nazarene.* The words in apposition are referred to as *appositives.*

article. A type of **determiner** that indicates whether a noun is definite or indefinite. Articles differ from other determiners in that they cannot stand alone in a phrase. In English *a, an, the* are articles, while *this, that, those* are not. We can say *I want this* but not *I want the.*

aspect. The way a language indicates the internal temporal nature of an action or situation (e.g., ongoing versus completed.) Aspect differs from **tense** in that the latter relates an action to external time factors (e.g., before the present, in the future). Biblical studies textbooks do not always distinguish aspect and tense in this way. *See* **aorist, imperfect,** and **perfect.** *Compare* **tense.**

asyndeton. The omission of conjunctions from closely related clauses where they would normally appear: *I won't be at school today;* (because) *I am expecting out-of-town guests. See also* **parataxis.**

attributive adjective. An **adjective** included in the **noun phrase** that gives an attribute of a noun: *the diligent student.* Also called a descriptive adjective.

auxiliary (verb). A verb form that is added to a main verb to show such information as **tense, aspect,** or **modality** for that verb: *We had gone. We were going. We should go.*

back vowel. A vowel sound made farther toward the back of the mouth, relatively speaking. The vowel sounds in the words *boot, foot, boat,* and *bought,* for example. *See also* **central vowel** and **front vowel.**

base. For biblical Hebrew it can be helpful to distinguish the "base" of a word from its **root.** The root consists normally of three or sometimes two consonants, while the base consists of the root plus vowels that are used for different types of nouns or verbs. The root *m-l-k* has a different base (underscored) in each of the following: *melek* "king," *mālak-tî* "I reigned," *yi-mlōk* "he will reign," *ma-mlek-et* "kingdom of."

bilabial. A sound made with both lips, such as *p, b, m,* or *w.*

binyanim. Another term for **verb patterns** in Hebrew studies.

bitransitive. *See* **ditransitive.**

bound morpheme. A **morpheme** that must be attached to another morpheme; a bound morpheme cannot stand alone as a separate word. Hebrew: *ʾēlay* "to-me" (with a bound form) versus *ʾel Yaʿăqōb* "to Jacob" (with *ʾel,* "to," as a free morpheme).

cardinal number. A number that counts how many of an item there are: *There are seven days in a week. Compare* **ordinal number.**

case. The way a language indicates grammatical relations within a clause, such as the **subject** or **object** of a **verb** or the **object of a preposition,** by morphological markers on the noun or its modifiers. Greek: *anthrōpos* (subject of a verb), *anthrōpon* (object of a verb), *diʾ anthrōpou* (object of the preposition *through*). Case can also be used within a noun phrase or a prepositional phrase.

causative. A semantic classification of a verb, which can be marked morphologically, indicating that an **agent** causes an action to happen. Hebrew: *rāʾâ* "he saw" becomes *hi-rʾâ* "he showed" ("show" = "cause to see").

central vowel. A vowel sound made toward the middle of the mouth, relatively speaking. The vowel sound in the word *but,* for example. *See also* **back vowel** and **front vowel.**

circumfix. An **affix** that has one part before and one part after the **root.** Hebrew: *tišmĕrî "you (fem. sg.) will watch"* in which the morpheme *ti-î* is a circumfix.

clause. A syntactic unit that (normally) contains both a **subject** and a **predicate:** *I studied Hebrew. Hebrew is an easy language.*

closed class. A group of words that belong together because of their similar morphological relationships but are limited to a fixed number of words. For example, **prepositions, articles, conjunctions,** and **pronouns.**

cognate (words). Words in two or more languages that originally came from the same source. For example: English *father,* German *Vater,* and Latin *pater* all come from the same Proto-European root.

cognate accusative. The **object** of a verb that is derived from the same **root** as the verb. Such expressions are common in Hebrew. Sometimes the term is also used for a **noun** or **noun phrase** that modifies the **verb.** Hebrew: *ḥālam ḥălôm* [he-dreamed a-dream] "He had a dream"; *yārēʾ yirʾâ gĕdôlâ* [he-feared a-fear great] "He was very much afraid."

cohesion. The linguistic means by which a larger unit of text (paragraph, chapter, book) is held together. Examples would be **anaphora** or the use of certain structuring **conjunctions** or phrases, such as *therefore* or *in the meantime: "In the beginning was the Word, and the Word was with God, and the Word was God. He was with God in the beginning. Through him all things were made; without him nothing was made that has been made"* (John 1:1–3). The underlined words help maintain the cohesion of the statements.

cohortative. A first person exhortation to oneself or to a group: *Let's go eat.* Hebrew: *ʾettĕnâ bĕrîtî* "I will establish my covenant"; *nilbĕnâ lĕbēnîm* "let us make bricks."

comment. A portion of a sentence that gives information regarding the **topic.** In general the **subject** corresponds to the topic and the **predicate** corresponds to the comment. *"The Lord is my shepherd"* (Ps. 23:1a KJV).

comparative. A morphological form of the **adjective** or **adverb** used in comparisons: *Saul was taller than the others.* "The foolishness of God is wiser than man's wisdom" (1 Cor. 1:25 NASB). *They finished sooner than we did.*

complementary distribution. In phonology, the fact that two or more similar sounds occur in different phonetic environments; they never **con-**

trast. In English the initial sound in *pot* and the second sound in *spot* are in complementary distribution. The two *p* sounds are said to complement each other.

compound. Composed of two or more equal parts. In a compound word, the equal parts are **free morphemes,** while in a compound sentence they are two clauses joined by a coordinating conjunction or by **asyndeton.** Hebrew: *ṣalmawet* is traditionally interpreted as *ṣal* "shadow" plus *māwet* "death," hence "shadow of death" is a compound word. *I won't be at school today;* (because) *I am expecting out-of-town guests* is a compound sentence.

concord. Shared grammatical information within a **noun phrase.** In Greek, the **article, adjective,** and **noun** exhibit concord of **person, number,** and **case:** *ho agath<u>os</u> anthrop<u>os</u>* "the good man."

conditional clause. A clause that consists of a circumstance or condition (**protasis**) that, if met, results in the outcome or conclusion (**apodosis**): "*<u>If we are children</u>, then we are heirs*" (Rom. 8:17).

conjugation. The pattern or **paradigm** of **inflectional** changes in a **verb.**

conjunction. A **lexical category** of words that join two items of the same syntactic category together, such as two words, phrases, or clauses: *Ruth <u>and</u> Naomi; very tall <u>but</u> extremely skillful; David planned the temple, <u>and</u> Solomon built it.*

connotation. The associations or feelings that attach to a word. Sometimes synonyms may be distinguished by connotations attached to one term that are not attached to another. The terms *ghost* and *spirit* are synonymous in some contexts, but *ghost* has a lot of folkloristic connotations that *spirit* does not. *See also* **denotation.**

consonant. A sound made with some restriction of the airflow. The sounds *p, d, s, w,* for example. Consonants normally occur at the beginning or end of a syllable. *Contrast* **vowel.**

constituent. A unit that is part of a larger whole. A **word** is a constituent of a **phrase;** a phrase is a constituent of a **clause;** and a clause is a constituent of a **sentence.**

construct phrase. A phrase that consists of a noun or adjective in the **construct state** followed by a modifying noun phrase. Hebrew: *<u>melek</u> Yiśrāʾēl* [king-of Israel] "king of Israel."

construct state. A term from Hebrew grammar applied to a noun or adjective when it is defined more precisely by a following noun phrase (or rarely, a verb phrase): Hebrew: *bêt Dāwîd* [house-of David] "David's house." *See also* **absolute state.**

content word. A word that has a lexical meaning. For example, *tree, large, run, quickly. Contrast* **function word.**

context. The words surrounding a particular form.

continuant. A sound produced without completely blocking the air coming through the vocal apparatus. Any **vowel** or **fricative** is a continuant. *Compare* **stop.**

contrast. In phonology, the relationship of two sounds that can occur in the same kinds of phonetic environments. The initial sounds in rhyming words such as *bat* and *pat* or the vowels in words such as *bat* and *bet* are in contrast because the change in sound changes the meaning of the word. *See also* **complementary distribution** and **minimal pair.**

coordinate clause. A **clause** that joins with another clause in a parallel relationship (rather than a **subordinate** relationship) to make up a broader sentence. More than two clauses may be coordinated: *"God called the light 'day,' and the darkness he called 'night'"* (Gen. 1:5). *"In the beginning was the Word, and the Word was with God, and the Word was God"* (John 1:1 KJV).

copula. A copula links a **subject** to a **predicate.** In English and Greek, this is generally done by an **intransitive** verb such as *to be* or *to seem,* but in Hebrew the copula may be a **personal pronoun** that agrees with the **subject:** *The Lord is our God. The Lord is good.* Hebrew: *YHWH hûʾ ʾĔlōhê haʾĕlōhîm* [the-Lord he God-of the-gods] *"The Lord your God is the God of gods."*

count (noun). A noun that can occur with a **number:** *two buckets, three books. Contrast* **mass noun.**

dagesh. In Hebrew grammar a dot placed within a letter to show that it is doubled or that it has a **plosive** sound or both: הַכָּבוֹד—*hakkāḇōḏ;* וְכָבוֹד—*wĕḵāḇôḏ* (the line under the consonant *k, b,* or *d* shows that the sound should be **fricative**).

dative (case). A morphological marker on a noun or its modifiers or on a pronoun marking the **recipient** of something or certain other syntactic functions such as **indirect object.** Greek: *tō̱ doulō̱* "(to) the slave."

declarative. The **mood** of an utterance that makes a statement. Also called the **indicative.** *It is important to study the biblical languages. Contrast* **imperative** and **interrogative.**

declension. The pattern or **paradigm** of inflectional changes in a **noun,** noun modifier (**adjective, article**), or **pronoun.** In Greek a noun arranged with all of its forms for the various **cases,** singular and plural, is its declension.

definite. A noun is said to be definite if it can be identified by the speaker or the person addressed and is marked for such specificity: *The house* (versus *a house*). *Contrast* **indefinite.**

demonstrative. A **lexical category** of words that make a noun **definite** as well as mark physical time or **discourse** location of the **referent:** *this man/that man* (physical), *this time/at that time* (time), *This is the account of Noah* (discourse).

denominative. A word derived from a noun: *to star in a play, to field a ball, to impact a mind.* Also called a denominal.

denotation. In semantics, the conceptual meaning of a word. The word *chair* denotes a type of furniture that someone sits on. *See also* **connotation.**

dependent clause. A clause that cannot stand alone as a complete sentence. Also called **subordinate clause:** *when I went home, after the ball was over. Contrast* **independent clause.**

deponent (verb). In Greek studies, a verb that has **passive** morphology but expresses an **active** idea. Greek *apokrinomai,* "I answer," has a passive ending but expresses an active idea.

derivation. The process of forming a new word by adding affixes. The word *unjust* is derived from *just,* and *joyous* is derived from *joy. Contrast* **inflection.**

determiner. A **lexical category** that limits the potential referents of a **noun (phrase).** In English, **indefinite** articles *(a, an),* **definite** articles *(the),* **demonstrative** pronouns *(this, that),* and possessives *(my, their)* are all determiners.

diachronic. Referring to the comparison of older and newer forms of a language. *Contrast* **synchronic.**

diacritic. A mark placed on a letter to indicate such information as pitch or **stress.** Also called diacritical marks. Greek places the rough-breathing mark (ʽ) as a diacritic over or in front of a word that begins with an aspirated **phoneme.**

dialect. A variety of a language spoken in a particular area or by a particular subgroup of society. Biblical Hebrew has a Judean (southern) and an Israelite (northern) dialect. English has numerous regional dialects.

digraph. A group of two letters used to represent one sound. English: *th, ch, sh.*

diphthong. A sequence of two vowel sounds that is considered to be one sound.

Typically the second part of the sound is the sound [i] or [u] and is relatively shorter. The vowel sounds in *how, hay,* and *toy* are diphthongs.

direct object. The **grammatical relation** of a noun phrase that completes the action of a **verb:** *I saw <u>her</u>. I greeted <u>the child</u>.*

direct quotation. A quotation that gives the exact words of a speaker: *She said, <u>"I will go."</u> John asked, <u>"Should she go?"</u> Contrast* **indirect quotation.**

discontinuous morpheme. A morpheme that is separated by other morphemes. Hebrew verb roots consist of three **radicals** that are kept in the same order but have different patterns inserted within the root: <u>*š*</u>*ā*<u>*m*</u>*a*<u>*r*</u> "he watched," <u>*š*</u>*ō*<u>*m*</u>*ē*<u>*r*</u> "one (masc.) watching," <u>*š*</u>*ā*<u>*m*</u>*û*<u>*r*</u> "one (masc.) watched."

discourse. A group of sentences that is considered to be a unit, such as a story or a discussion.

ditransitive. A **verb** that must take two **objects** (traditionally called the **direct** and **indirect** objects) to complete it: *She gave <u>him the Bible</u>. We sent <u>her the letter</u>.* Also called **bitransitive.**

doubling. Consonant doubling is not indicated in the pre-Masoretic writing system, but the Masoretes used a dot placed within a consonant to show that it was doubled. *See* **gemination** and **dagesh.**

dual. A **number** category referring to two people or objects. Hebrew has a limited use of a dual form, using it for units of time (*yômayim* "two days"), quantity (*ʾalpayim* "two thousand"), or things that naturally occur in pairs (*ʿênayim* "eyes"). For naturally paired items, the dual also serves as the normal plural (*raglayim* = "two feet" or "feet" in general).

elision. The process by which a sound is omitted in certain phonetic environments. This can occur at the end of a word or when two vowels occur next to each other. In Greek, the final sound of the word *dia* is dropped when the next word starts with a vowel: *dia autou* becomes *di' autou* "through him."

emphatic (consonant). *See* **velarized (consonant).**

etymology. The history of a word; that is, how it came to sound the way it does and mean what it does.

experiencer. A **semantic role.** The person who experiences an emotion or sensation: *<u>They</u> heard the noise. Compare* **agent.**

factitive. A **verb** that denotes an action or process that leads to a result. The verb *kill* is factitive because the act of killing leads to the result that someone is dead.

figurative. Nonliteral use of a word or phrase. A figurative use of *head* refers to being a leader.

finite verb. Traditionally defined as a verb that is marked for person, number, and tense (i.e., all available inflectional markers of the language). More generally, any verb that can occur in a simple declarative clause. English has very limited person and number markers: *She studies; he reads.* Greek: *legō* "I read," *legomen* "we read." *Contrast* **infinitive.**

first person. Relating to the speaker(s). English: *I, we; me, us; my, our.*

formative. Another term for an **affix** in biblical language studies. Also used instead of **morpheme** in some circles.

free morpheme. A morpheme that can occur by itself; it does not need other morphemes. In English most root morphemes are free; but in Greek, nouns, adjectives, and verbs cannot occur without additional affixes. Affixes are always bound. *Contrast* **bound morphemes.**

fricative. A sound made with the airstream constricted in such a way that the friction of the air is audible. English: *f, v, th.*

front vowel. A vowel sound made by placing the tongue relatively forward in the mouth. The vowel sounds in *beet, bit, bait, bet,* and *bat. See also* **back vowel** and **central vowel.**

function word. A word that has no separate reference or denotation; it relates to other words in the clause. Prepositions, conjunctions, and determiners are all function words. *Contrast* **content word.**

geminate(s). A class of Hebrew roots that have the same root consonant for the second and third root position: *sbb* "to go around," *qll* "to curse," *mdd* "to measure," *rvv* "to be bad, evil."

gemination. Another term for consonant **doubling.**

gender. A grammatical feature of nouns that indicates one of several classes of nouns; there is not necessarily a physiological relationship to male and female. Greek has three "genders": masculine, feminine, neuter.

genitive (case). A morphological marker on a noun or its modifiers indicating a relationship with another noun. In *Jan's book* the suffix *-'s* is a genitive marker. Also called possessive, but the relationship between the two nouns is not always that of ownership; for example, *Jan's doctor* and *Jan's church.*

glide. A consonant sound that is produced in the same way as a vowel but acts as a consonant. Also called a *semivowel.* The initial sounds in *wet* and *yet* are glides.

glottal. Sound made with the glottis; e.g., the **glottal stop.**

glottal stop. A sound made by stopping the airstream by closing the glottis. The "sound" made in the middle of *uh-oh.*

goal. A **semantic role.** The person or object toward which the action of a verb is directed: *They went to the church. They went to their parents. Compare* **recipient.**

grammar. The patterns or rules of a language, including the sounds, words, and clauses.

grammatical. Following the accepted patterns of a language.

grammatical relation. The role of a noun phrase or complement clause as it relates to the verb. *See* **subject** and **object.**

guttural. The term *guttural* is often applied by Hebrew grammar books to the **laryngeals, pharyngeals,** and **glottals,** which include *aleph, he, chet,* and *ayin.*

head. The part of a **phrase** that determines the overall characteristics of the phrase. In the noun phrase *the two large books,* the noun *books* is the head. The head of an English noun phrase is the noun that refers to the same entity the whole phrase refers to.

high vowel. A vowel sound made by placing the tongue relatively close to the roof of the mouth. The vowel sound in *beat* and *boot,* for example.

homonym. A word that is pronounced the same as another word that has a different meaning. The words *bat* (a wooden object) and *bat* (a winged rodent) are homonyms.

homorganic (consonants). Consonant sounds that are made at the same **place of articulation.** For example, *mp, mb, nt, nd.*

idiom. A construction whose meaning cannot be deduced from the meanings of its parts: *Fly off the handle. They spilled the beans about the party.*

imperative. The **mood** used to express a command. Also an utterance that expresses a command. Typically, only with the second person *(you):* e.g., *Open your book! Contrast* **indicative, optative,** and **subjunctive mood** and **declarative** and **interrogative.**

imperfect. The **tense** that indicates that an action is viewed as being extended over a period of time in the past; a "past progressive": *I was studying when you came.* In most Hebrew grammar books the term refers to the form of the verb with prefixes for the person, gender, and number. *See* **prefix conjugation.** It also refers to the **imperfective** aspect as well as the imperfect tense.

imperfective. The **aspect** that denotes an action or event that is viewed as extending over a period of time. *Contrast* **perfective.**

indefinite. Not referring to a previously identified item or person: *a chair, some students. Contrast* **definite.**

independent clause. A **clause** that can stand alone as a complete sentence: *I studied for the test. When I went home, I studied for the test. Contrast* **dependent clause.**

indicative. The **mood** used in simple statements. Also called **declarative:** *You did well on the exam. Contrast* **imperative, optative,** and **subjunctive.**

indirect object. The **grammatical relation** of the noun phrase that expresses the semantic **recipient:** *They gave an offering to the church.*

indirect quotation. A report of what someone said that does not use the exact words: *She said she would go. Contrast* **direct quotation.**

infinitive. A verb form that has the minimum verbal morphology allowed in a language. In English, the infinitive is the basic root of the verb: *The teacher made the student study.* In Greek, the infinitive is marked for tense, but not for person or number: *luein* "(to) loose" (present tense); *lusein* "(to) loose" (future tense). *Contrast* **finite verb.**

infix. A **morpheme** that is inserted within a **root.** Either a long *i* or a long *e* occurs between the second and third root letters in most forms of the *hiphil* verb pattern in biblical Hebrew.

inflection. Variation in the form of a word, typically by means of an affix, that expresses a grammatical contrast that is obligatory in a particular grammatical context. In English, inflection can be indicated on verbs *(He comes* versus *they come),* nouns *(book, books),* and adjectives *(smart, smarter, smartest).*

injunctive. A verbal form used to express prohibitions. Hebrew: *lōʾ tignōb* "thou shalt not steal."

instrument. A **semantic role.** The noun that is used as a tool to do an action: *They ate ice cream with their spoons.*

interdental. A sound made by placing the tongue tip between the top and bottom teeth. The initial sound in *this* and *thin* and the last sound in *breath* and *breathe.*

interjection. A **lexical category** of words that are used most often as exclamations or parts of exclamations: *Ugh! Oh!*

interrogative. The **mood** of an utterance that asks a question: *Is it important to study the biblical languages? Contrast* **declarative** and **imperative.**

intonation. The way a speaker's voice goes higher or lower within a clause or sentence. In English *Jan went to school* and *Jan went to school?* are distinguished by the differing intonation patterns of **declarative** and **interrogative** sentences.

intransitive. A **verb** that may not occur with an **object:** *I hiccuped. I fell. Contrast* **transitive.**

irregular. A form that does not follow the standard inflectional patterns of a language. *See also* **weak verb.**

iterative. The **aspect** that indicates repeated action.

jussive. A command referring to a third person *(him/her/them)* rather than to the second person *(you).* Also referred to as "third person imperative": *Let them eat cake!*

labial. A sound made with at least one lip. The English sounds *p, b, m,* and *w,* as well as *f* and *v. See also* **bilabial** and **labiodental.**

labiodental. A sound made by placing the upper teeth against the lower lip. The initial sounds in *fat* and *vat* and the last sounds in *roof* and *groove.*

laryngeal. Sound made in the larynx, also known as a **glottal;** e.g. the **glottal stop** [ʔ] and [h].

lateral. A sound in which the air flows over the sides of the tongue rather than over the middle. The initial sound in *late* and the last sound in *tell.*

length. The amount of time it takes to utter a vowel or consonant. Long vowels take more time to say than short vowels. (This is not the same as how some teachers use the terms *long* and *short vowels* in English.)

lexical category. Words that share common morphological or syntactic traits, such as noun, verb, or adverb. Also called **part(s) of speech** or **word class.**

lexicon. A list of the morphemes and words of a language.

liquid. A sound made with moderate obstruction of the airstream in the middle of the mouth. This includes **lateral** sounds and **rhotic** sounds. The initial sound in *late* and *rate.*

location. A **semantic role** that expresses where something occurs: *The book is on the table. We are in the house.*

low vowel. A vowel sound made by placing the tongue relatively low in the mouth. The vowel sound made when the doctor asks a patient to say "ah."

main clause. A **clause** that is not a part of another clause. Also called an **independent** clause: *After she read the lesson, she understood the idea. Contrast* **subordinate** or **dependent** clause.

manner of articulation. The way in which a sound is made. For example, stops, fricatives, and nasals.

marked. The fact that grammatical information is indicated on a word. A Greek verb is "marked" for the person and number of the subject. Also used in reference to forms that are not the "default" forms. In English, *actress* is more "marked" than *actor* because the latter can be understood to include males and females, while the former can refer only to females.

mass (noun). A noun that cannot be counted, such as *sand* or *joy.*

matres lectiones. *See* **vowel letters.**

metaphor. The nonliteral expression comparing one concept to another concept, where there is some similarity or correlation between the two: *You were my rock today. Jesus is the Good Shepherd.*

metathesis. A change in the order of sounds in a word. Hebrew: *kebeś* or *keśeb* "young ram."

middle (voice). A morphological indication on a verb that the **subject** is acting on or for him- or herself. There is no middle voice in English. Greek: *Satanas metaschēmatizetai* "Satan disguises himself" (2 Cor. 11:14). *Contrast* **active** and **passive.**

minimal pair. Two words that are identical in pronunciation except for one sound and have different meanings: *pair* and *peer, pat* and *bat, bus* and *buzz.*

modal. A word that expresses **mood.** In English the modal verbs are *can, could, must,* and *should.* These English verbs do not act like finite verbs: they are not inflected for person, number, or tense.

modifier. A word that describes or classifies another word; for example, an **adjective** modifies a **noun,** and an **adverb** modifies a **verb:** *the large class; learn rapidly.*

mood. A grammatical concept that expresses how a clause is related to reality. **Indicative, imperative, subjunctive,** and **optative** are moods.

morpheme. The minimal grammatical unit of a language; a form that has a meaning.

morphology. The study of how words are formed.

nasal. A sound in which the air passes through the nasal cavity: the initial sounds in *mouth* and *now;* the final sounds in *some, sun,* and *sung.*

nominal. A word with nounlike properties. In *The poor are many* the word *poor* is a nominal. It functions as a noun in this sentence; however, it cannot be pluralized. Also called a **substantive.**

nominative (case). A morphological marker on a noun or its modifiers typically indicating the subject of a clause. In Greek *anthropos,* "man," is the nominative form of the word.

noun. A lexical category of words that typically express objects and people. Nouns are defined in each language by morphological and syntactic properties. In English most nouns can be pluralized *(language—languages)* and may occur in particular patterns such as after a **determiner** *(the language)*.

noun phrase. A phrase that has at least a noun; it may also have other modifiers: *the three wise men, the incredible opportunity to learn the biblical languages.*

number. A grammatical category that indicates quantity. **Singular, dual,** and **plural** are number categories.

numeral. A **lexical category** of words that refer to a specific quantity: *two books.*

object. *See* **direct object** and **indirect object.**

object of a preposition. A **noun** that is an argument of a preposition. English: *in the house; from Jerusalem.* In Greek, nouns that are objects of prepositions are marked for **case:** *para tou theou* "from God," *para tō theō* "with God."

obstruent. A consonant sound made by blocking the airflow somewhere in the mouth without any air going through the nasal cavity. All **stop, fricative,** and **affricate** sounds. *Contrast* **sonorant.**

open class. A class of words to which new words can be regularly added. **Nouns** and **verbs** are open classes. *Contrast* **closed class.**

optative. The **mood** that expresses a wish. Greek: *ho theos . . . hagiasai humas* "May God sanctify you" (1 Thess. 5:23). *Contrast* **imperative, indicative,** and **subjunctive.**

ordinal number. An **adjective** form of a number. An ordinal number gives information about the "order" of a noun in a group: *God rested on the seventh day. Compare* **cardinal number.**

palatal. A sound made by placing the middle of the tongue on or near the hard palate. The initial sound in *yes.*

palatalization. In phonology, the process of a sound moving to or toward the palatal area.

paradigm. A group of words based on the same **root** that have different **inflectional** affixes. *See* **conjugation** and **declension.**

parataxis. Clauses which are not structurally imbedded in other clauses and can be juxtaposed, either with or without conjunctions. Hebrew is often called a "paratactic" language.

part of speech. *See* **lexical category.**

participle. A form of a verb that acts as an adjective. In English participles can be present *(the sleeping dog)* or past participles *(the used cars)*. Greek participles have gender and case like an adjective and tense and voice like a verb. In Hebrew participles can act like a verb predicate, having a subject noun or pronoun and taking an object.

particle. Any of a number of words that have only one form. They are not derived from other forms and do not take inflection. **Conjunctions** and **prepositions** are particles in English.

passive (voice). A syntactic construction in which the grammatical **subject** is the **patient/undergoer** of the verb: *The teacher was helped by the student.* Greek has affixes within the verb to indicate **passive** voice. *Contrast* **active** and **middle.**

patient. A **semantic role.** The person or object that receives the action of a verb. Also called **undergoer:** *They bought the book. The book was bought by the students.*

penult. The second to last syllable in a word. Normally regarding **stress** patterns: *enthusiastic, semantics.*

perfect. The **aspect** that indicates the results of an action that took place in the past. Also used to identify a tense morpheme that indicates this meaning. In most Hebrew grammar books the term applies to the form of the verb that uses suffixes for the person, gender, and number. *See* **suffix conjugation.** It is also used for the **perfective** aspect as well as the perfect aspect. *Contrast* **imperfect.**

perfective. The aspect that denotes an action or event as viewed in its entirety, without regard for tense. *Contrast* **imperfective.**

performative. An utterance by which a speaker does an action: *I dare you to . . .; I blame you.*

person. A grammatical category that distinguishes people in relation to the speaker. *See* **first, second,** and **third person.**

personal pronoun. A **pronoun** that expresses the difference between the speaker and others: *I, we, you, they.*

pharyngeal. A sound made inside the pharynx. Hebrew: *chet* and *ayin* in their ancient pronunciation.

phoneme. A speech sound and its variations. The sounds of the *t* in *top* and *stop* are one phoneme in English, even though they are slightly different phonetically.

phonetics. The study of the sounds used in human languages.

phonology. The study of the way sounds are used in a language. Phonology looks for patterns within a language, such as which sounds can begin and end a word and which sounds can occur next to each other.

phonotactics. The patterns of sound sequences in a language. English allows consonants to occur next to each other at the beginning of words such as *splash* and *scratch,* but these combinations cannot end a word.

phrase. One or more words that form a unit or **constituent.** Phrases can be **noun phrases** (the big book), **prepositional phrases** *(to the end of the lesson),* **adjective phrases** *(very, very good),* and so forth.

phrase structure rule. A summary statement of the grammatical patterns of a language. For example, in English the **noun phrase** consists of an optional **determiner** followed by an optional **adjective** and a **noun.** This can be summarized as: NP → (Determiner) (Adjective) Noun.

phrase structure tree. A graphic representation of the structure of a phrase or clause.

place of articulation. The location within the vocal tract where a sound is made: **bilabial, alveolar, velar,** and so forth.

pleonastic. Redundant forms of speech: *female women.*

plosive. *See* **stop.**

pluperfect. A form that combines **past tense** and **perfect** aspect: *I had written the letter before lunch.*

plural. A **number** category referring to more than one person or object: *books, women, children.*

pointing. The vowel "points" added to the letters of the received text by the Masoretes (Jewish scribes of the Middle Ages) to preserve a more exact pronunciation. דבר → דָבָר [*d b r* → *dā-bā-r*] *dābār* "word."

polysemy. More than one meaning of the same word: *He used his head to head the ball into the goal.*

pragmatics. The study of meaning as related to the social and physical context of speech.

predicate. The part of a clause that adds information about the subject: *They studied a long time; they are good students.*

predicate adjective. In English an **adjective** that follows a **copula,** or linking verb, such as *be, seem,* and *appear: They are tired. They seem happy.* In Hebrew and Greek, predicate adjectives may occur without a linking verb. Hebrew: *tōb haddābār* "the word (is) good"; Greek: *ho anthrōpos agathos* "the man (is) good."

predicate nominative. A **noun** (phrase) that follows a **copula:** *They are stu-*

dents. *They were the best students of the year.* Hebrew and Greek allow nominals to occur without a linking verb. Hebrew: *hûʾ hāʾĕlōhîm* "He (is) God." Greek: *martus gar mou ho theos* (literally: "witness for my the god") "For God (is) my witness" (Phil. 1:8).

prefix. A **morpheme** that precedes a **root:** *pre-history, un-happy, multi-national.*

prefix conjugation. The **verb conjugation** in Hebrew formed by adding a **prefix** to show changes of personal subject. This form is called **imperfect** in many Hebrew grammars: *ʾe-šmōr* "I will watch," *ti-šmōr* "you (masc. sg) will watch," *yi-šmōr* "he will watch."

preposition. A **lexical category** of words that express relationships between nouns and other words. For example: *in, of, with.* In Hebrew the prepositions are sometimes attached to the noun they modify.

prepositional phrase. A phrase that begins with a **preposition:** *in the book, under the tree.*

preterite. The simple past tense form of a verb. In biblical Hebrew the form otherwise known as "*waw*-consecutive with imperfect" is sometimes said to be preterite in function.

principal part(s). The basic forms of a verb used to construct the various inflected forms. In English the present, simple past, and the past participle are the three principle parts of a verb; for example, *eat, ate, eaten; sing, sang, sung.* Greek verbs have six principal parts.

progressive. The **aspect** that expresses the ongoing action of a verb. Also called **imperfective** or continuous.

prohibitive. *See* **injunctive.**

pronoun. A **lexical class** of words that can take the place of a **noun phrase:** *The students study Greek, and they enjoy it.*

proper noun. The name of a person or place.

protasis. A **conditional clause:** *If you study Greek, you will understand the New Testament better. Contrast* **apodosis.**

quiescent. Referring to a letter that becomes silent in pronunciation but shows up in the spelling. In the Hebrew word *lē(ʾ)mōr,* the letter *aleph (ʾ)* has become silent but is still written in the text.

radical. Often referring in Hebrew grammars to a root letter. Each root letter is called a radical. Root *ktb* ("to write"): 1st radical—*k,* 2d radical—*t,* 3d radical—*b.*

recipient. A **semantic role.** The person who receives something. *I gave the book to my friend. I gave my friend the book. Compare* **goal.**

reciprocal. Two or more people performing an action on each other: *they helped each other.*

reduplication. A repeating of a root consonant within a word. It differs from **doubling** in that a vowel separates the repeated consonant. Some Hebrew **roots** form a verb **base** by reduplicating the last root letter: *šûb* "to go back," *šôbēḇ* "to bring back." Greek also has some reduplicated forms: *luō* "I loose," *leluka* "I have loosed."

referent. The **antecedent** for a **pronoun** or the real world correspondent to a word or phrase: *I saw Tom. He didn't see me.*

reflexive. A form that refers to the same person as both subject and object of an action: *I cut myself.*

regular (verb). A **verb** that follows the normal patterns of a language. *Contrast* **irregular.**

relative clause. A **subordinate clause** that modifies a noun. A restricted relative clause identifies the noun; an unrestricted relative clause provides additional information about the noun: *The student who sat in the front row was very intelligent. His brother, who lived in Chicago, came to visit.*

relative pronoun. A **pronoun** that begins a **relative clause.** English: *who, whose, whom;* Greek: *hos, hē, ho.*

root. The simplest possible form of a lexical morpheme from which other forms are made. In English, the root of *runners* is *run.*

second person. Relating to the hearer. English: *you, your, yours.*

secondary sense. A meaning closely related to the literal or primary meaning of a word. A secondary sense of *head* is *authority. Compare* **figurative sense.**

semantic role. The semantic function of a noun phrase in a situation. **Agent, patient,** and so on. Also called **thematic role.**

semantics. The study of meaning as it relates to language.

sense. One of the meanings of a word; the primary, secondary, or figurative meaning.

sentence. A grammatical construction that is considered to be a complete thought. It may consist of one or more clauses.

sibilant. A sound that has a "hissing" noise. The initial sounds of *sue, zoo,* and *shoe,* for example.

simile. In English a **metaphor** that includes the word *like* or *as: You were like a rock to me today.*

simple sentence. A sentence that consists of only one clause.

singular. A **number** category referring to one person or object.

sonorant. A sound made with relatively little blockage of the airflow. All vowels and such sounds as the English *n, m, r, l, w,* and *y. Contrast* **obstruent.**

source. A **semantic role.** The person, place or thing from which an action initiates: *I come from Alabama with a banjo on my knee. I received a letter from him.*

spirant. *See* **fricative.**

spirantization. Changing a **stop** to a **spirant** or **fricative,** generally due to the presence of a **vowel** sound. In biblical Hebrew (Masoretic form) the **stops** *b, g, d, k, p, t* were spirantized when they occurred after a vowel. For example, *bêt* "house of" plus *ʾēl* "God" becomes *Bêt-ʾēl,* pronounced "Bethel." The pronunciation with *th* is due to **spirantization** of the *t* following the vowel *ê*.

stative. An **aspect** that expresses a state or condition, as opposed to an activity or action. English expresses most statives with predicate adjectives: *They are old.* Hebrew has many stative verbs that express these kinds of ideas. An English translation has to use a linking verb and an adjective, but the Hebrew forms are verbs: *kābēd* "he is heavy," *zāqēn* "he is old."

stop. A sound made by completely blocking the airflow. Also called a **plosive.** The English sounds *b, g, d, k, p,* and *t.*

stress. Emphasis on a syllable. Stress is often a combination of intensity, higher pitch, and length.

strong verb. In Hebrew grammar books, this term is used to refer to **regular** verbs. Strong verbs follow the patterns associated with *qāṭal* "he killed" or *šāmar* "he watched."

subject. The **grammatical relation** of a noun (phrase) that agrees with the verb. In active clauses, the subject typically serves as the **agent** or **experiencer** of the verb: *The students did their homework. The students enjoy their classes.*

subjunctive. The **mood** that indicates that an action is not (yet) a reality. Greek uses the subjunctive in several ways, including conditional clauses: *ei de pneumati agesthe* "if you are being led by the Spirit" (Gal. 5:18). *Contrast* **imperative, indicative,** and **optative.**

subordinate (clause). *See* **dependent clause.**

substantive. A noun or any word or phrase used as a noun: *The good, the bad, and the ugly; to die is better than to be enslaved.*

suffix. A **morpheme** that comes after a root. English: *walk-s, walk-ed, walk-er.*

suffix conjugation. The **verb conjugation** in Hebrew formed by adding a

suffix to show changes of personal subject. This form is called **perfect** in many Hebrew grammars: *šāmar-tî* "I watched," *šāmar-tā* "you watched," *šāmar-nû* "we watched."

superlative. The maximum degree of an **adjective** or **adverb.** English: *tallest, wisest.*

suppletion. The use of multiple roots for the same word. English *be* has suppletive forms *am, was,* and *are.*

syllable. A sound unit consisting minimally of a vowel sound. There also may be consonants before and after the vowel, depending on the patterns of the language. English: *strength* is one syllable; *stronger* is two syllables.

synchronic. Referring to the study of a language using data from the same time period. *Contrast* **diachronic.**

synonym. A word that has approximately the same meaning as another word, at least in most contexts. English: *large* and *big.*

syntax. The patterns of **phrases, clauses,** and **sentences.**

tense. A grammatical category related to time; normally in relation to the present. Past, present, and future are tenses. In morphology, any forms (e.g., affixes) that indicate these time relationships. *Compare* **aspect.**

thematic role. *See* **semantic role.**

theme. *See* **patient.**

third person. Relating to someone besides the speaker and hearer. English: *he, she, it; they, them, their.*

tone. In some Hebrew grammars an alternate term for **stress** or **accent.** The tone syllable always has the main or primary stress, never a secondary stress. In other linguistic materials, tone refers to the pitch of a syllable, especially in relation to meaning. Mandarin is a tone language.

topic. The "known" information of a clause or what the clause is "about"; typically the subject: "*The Lord is my shepherd*" (Ps. 23:1 KJV).

transitive. A verb that has a **direct object:** *We carried our books. They described their studies. Contrast* **intransitive.**

ultima. The last syllable of a word. Normally regarding **stress** patterns. Most Hebrew words (Tiberian pronunciation) are stressed on the ultima: *dā-bār* "a word"), *šā-mar* "he watched." English: *undo.*

undergoer. *See* **patient.**

universals. General truths about the languages of the world based on linguistic studies.

uvular. A sound made by placing the back of the tongue on or near the uvula (the flap of tissue that hangs in the back of the throat).

velar. A sound made by placing the back of the tongue on or near the velum (soft palate). The initial sound in the words *cut* and *gut;* the final sound in *lack, log,* and *long.*

velarized (consonant). A sound made with the tip of the tongue touching some part of the mouth forward of the **velum** but with the back part of the tongue touching the velum simultaneously. Also called **emphatic (consonant).**

verb. A **lexical category** of words that typically express an action, event, or state. Verbs also can be defined by morphological and syntactic characteristics of a language. In English a verb can have the progressive suffix *-ing (walk-ing)* or the past-tense suffix *-ed (walk-ed).*

verb patterns. The Hebrew verb can occur in certain formations with a consistent variation that correlates with certain semantic meanings. These formations are called verb patterns or **binyanim.** *Qal* pattern (simple): *mālak-tî* "I reigned," *mālak* "he reigned"; *Hiphil* pattern (causative): *hi-mlak-tî* "I caused to reign," *hi-mlîk* "he caused to reign."

verb phrase. A **phrase** in which a **verb** is the main part. Other words also may appear in the phrase: *They fell. They are good students. They understand the main ideas. Compare* **predicate.**

vetitive. In Hebrew studies, a negative command. Hebrew: *tēlēk* "you will go," *ʾal-tēlēk* "do not go." *Compare* **injunctive.**

vocative (case). A morphological marker on a noun or pronoun marking the person being spoken to. Greek: *anthrōpe* "O man."

voice. A syntactic category used to describe the relationship between the grammatical **subject** and its **semantic role.** *See* **active, middle, passive.**

voiced. A sound made while the vocal cords are vibrating. The initial sound in *zoo, then,* and *bat;* the final sound in *buzz, bathe,* and *cab.*

voiceless. A sound made without any vibration of the vocal cords. The initial sound in *sue, thin,* and *pat;* the final sound in *bus, bath,* and *cap.*

vowel. A sound made with little restriction of the airflow. Vowels function as the central part of a **syllable.** The sounds *a, e, o, u. Contrast* **consonant.**

vowel letters. In Hebrew studies, referring to one of the letters, *waw, yod, he,* or occasionally *aleph,* used to stand for a vowel. Also called **matres lectiones.** Spelling: *byt;* pronunciation: *bêt.* Spelling: *sws;* pronunciation: *sûs.* Spelling: *twrh;* pronunciation: *tôrâ.*

weak verb. A term used in many Hebrew grammars for verbs that do not follow standard patterns.

word. A grammatical unit that can stand alone.

word classes. *See* **lexical category.**

For Further Study

There are many resources that provide definitions of linguistic terms.

Braun, Frank X. *English Grammar for Language Students.* Ann Arbor, Mich.: Ulrich's Books, 1947. A short overview (23 pages) of linguistic terms with English examples.

Crystal, David. *A Dictionary of Linguistics and Phonetics.* 3d ed. Oxford: Blackwell, 1991.

———. *An Encyclopedic Dictionary of Language and Languages.* Oxford: Blackwell, 1992.

DeMoss, Matthew S. *Pocket Dictionary for the Study of New Testament Greek.* Downers Grove, Ill.: InterVarsity, 2001. Over 1700 terms regarding linguistics, textual criticism, and exegesis.

Matthews, Peter. *The Concise Oxford Dictionary of Linguistics.* Oxford: Oxford University Press, 1997. Over 3000 terms regarding linguistics and semantics.

Porter, Stanley, E. *Idioms of the Greek New Testament.* 2d ed. Sheffield: Sheffield Academic Press, 1994. Includes a glossary of over ninety terms used to discuss Greek grammar.

Trask, R. L. *A Student's Dictionary of Language and Linguistics.* London: Arnold, 1997. Over 2000 terms regarding linguistics and semantics.

Internet Resources

SIL maintains an extensive database of linguistic terms at http://www.sil.org/linguistics/GlossaryOfLinguisticTerms/.

References

References to Linguistics in General

Aitchinson, Jean. *Language Change: Progress or Decay?* New York: Universe Books, 1985.

Braun, Frank X. *English Grammar for Language Students.* Ann Arbor, Mich.: Ulrich's Books, 1947.

Brewster, Thomas, and Elizabeth E. Brewster. *Language Acquisition Made Practical.* Pasadena, Calif.: William Carey Library, 1984.

Bright, William, ed. *International Encyclopedia of Linguistics.* Oxford: Oxford University Press, 1992.

Brown, H. Douglas. *Breaking the Language Barrier.* Yarmouth, Me.: Intercultural Press, 1991.

———. *Principles of Language Learning and Teaching.* 3d ed. Englewood Cliffs, N.J.: Prentice Hall Regents, 1994.

Bussman, Hadumod. *Routledge Dictionary of Language and Linguistics.* London: Routledge, 1996.

Campbell, George L. *Handbook of Scripts and Alphabets.* London: Routledge, 1997.

Collinge, N. E., ed. *An Encyclopaedia of Language.* London: Routledge, 1990.

Comrie, Bernard. *Language Universals and Linguistic Typology.* 2d ed. Chicago: University of Chicago Press, 1989.

Coulmas, Florian. *The Writing Systems of the World.* Oxford: Basil Blackwell, 1991.

Crowley, Terry. *An Introduction to Historical Linguistics.* Oxford: Oxford University Press, 1992.

Crystal, David, ed. *The Cambridge Encyclopedia of Language.* Cambridge: Cambridge University Press, 1987.

———. *A Dictionary of Linguistics and Phonetics.* 3d ed. Oxford: Blackwell, 1991.

———. *An Encyclopedic Dictionary of Language and Languages.* Oxford: Blackwell, 1992.

Daniels, Peter T., and William Bright, eds. *The World's Writing Systems.* New York: Oxford University Press, 1996.

Diringer, David. *The Alphabet: A Key to the History of Mankind.* 2 vols. 3d ed. New York: Funk & Wagnalls, 1968.

Dixon, R. M. W. "Where Have All the Adjectives Gone?" *Studies in Language* 1, no. 1 (1977): 19–80.

Dooley, Robert A., and Stephen H. Levinsohn. *Analyzing Discourse: A Manual of Basic Concepts.* Dallas: SIL International, 2001.

Eastman, Carol M. *Aspects of Language and Culture.* 2d ed. Novato, Calif.: Chandler and Sharp, 1990.

Fuller, Graham E. *How to Learn a Foreign Language.* Friday Harbor, Wash.: Storm King Press, 1987.

Goddard, Cliff. *Semantic Analysis: A Practical Introduction.* Oxford: Oxford University Press, 1998.

Greenberg, Joseph, ed. *Universals of Human Language.* Cambridge, Mass.: MIT University Press, 1966.

Lakoff, George. *Women, Fire and Dangerous Things: What Categories Reveal About the Mind.* Chicago: University of Chicago Press, 1987.

Lakoff, George, and Mark Johnson. *Metaphors We Live By.* Chicago: University of Chicago Press, 1980.

Larson, Donald N., and William A. Smalley. *Becoming Bilingual: A Guide to Language Learning.* New York: University Press of America, 1984.

Lawrence, Gordon. *People Types and Tiger Stripes: A Practical Guide to Learning Styles.* 2d ed. Gainesville, Fla.: Center for Application of Psychological Types, 1982.

Lehmann, W. P. *Historical Linguistics: An Introduction.* 2d ed. New York: Holt, Rinehart and Winston, 1973.

Luria, A. R. *The Man with the Shattered World.* Cambridge, Mass.: Harvard University Press, 1972.

Malmkjaer, Kirsten, ed. *The Linguistics Encyclopedia.* London: Routledge, 1991.

Marshall, Terry. *The Whole World Guide to Language Learning.* Yarmouth, Me.: Intercultural Press, 1989.

Matthews, Peter H. *Morphology: An Introduction to the Theory of Word Structure.* 2d ed. Cambridge: Cambridge University Press, 1991.

———. *The Concise Oxford Dictionary of Linguistics.* Oxford: Oxford University Press, 1997.

O'Grady, William, Michael Dobrovolosky, and Mark Aronoff. *Contemporary Linguistics: An Introduction.* 2d ed. New York: St. Martin's, 1993.

Payne, Thomas A. *Describing Morphosyntax: A Guide for Field Linguists.* Cambridge: Cambridge University Press, 1997.

Pike, Kenneth L. *Linguistic Concepts.* Lincoln, Neb.: University of Nebraska Press, 1982.

Pinker, Steven. *The Language Instinct.* New York: William Morrow and Company, 1994.

———. *Words and Rules.* New York: Basic Books, 1999.

Rheingold, Howard. *They Have a Word for It: A Lighthearted Lexicon of Untranslatable Words and Phrases.* Los Angeles: Jeremy P. Tarcher, 1988.

Rubin, Joan, and Irene Thompson. *How to Be a More Successful Language Learner.* Boston: Heinle & Heinle Publishers, 1994.

Schaller, Susan. *A Man Without Words.* Berkeley: University of California Press, 1995.

Stewart, Thomas W., Jr., and Nathan Vaillette, eds. *Language Files: Materials for an Introduction to Language and Linguistics.* 8th ed. Columbus: Ohio State University Press, 2001.

Trask, R. L. *A Dictionary of Grammatical Terms in Linguistics.* London: Routledge, 1993.

———. *A Student's Dictionary of Language and Linguistics.* London: Arnold, 1997.

Trask, R. L., and Bill Mayblin. *Introducing Linguistics.* New York: Totem Books, 2001.

Trudgill, Peter. *Sociolinguistics: An Introduction to Language and Society.* New York: Viking Penguin, 1983.

Wilson, Clifford A., and Donald McKeon. *The Language Gap.* Grand Rapids: Zondervan, 1984.

References to Linguistics and the Bible

Barnwell, Katharine. *Introduction to Semantics and Translation.* 2d ed. Dallas: SIL, 1980.

Barr, James. *The Semantics of Biblical Language.* Oxford: Oxford University Press, 1961.

Caird, George Bradford. *The Language and Imagery of the Bible.* Grand Rapids: Eerdmans, 1980.

Callow, Katherine. *Discourse Considerations in Translating the Word of God.* Grand Rapids: Zondervan, 1974.

Cotterell, Peter, and Max Turner. *Linguistics and Biblical Interpretation.* Downers Grove, Ill.: InterVarsity, 1989.

Nida, Eugene A. "Sociolinguistics and Translating." *Sociolinguistics and Communication,* edited by Johannes P. Louw, 1–49. UBS Monograph Series, no. 1. London: United Bible Societies, 1986.

———. *Signs, Sense, Translation.* Cape Town: Bible Society of South Africa, 1984.

Pike, Kenneth L. "The Linguist and Axioms Concerning the Language of Scripture." *Journal of the American Scientific Affiliation* 26, no. 2 (1974): 47–51.

Porter, Stanley E. "Studying Ancient Languages from a Modern Linguistics Perspective." *Filologia Neotestamentaria* 2 (1989): 147–72.

Silva, Moisés. *Biblical Words and Their Meaning: An Introduction to Lexical Semantics.* Grand Rapids: Zondervan, 1983.

———. *God, Language and Scripture: Reading the Bible in the Light of General Linguistics.* Grand Rapids: Zondervan, 1990.

Webb, V. N. "Some Aspects of the Sociolinguistics of Bible Translation and Exegesis, and of Religious Language." *Sociolinguistics and Communication,* edited by Johannes P. Louw, 50–82. UBS Monograph Series, no. 1. London: United Bible Societies, 1986.

References to New Testament Greek

Black, David Alan. *It's Still Greek to Me.* Grand Rapids: Baker, 1998.

———. *Learn to Read New Testament Greek.* Expanded ed. Nashville: Broadman and Holman, 1994.

———. *Linguistics for Students of New Testament Greek.* 2d ed. Grand Rapids: Baker, 1995.

———. *Using New Testament Greek in Ministry: A Practical Guide for Students and Pastors.* Grand Rapids: Baker, 1993.

Black, David Alan, ed. *Linguistics and New Testament Interpretation: Essays on Discourse Analysis.* Nashville: Broadman Press, 1992.

Blass, F., A. Debrunner, and R. W. Funk. *A Greek Grammar of the New Testament.* Chicago: University of Chicago Press, 1961.

DeMoss, Matthew S. *Pocket Dictionary for the Study of New Testament Greek.* Downers Grove, Ill.: InterVarsity, 2001.

Dobson, John H. *Learn New Testament Greek.* 2d ed. Grand Rapids: Baker, 1993.

Easley, Kendell H. *User-Friendly Greek: A Common Sense Approach to the Greek New Testament.* Nashville: Broadman and Holman, 1994.

Goetchius, Eugene van Ness. *The Language of the New Testament.* New York: Charles Scribner's Sons, 1965.

Healey, Phyllis, and Alan Healey. "Greek Circumstantial Participles: Tracking Participants with Participles in the Greek New Testament." *Occasional Papers in Translation and Textlinguistics* 4, no. 3 (1990).

Levinsohn, Stephen H. *Discourse Features of New Testament Greek: A Coursebook.* Dallas: SIL International, 1992.

Louw, J. P. *Semantics of New Testament Greek.* Philadelphia: Fortress Press, 1982.

Louw, Johannes P., and Eugene A. Nida, eds. *Greek-English Lexicon of the New Testament Based on Semantic Domains.* New York: United Bible Societies, 1988, 1989.

Metzger, Bruce M. *Lexical Aids for Students of New Testament Greek.* 3d ed. Grand Rapids: Baker, 1998.

Porter, Stanley E., and D. A. Carson, eds. *Biblical Greek Language and Linguistics: Open Questions in Current Research.* Journal for the Study of the New Testament Supplement Series 80. Sheffield: JSOT Press, 1993.

———. *Discourse Analysis and Other Topics in Biblical Greek.* Sheffield: Sheffield Academic Press, 1995.

Wilson, Mark, with Jason Oden. *Mastering New Testament Greek Vocabulary Through Semantic Domains.* Grand Rapids: Kregel, 2003.

Young, Richard A. *Intermediate New Testament Greek: A Linguistic and Exegetical Approach.* Nashville: Broadman and Holman, 1994.

References to Biblical Hebrew

Bergen, Robert D., ed. *Biblical Hebrew and Discourse Linguistics.* Dallas: SIL International, 1994.

Bodine, Walter R., ed. *Linguistics and Biblical Hebrew.* Winona Lake, Ind.: Eisenbrauns, 1992.

———. *Discourse Analysis of Biblical Literature: What It Is and What It Offers.* Semeia Studies. Atlanta: Society of Biblical Literature, 1995.

Buth, Randall John. "Word Order Differences Between Narrative and Non-narrative Material in Biblical Hebrew." In *Proceedings of the 10th World Congress of Jewish Studies,* 9–16. Jerusalem: Magnes Press, Hebrew University, 1990.

———. "Language Use in the First Century: Spoken Hebrew in a Trilingual Society in the Time of Jesus." *Journal of Translation and Textlinguistics* 5, no. 4 (1992): 298–312.

———. Review of *Speaking of Speaking: Marking Direct Discourse in the Hebrew Bible,* by Samuel A. Meier. *Themelios* 20 (1994): 25–26.

Chisholm, Robert B., Jr. *From Exegesis to Exposition: A Practical Guide to Using Biblical Hebrew.* Grand Rapids: Baker, 2000.

Dobson, John H. *Learn Biblical Hebrew.* Dallas: SIL International, 1999.

Landes, George M. *Building Your Biblical Hebrew Vocabulary: Learning Words by Frequency and Cognate.* Society of Biblical Literature Resources for Biblical Study, no. 41. Atlanta: Society of Biblical Literature, 2001.

Long, Gary A. *Grammatical Concepts 101 for Biblical Hebrew: Learning Biblical Hebrew Grammatical Concepts Through English Grammar.* Peabody, Mass.: Hendrickson, 2002.

Mitchel, Larry A. *A Student's Vocabulary for Biblical Hebrew and Aramaic.* Grand Rapids: Zondervan, 1984.

Parker, Don. *Using Biblical Hebrew in Ministry: A Practical Guide for Pastors, Seminarians, and Bible Students.* New York: University Press of America, 1995.

Sáenz-Badillos, Angel. *A History of the Hebrew Language.* Translated by John Elwolde. Cambridge: Cambridge University Press, 1993.